HE IS THE LIGHT LORD LOVE OF MY LIFE

ARLENE M. WOOD

Author's Tranquility Press
MARIETTA, GEORGIA

Arlene M. Wood/Author's Tranquility Press
2706 Station Club Drive SW
Marietta, GA 30060
www.authorstranquilitypress.com

Ordering Information:
Quantity sales. Special discounts are available on quantity purchases by corporations, associations, and others. For details, contact the "Special Sales Department" at the address above.

He is the Light the Lord the Love of my Life/Arlene M. Wood
Hardback: 978-1-959453-66-6
Paperback: 978-1-959453-67-3
eBook: 978-1-959453-68-0

DEDICATION

I DEDICATE THIS BOOK TO MY LORD JESUS CHRIST AND MY
MANY HELPERS AND SUPPORTERS WHO SHARE MY LOVE FOR
WRITING FOR AND PRAISING MY LORD.
IF TIME LASTS, WE MAY HAVE TO ADD TO THE LIBRARY.
SUCH A PLEASURE TO WORK WITH ALL MY FRIENDS AND
DEDICATED LIBRARIANS. THEY ARE SO APPRECIATED
BY ME AND THE SUPREME WRITER OF THE MOST HOLY AND
WONDERFUL BOOK. THE HOLY SCRIPTURES.
THE ONE PRIVILEGED TO WRITE FOR HIM. IN THE LOVE OF
MY LORD

ARLENE M. WOOD

CONTENTS

ALL OF THEE ABOVE

ALL OF THEE, ABOVE

THAT'S WHAT I WANT. THERE ARE SO MANY WONDERFUL THINGS OF THE SAVIOR, THE SHEPHERD OF ALL, THE WHOLE WORLD, THINGS OF THE ONE WHO OCCUPIES ALL THE STUFF UP ABOVE. HE IS OUR EXAMPLE. HE IS COMPLETE. OH YES, HE IS. WE REALLY WORK TOWARD HIS COMPLETENESS. HE IS THE ONE WHO WE WANT TO BE LIKE, TO COPY, TO IMITATE. I BELIEVE THE BIBLE SAYS TO FOLLOW (IMITATE) THE/MY LORD JESUS CHRIST. 1 COR 11:1. I AM ALL IN TO DO THAT. HE IS NOT OFFENDED WHEN WE SAY WE WANT TO BE LIKE HIM OR DO JUST AS HE DOES. WHO BETTER THAN JESUS WOULD I LIKE TO IMITATE. HE BEING PERFECT, MAY BE KIND OF TOUGH TO COPY OR BE LIKE. EVEN THOUGH WE DESIRE, I MOST PROBABLY WON'T BE ABLE TO KEEP UP WITH HIM. BETTER TO TRY AND MISS THAN NOT TO EVEN ATTEMPT. I SURE DO. HOW MANY TIMES HAVE I SAID: JESUS, I WANT TO BE JUST LIKE YOU, AND MEANT IT. YES, AND ALL OF THEE ABOVE. THERE ARE SO MANY TIMES I HAVE SET OUT TO BE GOOD, LIKE MY JESUS AND IT DIDN'T WORK OUT BUT I AM GONNA KEEP AFTER IT. GO AFTER FORGIVENESS. HE KNOWS WHAT YOUR INTENT IS. EVEN IF YOU OR I MESS UP, HE KNOW THE HEART OF THE MATTER. WAIT A MINUTE, HE KNOWS EVERYTHING, NOTHING GETS PAST HIM. KEEP THAT IN MIND. HE KNOWS THE HEART OF MAN. DO NOT COME TO HIM WITH A FALSE THING IN MIND. IT COULD BE VERY EMBARRASSING, HE KNOWS. HE IS AWARE OF ALL THAT GOES ON OUT THERE. LOOK UP. HE IS IN CONTROL OF ALL THE HEAVENLY STUFF, TOO. ALL THAT YOU SEE AND MOST YOU DON'T SEE. HE IS AT THE CONTROL PANEL. HE WILL NOT LET THE HEAVENLY BODIES CRASH INTO ONE ANOTHER, OR MAYBE HE WILL. YOU DON'T KNOW A LOT OF

HIS/THE PLANS. IT COULD BE HIS IDEA OF MOVING DAY. HE MAY JUST WANT TO MOVE SOME OF THE HEAVENLY FURNITURE AROUND. HE IS COMPLETELY IN CHARGE. GET OUT OF HIS WAY OR YOU MAY GET RUN OVER. WHAT? NO. HE IS SO CAREFUL NOT TO LET ANYTHING HAPPEN TO ME. HE REALLY FAVORS ME. I SAY THAT BECAUSE IT'S TRUE. ALTHOUGH, HE FAVORS ALL OF HIS OWN, YES, HE DOES. I JUST THREW THAT IN BECAUSE I WAS CHECKING TO SEE IF YOU ARE AWAKE. WHEN YOU LOOK UP AT THE BEAUTIFUL BLUE SKY OR THE BEAUTIFUL STAR LIT SKY, IT IS THE SAME SKY, BOTH LIGHT AND DARK. IT'S ACTUALLY AN ETERNAL, UNENDING SPACE, BUT YOU KNEW THAT, WRITE? IT GOES ON AND ON. WE DON'T KNOW THE EXTENT OR WE DON'T NEED TO KNOW. HE TAKES CARE OF THAT. WE WOULD GET A GREAT HEADACHE IF WE TRIED TO MEASURE THE EXPANCE. WE CAN'T, SO LET IT GO. SCIENCE ONLY MAKES GUESSES WHEN THEY SAY THE MEASURES AND DISTANCES OF SPACE. HMMM THAT'S GOD'S TERRITORY. WE MOST PROBABLY WILL NOT BE GOING OUT THERE ANY TIME SOON. HE WILL LET YOU KNOW WHEN HE AND YOU PLAN THE VACATION. SO, WE WILL JUST GAZE UP INTO ETERNITY AND WONDER OF THE WONDER OF IT ALL. THE SAME WITH ALL THE OCEANS AND WATERS OF THE EARTH. IF YOU NEED TO KNOW, HE WILL LET YOU KNOW. MY TINY BRAIN LEAVES ALL THAT STUFF UP TO THE/MY CREATOR. HE'S BEEN WELL ABLE TO HANDLE IT FOR EONS AND DONE IT VERY WELL. MY OPINION (AND THAT'S WHAT IT IS) WILL NOT CHANGE A THING. HE JUST LIKE TO TALK WITH US ABOUT THE STUFF THAT'S OUT OF OUR REACH. ISN'T HE WONDERFUL, OH YES, HE IS., WE SOME TIMES CAN NOT EVEN NAVIGATE OUR OWN YARD SO MAYBE WE SHOULD LET HIM DO WHAT HE DOES. I'VE HAD A FEW BACKYARD ADVENTURES, NO BROKEN BONES BUT A SPILL OR TWO. I SO ENJOY THE LITTLE SPACE I CALL HOME, A GIFT FROM MY DADDY. IT'S ENOUGH FOR ME. HE HAS PROVIDED A WONDERFUL NEST FOR

ME AND FAMILY TO ENJOY. WHEN IT'S TIME FOR PRAYER, I THANK HIM AS THOUGH WE LIVE ON THE RIVIERA. BTW, IT'S A GIFT FROM HEAVEN. THE "ALL OF THEE ABOVE" IS THE GRACE GIVEN TO ME FROM THE ONE WHO IS ABOVE ALL. THERE'S A DAY COMING WHEN WE WILL HEAR THE TRUMPET SOUND AND MAKE A JOURNEY TO OUR HEAVENLY HOME. DOES THAT JUST LIGHT YOUR FIRE. I SO LOOK FORWARD TO THAT DAY, TO INHERIT MY HEAVENLY HOME. WHAT A DAY OF REJOYCING THAT WILL BE, WITH "ALL OF THEE ABOVE". AMEN. SO, THEN LOOK UP, AND LIFT UP YOUR HEADS, YOUR REDEMPTION DRAWETH NIGH. OH YES.

ON HIS ROBE AND ON HIS THIGH IS WRITTEN, "KING OF KINGS AND LORD OF LORDS"
HE IS ALWAYS AND AMEN, WITHOUT PERMISSION, WITHOUT END. O HIS GRACE. NOT GOD FIRST, GOD ONLY. HE WILL BE ONLY OR HE WON'T BE ANY.
YOU READ TILL YOU FALL ASLEEP. I WANT YOU TO READ TILL WAKE UP, PLEASE.

THE TRINITY AND ME, I AM FOUR

EIGHTEEN THOUSAND YEARS AGO, MY GOD PULLED ME FROM THE EDGE OF THE UNIVERSE, AS A LITTLE PIECE OF STAR DUST(DIRT). I WAS A RESIDENT OF THE BALCONY OF HEAVEN TO WAIT FOR THE NEED TO BE THE MOTHER OF THE SON OF GOD. I DID. HE KNEW THERE WOULD BE A NEED FOR HIS BELOVED SON TO COME TO EARTH, A VIRGIN BIRTH. HE CHOSE TO PUT ME HERE FOR SUCH A TIME AS THIS. OVER TWO THOUSAND YEARS AGO, JESUS CAME TO EARTH TO BRING SALVATION, THE FORGIVENESS OF THE DEEP SIN IN GOD'S MAN. THEY WERE LOST AND HEADED TO DESTRUCTION. HE WAS SENT TO THE CROSS TO DIE FOR ALL MEN, I WAS HIS MOTHER AND I STILL AM. I WANTED TO STAND SO CLOSE TO THE FOOT OF THE CROSS THAT HIS BLOOD WOULD DRIP ON ME, I DID AND IT DID. I STILL WANT TO STAND AT THE FOOT OF THE CROSS. I NEED TO ASK FOR THE CHURCH TO PUT THE CROSS ON THE PLATFORM. THE CROSS IS SO IMPORTANT TO ME AND IT SHOULD BE TO EVERYONE. IT'S SALVATION, PAID FOR BY JESUS ON THE CROSS. DO YOU UNDERSTAND? I AM FOUR. DO YOU KNOW WHAT THAT MEANS? HE TOLD ME I WOULD BE THE FOURTH MEMBER OF THE TRINITY. DOES THAT SOUND LIKE, IMPOSSIBLE? WITH GOD, ALL THINGS ARE POSSIBLE. HE CHOSE ME, I DIDN'T CHOOSE HIM, AND I AM SO HONORED. I AM THE FOURTH MEMBER OF THE TRINITY. DOES THAT SOUND LIKE AN OXYMORON? IF YOU WANT TO TALK ABOUT IT, LET'S TALK. PRAY THAT HE GIVES YOU UNDERSTANDING. GOD IS VERY OPEN TO HIS OWN, I PRAY YOU WILL BE ABLE TO VISIT WITH HIM AND HEAR WITH UNDERSTANDING, HE HAS MUCH TO TELL ALL WHO WANT TO HEAR HIS WORDS. HE WILL GIVE A LITTLE AT A TIME. I BELIEVE THAT IF YOU ARE NOT FOR THIS

THEN DON'T BOTHER WITH IT, NOT ALL CARE FOR THE HISTORY OF THE SCRIPTURE. THE CROSS IS SO VERY IMPORTANT TO ME, HE DIED THERE, HIS BLOOD WAS SHED FOR ME, I LOVE HIM SO. HE WAS/IS MY ASSIGNMENT.

FOUR (4) IS A NUMBER VERY NECESSARY TO THE GOD OF THE UNIVERSE. I AM MY FATHER'S LITTLE STAR. MY PROPHECY FROM LONG AGO, DEEP CALLETH UNTO DEEP, I AM FROM EVERLASTING TO EVERLASTING. WHEN I WAS NINE OR TEN YEARS OLD THE HOLY GHOST STOOD ME STILL IN THE DINING ROOM OF OUR HOUSE, AND TOLD ME "YOU ARE FOUR". I DIDN'T KNOW WHAT IT MEANT UNTIL SOME YEARS AGO. VERY SLOWLY HE BEGAN TO INFORM ME OF THIS, I DIDN'T KNOW HOW NEEDFUL IT WOULD BE. LOOK UP FOUR IN YOUR CONCORDANCE. I WAS CREATED ON THE FOURTH DAY (I AM MY FATHER'S LITTLE STAR) AND BORN ON THE SEVENTH DAY, THE DAY GOD RESTED. I GREW UP ON FOURTH STREET. 207 4TH STEET, N E, PIPESTONE, MN. THE SIGNIFICANCE OF '207' IS THE SECOND (2) OF SEVEN (7). I AM THE SECOND BORN OF SEVEN.

MY CREATED NAME IS MEZZECHAH, THE NAME WRITTEN IN THE LAMB'S BOOK OF LIFE. IF GOD CAN NAME ALL THE STARS AS HE CREATED THEM, HE CAN NAME ME. I HAVE MY WHITE STONE, MY NAME IS ON IT. A FRIEND GAVE ME A PLANT MANY YEARS AGO, IT IS "MOTHER OF A THOUSAND", DO YOU KNOW THAT PLANT? I AM MOTHER OF THOUSANDS. GENESIS 24:60. SCRIPTURE SAYS THOUSANDS OF MILLIONS. I HAD A LOT OF PRACTICE VIA MANY ASSIGNMENTS AND PRACTICE, TO BE THE PERFECT MOMMY FOR BABY JESUS. JESUS IS MINE, MY LITTLE PRINCE, BUT NOW MY KING OF KINGS. I AM OF THE TRIBE OF JUDAH, 4TH GENERATION FROM ABRAHAM, 4TH SON OF JACOB. THIS IS THE LINEAGE OF JESUS.

I DID BEGIN THIS LATEST LEARNING PATH IN 2014. EARLY MORNING, MARCH 14,2014, HE (GOD) SAID "I WILL SHAKE THE EARTH FOR YOU, AND HE DID", FOUR DAYS LATER. MARCH 17, 2014, EARLY MORNING IN W. LOS ANGELES EARTHQUAKE 4.4

MAGNITUDE. I DID CALL MY BROTHER TO TELL HIM WHAT HAPPENED, HIS RESPONSE WAS "WHO DO YOU THINK YOU ARE"? HE, I THOUGHT, WOULD BE INTERESTED SINCE I THOUGHT HE WAS A CHRISTIAN, HE WAS ANGRY. WE DON'T HAVE MUCH TO TALK ABOUT ANY MORE, HMMMM, I WONDER WHY? GO AHEAD AND GOOGLE IT, THE 4.4. FOUR IS THE TRINITY AND ME. IS THAT HARD TO UNDERSTAND? THAT'S A LOT OF FOURS, HUH. THERE ARE A LOT OF FOURS IN THE SCRIPTURES. GOD LOVES THE NUMBER FOUR. GOD LOVES ME. HE LOVES ALL OF HIS CHILDREN. YOU HAVE AN ASSIGNMENT, DO YOUR BEST.

WHEN HE CAME, I SCREAMED AND CRIED, WHEN HE DIED, I SCREAMED AND CRIED. YOU READ TILL YOU FALL ASLEEP, I WANT YOU TO READ TILL YOU WAKE UP. WHEN HE SITS ME DOWN TO WRITE FOR HIM, I AM HIS TO USE. I AM HIS, ALWAYS.

HOW LONG O LORD?

WE, IT SEEMS, HAVE BEEN WAITING FOR SO LONG FOR THE RETURN OF OUR SAVIOR. MOST ARE GETTING SO IMPATIENT. ME TOO. I GUESS BECAUSE THE WORLD IS SO MESSED UP. SO MANY HIDEOUS GOINGS ON OUT THERE. WE ARE SO FED UP WITH ALL THE WARS, AND SO MANY PEOPLE DYING, NEEDLESSLY. THE HORROR OF THE INSANE DOING STUFF THAT JUST BAFFLES THE MIND. YES, I HAVE ASKED MANY TIMES "HOW LONG O LORD? HE, SOMETIMES WILL ANSWER. BE PATIENT. I WILL COME AT THE APPROPRIATE TIME. MY OWN HAVE ASKED OF ME FOR MANY YEARS, WANTING TO KNOW WITH DESPERATION THE DAY OF THE LORD. THE DAY WE WILL HEAR THE TRUMPET AND HE WILL DESCEND FROM HEAVEN TO GATHER HIS OWN. I AM SOMETIMES IN WONDER, ASKING "WHY SO LONG O' LORD"? CHILDREN BEING KILLED BY ABORTION, CHILDREN AS VICTIMS OF STREET KILLINGS. IT'S AN UNTHINKABLE CRIME. I DO KNOW THEY ARE INNOCENT AND WILL IMMEDIATELY WITH THE FATHER IN HEAVEN. THEY DO NOT HAVE UNDERSTANDING YET, THOUGH THEY SUFFER, OR NOT. YOU KNOW THEY ARE NOT ABLE TO GRASP THE MEANING OF SUCH HORROR. I SAY THAT THEY MUST BE SAYING "WHY ME, WHAT DID I DO"? SO INNOCENT. EVEN THE ADULTS WHO ARE KILLED BY SOME CRAZY MUST ENQUIRE 'WHY ME'? HOW DO YOU ANSWER THEIR CRIES? I KNOW THEY ARE WITH YOU IN THEIR INNOCENCE. WHEN I SEE IT OR JUST HEAR ABOUT IT, IT GIVES ME THE WILLIES. THEY MUST SO SUFFER WAITING TO GO INTO DEATH. THE ONE WHO PERFORMS THE TRAGIC EVENT MOST LIKELY KILLS HIM/HER SELF AS THEY CAN'T FACE THE AFTERMATH. IT'S THE GREAT POPULATION WHO CRIES OUT "WHAT IS GOD THINKING"? IT'S

NOT GOD, SATAN IS THE CAUSE OF THE HORROR THERE ARE SOME OF US WHO ARE SANE AND CHRISTIANS WHO ARE SOMETIMES ASKING THE SAME QUESTIONS. I LOVE THE BEEJEEBIES OUT OF MY GOD, MY MAKER, MY MOST GLORIOUS HEAVENLY FATHER. I HAVE BEEN ASKED BY SOME WHO ARE NOT OF OUR LORD JESUS CHRIST, UNSAVED, WHY DOES GOD NOT PUT AN END TO THIS HORRENDOUS STUFF? GOD KNOWS AND HE IS IN CHARGE OF ALL THE DETAILS. YOU KNOW I AM IN A PLACE WHERE I AM A CHRISTIAN AND SOME WOULD LIKE TO BEAT ME UP BECAUSE MY FATHER DOESN'T DO SOMETHING ABOUT THE STUFF THAT'S GOING ON. IT'S THE REASONING OF THE WORLD, AS IF I MUST HAVE A PART IN THE TORMENT. WHAT A FRIGHTENING SITUATION. THE WORLD JUST WANTS SOMEONE TO PICK ON OR BLAME OR BEAT'UP ON. I BELIEVE THAT'S BEEN GOING ON SINCE TIME BEGAN. HMMM. I AM HIS TOO AND I DON'T AGREE THAT THESE THINGS SHOULD HAPPEN, BUT IT'S NOT MY FAULT. I DON'T AGREE WITH THE CRAZIES OUT THERE REEKING HAVOC ON THE INNOCENT. I PRAY FOR PEACE AND MERCY ON ALL OF GOD'S OWN. I LOVE ALL OF HIS CHILDREN AND FORGIVE AS HE SAYS, WHEN I AM ABLE, SOMETIMES IT'S TOUGH. I AM TO FORGIVE AS HE HAS FORGIVEN ME, AND THAT'S A WHOLE BUNCH. I HAVEN'T KILLED ANYBODY, BUT I HAVE THOUGHT ABOUT IT. I WOULD HOPE THAT I COULDN'T DO SUCH A THING. THE REAL CHURCH IS AT THE FEET OF JESUS, AND DON'T FORGET IT. IT IS THE REMINDER OF THE PRICE HE PAID FOR MY AND YOUR REDMPTION AND SALVATION. HE WENT TO AN AWFUL DEATH ON THAT CROSS FOR ME, FOR THE WHOLE WORLD. THOUGH THE WHOLE WORLD DOESN'T FESS UP TO THE SACRIFICE OFFERED ON CALVERY, DOESN'T CHANGE WHAT HE DID. IT WILL FOREVER STAND AS THE MOST WONDERFUL THING DONE FOR MANKIND. IT WAS/IS THE MOST GENEROUS ACT OF GOD'S GRACE AND FORGIVENESS. HOW CAN WE NOT GET UP EVERY DAY AND BE REMINDED OF THE DEED AND THANK HIM

FOR HIS GOODNESS. DEAREST GOD, SHOW THE MERCY THAT WAS SHONE TWO THOUSAND YEARS AGO. HE FAVORED ALL OF THE BELIEVERS WHILE JESUS HUNG ON THE CROSS PAYING MY DEBT. WHEN THE PAYMENT WAS FINISHED, HE, JESUS, SAID "IT IS FINISHED". PAID IN FULL. GLORY TO GOD. YES, AND AMEN. JESUS PAID IT ALL, THANK YOU MY PRECIOUS SAVER. NOW THE BEST IS YET TO COME AND I AM SO THRILLED THAT AT LAST, WE WILL SEE OUR SAVIOR FACE TO FACE. O' WHAT A DAY OF REJOICING THAT WILL BE. O' HALLELUJAH, LETS ALL BOW AND BLESSS THE KING OF KINGS AND LORD OF LORDS. WE WILL ALL WORSHIP, WE WILL SHOUT HALLELUJAH, WITHOUT END, FOREVER. GOD HAS A PLAN AND WON'T CHANGE IT. AMEN.

I WAS WITH GOD 18,000 YRS AGO, AFTER CREATION. I WAS WITH GOD 13,000 YRS AGO, DURING CREATION. I WAS WITH GOD 6,000 YRS AGO, AFTER SECOND CREATION. 2,000 YRS AGO I GAVE BIRTH TO HIS SON. I HAVE BEEN IN AND OUT OF THIS WORLD MANY TIMES IN THE LAST 6,000 YRS.

THE OFFERED AND THE SACRIFICE

OFFERED. HMM? IS THAT THE SAME AS A SACRIFICE. NOT NECESSARLY. TO OFFER IS GENEROUS. IF YOU PUT MONEY IN THE PLATE ON SUNDAY MORNING, IT'S AN OFFERING. TO OFFER A SACRIFICE IS A LITTLE MORE EXPENSIVE. TO SACRIFICE IN THE SCRIPTURE IS TO KILL, USUALLY AN ANIMAL. OUR LORD WAS A SACRIFICE, HE WENT TO THE CROSS, AND WAS KILLED. HE WAS A SACRIFICE FOR THE WHOLE WORLD. HIS BLOOD WAS SHED AND HE WAS KILLED FOR A WORLD BURIED IN SIN. TO BE FORGIVEN FOR YOUR SIN THERE MUST BE A DEATH. BLOOD MUST BE SHED. THAT IS OLD TESTAMENT. IN THE DAYS OF OLD THE SINNER WOULD BRING A LAMB OR SOME VALUED CRITTER TO BE KILLED AS PAYMENT FOR FORGIVENESS. IT SOMETIMES WOULD DEPEND ON THE WEALTH OF THE SINNER. GOD OFFERED HIS SON TO BE THE SACRIFICE FOR THE WHOLE WORLD. NOT ALL AGREED WITH THAT. I DO ACCEPT THAT BECAUSE IT WAS LONG BEFORE I CAME INTO THIS WORLD. ALL MY SIN WAS FORGIVEN BEFORE I KNEW WHAT WAS GOING ON. I AM SO HAPPY WITH THAT DECISION MADE BY MY LORD. I, HOWEVER, DIDN'T UNDERSTAND WHAT ALL THAT MEANT. I JUST HAD TO BELIEVE, AND I DID. I DID GIVE JESUS MY HEART LONG AGO. I GREW UP UNDER THE TEACHING OF THE BIBLE, AND GLADLY SO. THERE ARE SERVICES IN CHURCH WHERE PARENTS BRING THEIR CHILDREN TO OFFER THEM TO THE LORD. THAT IS TO SAY WE WILL GROW OUR CHILDREN TO SERVE THE LORD. MOST, IF NOT ALL, REALLY MEAN IT. THEY CALL IT DEDICATION TO GOD. IT'S AN OFFERING. SOMEWHERE ALONG THE WAY THEY LOST THE WILL TO LIVE FOR THE FATHER AND HIS SON. TOO BAD. ALL CHILDREN SHOULD BE DEDICATED TO

GOD SO AS TO GROW UP IN THE ADMONITION OF THE LORD. BUT THEN, YOU MUST FOLLOW UP WITH HOW GOD WANTS THE LITTLE ONES TRAINED. IT'S A LIFETIME OF DOING IT GOD'S WAY. IT'S NOT THAT HARD, JUST DO IT. BLESS HIS HOLY NAME. WHAT IF YOU RAISE UP A CHILD WHO WILL NOT BE A TROUBLED SOLE. STAYING IN THE GOOD GRACES OF GOD. YOU REALLY DO WANT A CHILD DEDICATED TO A WHOLESOME LIFE. IF YOU TRULY LOVE THAT YOUNGSTER, YOU WILL TEACH THEM TO FOLLOW A RIGHT PATH. WALK THE STAIGHT AND NARROW IS A GOOD THING. FOLLOW THE PATH TO A GOOD LIFE. THERE ARE PEOPLE ON BOTH SIDES OF THE ROAD. SOME COME UP IN SPITE OF THE WAY THEY ARE RAISED. IF YOU LOVE THEM SHOW THEM THE RIGHT WAY. GET A BIBLE AND FOLLOW THEIR IN. PUT THEM IN GOOD (GOD) HANDS. THEY MAY TELL YOU A STORY FROM THE BIBLE, WHERE JESUS DISOBEYED HIS PARENTS AND GOT IN TROUBLE. HE WAS TO GO HOME WITH THEM BUT FELT HE WANTED TO HANG BACK TO TALK WITH THE HOLY MEN IN THE TEMPLE. HE WAS SCOLDED BY HIS PARENTS BECAUSE OF BAD COMMUNICATION. THEY ALL SURVIVED, THO. HE WAS KNOWN AS THE LAMB OF GOD WHO TAKES AWAY THE SIN OF THE WORLD. AND HE WAS AND STILL IS. HE WAS AS PEACEFUL AS A BABY SHEEP, A LAMB. SO, SO BEAUTIFUL. NOW LET'S GET THE WHOLE HOUSEHOLD SAVED. CONFESS HIM AS THE LORD OF YOUR HEART AND LIFE. DO GET BAPTIZED IN THE WATER AND IN THE HOLY GHOST WITH EVIDENCE OF SPEAKING IN OTHER TONGUES. GET ALL IN. DO IT. THAT'S JUST THE BEGINNING, NOW LIVE IT. JESUS WILL WALK WITH YOU AND YOU WILL HEAR HIS VOICE. IT'S A GOTTA DO. JUST DO IT, PLEASE. I AM A BORN'AGAIN AND THAT'S WHAT I WANT FOR MY WHOLE FAMILY, MY NEIGHBOR, THE MAIL MAN, ALL THE WHOSOEVERS. DO NOT RISK HELL, WITH ALL THE LOVE AROUND YOU. GO AND GROW WITH JESUS. YOU COULD LEAD A WHOLE BUNCH OF PEOPLE TO THE LORD. THEY WILL LOVE YOU FOR IT. MY SUNDAY

SCHOOL TEACHER TAUGHT ME MORE THAN ANY. THANK YOU, MRS. CHANEY. CAN'T WAIT TO SEE YOU. WE ARE ALL BORN AS BAPTISTS BUT NOW I AM PENTECOSTAL. HAVE I BENT YOUR EAR LONG ENOUGH. DON'T BE ONE WHO IS LOST. JESUS LOVES YOU AND IS PLEADING WITH YOU TO COME INTO THE KINGDOM OF GOD. SALVATION IS FREE, BORN'AGAIN IS FREE, SO NOW JUST DO IT. YOU WILL BE SO GLAD WITH YOUR CHOICE. JESUS IS THE BEST CHOICE.

YOU MUST BE BORN AGAIN, INTO THE KINGDOM OF GOD.
IT'S ALL FREE. HE'S WAITING FOR YOU.
O' LAMB OF GOD, I COME TO YOU. I COME. AMEN.

SHEPHERD OF THE WORLD

I AM THE GOOD SHEPHERD: THE GOOD SHEPHERD GIVETH HIS LIFE FOR THE SHEEP. JOHN 10:11

WE ALL KNOW WHO THIS IS. CAN YOU GUESS WHO IT IS? IF YOU SAY THAT IT IS THE SAVIOR SENT FROM HEAVEN, YOU ARE SO RIGHT. THE WONDERFUL SHEPHERD SENT BY GOD SAW THAT THE WHOLE WORLD WAS TURNING TO IDOLS FOR WORSHIP. THEY WERE MAKING OR HAVING IDOLS MADE BY IDOL MAKERS TO PROTECT THEIR HOMES OR DWELLINGS BY MEN WHO HAD BUSINESSES TO CREATE IDOLS TO PLEASE THE RELIGIOUS PUBLIC. WHAT EVER THE WORSHIPPER WANTED. WOOD, STONE, GOLD, SILVER, MADE TO THE SPECIFICATIONS ACCORDING TO WHAT THE CUSTOMER WANTED. YOU NAME IT, THEY WOULD MAKE IT. THEY WOULD USE THEIR IMAGINATION TO COME UP WITH THE WILDEST THINGS. THE IDOL MAKERS WERE UP FOR PLEASING THE ORDER OF THE CUSTOMERS WILDEST VISIONS. WHAT WAS SOMETIMES VERY FRIGHTENING WAS WHAT THEY WOULD ASK FOR. IT WAS TO SCARE AWAY DEMONS OR TO INVITE DEMONS INTO THERE HOMES. IT MAY BE TO BRING FAVOR OR NOT. THE THOUGHT GIVES ME THE WILLIES. SOME MADE IDOLS TO WELCOME FAVORITE GODS OF GOOD FORTUNE. NAME IT AND CLAIM IT. IF THE NEIGHBORS HAD A BIG IDOL THE BUYER WOULD ASK FOR A BIGGER IDOL. THEY WOULD TRY TO OUT DO EACH OTHER. I BELIEVE THAT THE FOUR HUNDRED YEARS (?) BETWEEN THE OLD AND NEW TESTAMENT WAS A TIME FOR THE IDOL MAKER TO BE VERY BUSY WITH THEIR TRADE. THE PEOPLE LOST SIGHT OF THE GOD OF HEAVEN AND LOST FAVOR OF HIM ALSO. MY GOD WAS QUIET FOR A TIME, PROBABLY NOT SO PLEASED THAT HIS WONDERFUL CREATION TURNED AWAY FROM WORSHIP AND DIDN'T HAVE A NEED FOR THE GOD OF

HEAVEN. I AM SURE OUR WONDERFUL GOD OF HEAVEN MUST HAVE LEFT OFF WATCHING THIS 'ON GOING' CIRCUS. HIS WONDERFUL MAN WAS TURNING HIS BACK ON THE CREATOR FOR AN UGLY STATUE TO BOW DOWN TO. OF COURSE, MANY WENT TO THEIR GRAVES NEVER RETURNING TO THE GOD OF HEAVEN. MOST PROBABLY, THEY WERE BURIED WITH THEIR IDOLS. I BELIEVE THAT THERE IS STILL A MARKET FOR IDOLS. PROBABLY NOT AS BEFORE. THE NEED TODAY IS A LITTLE BIT MORE SOPHISTICATED. THERE ARE CARS, YACHTS, SOUND SYSTEMS, THE GREATEST CELL PHONES, REALLY WONDERFUL SPORTING EQUITMENT. WHAT EVER DRIVES THEIR FANCY. GOD DOESN'T GIVE UP THOUGH, HE IS SO PATIENT. HE STILL IS WAITING FOR THE RETURN OF HIS BELOVEDS. HE IS ETERNAL SO HE CAN OUT'WAIT, EVEN OUT LIVE ALL OF THE ABOVE. HIS SON IS THE GOOD SHEPHERD OF THE WHOLE WORLD. HE IS THE ONE WHO GOD PUT IN PLACE TWO THOUSAND YEARS AGO. I, BTW, WAS THE ONE HE CHOSE TWO THOUSAND YEARS AGO TO BIRTH HIS SON. WHAT A GIFT. HE HAD TO GIVE HIS SON TO SHEPHERD HIS PEOPLE BACK TO HIM. JESUS, GOD'S BELOVED IS THE GOOD SHEPHERD. MY WRITES ARE AN EXTENTION OF SCRIPTURE. THE WALL THAT ALL GATHER TO IN JERUSALEM IS A LEFTOVER OF THE IDOL AGE. THEY STILL GO TO THE WALL AND BOW, A REALLY BIG IDOL. THEY WRITE NOTES TO LEAVE WITH THE IDOL. READ EZE 38:20. GOD DID TAKE THE ARK OF THE COVENANT TO HEAVEN, AS NOT TO LET IT BECOME AN IDOL. READ REVELATION 11:19 ON MARCH 14, 2014 HE TOLD ME HE WOULD SHAKE THE EARTH FOR ME AND HE DID. FOUR DAYS LATER, ON MARCH 17, 2014 HE DID, THERE WAS AN EARTHQUAKE, THE MAGNITUDE WAS 4.4. THE SIGNIFICANCE IS THE 4. I AM THE FOURTH MEMBER OF THE TRINITY. HE HAD TO GIVE HIS SON TO SHEPHERD HIS PEOPLE BACK TO HIMSELF. THAT IS A LOT TO TAKE IN, TO WRAP YOUR HEAD AROUND. OUR GOD IS IN CHARGE, STAY WITH HIM. HE WILL BRING YOU TO THE EXPECTED END. I WAS CREATED ON

THE FOURTH DAY, I AM MY DADDY'S LITTLE STAR. HE DID REACH OUT TO THE EDGE OF THE UNIVERSE TO TAKE A LITTLE PIECE OF DUST FROM A STAR FOR MY CREATION ON THE FOURTH DAY. I AM A BELOVED OF MY FATHER AND SO GRATEFULL FOR HIM. ALL THIS INFORMATION CAME FROM ABOVE TO EDIFY (PROVE) THE INFORMATION HE HAS GIVEN ME. WE ARE BEING TAUGHT ALL THIS SO TO BETTER UNDERSTAND THE GOODNESS OF GOD. AS I SIT TO LISTEN OF ALL HIS WISDOM, I HEARD LOVE THAT IS ETERNAL, THAT WILL NEVER GIVE UP ON HIS BELOVED'S CREATION. YOU ARE SO SPECIAL TO THE FATHER, SO HE SENT THE GOOD SHEPHERD, HIS BELOVED SON TO YOUR RESCUE, SAVE YOU. THE ONLY SHEPHERD HE COULD TRUST TO BRING HIS LAMBS INTO THE FOLD, HIS REDEMPTION AND SALVATION.

HE LOVES YOU SO LOVE HIM BACK. HE DID SO LOVE THE WORLD THAT HE GAVE HIS ONLY BEGOTTEN SON, THAT WHOSOEVER BELIEVES IN HIM SHALL NOT PARISH, BUT HAVE EVERLASTING LIFE. HE TRULY IS THE SHEPHERD OF THE WHOLE WORLD. YES, AND AMEN.

GOD INTOXICATED

DRUNK WITH THE HOLY WINE OF THE TRIUNE GOD, FATHER, SON AND HOLY GHOST, HIS PRESENCE AND HIS ESSENCE

YE HAVE NOT YET RESISTED UNTO BLOOD. I, MEZZECHAH, ANCHOR OF MY SOUL, OF MELCHIZEDEK ALSO ANCHOR OF THE SOUL. I AM AN ANCHORITE, NO. I HAVE MY WHITE STONE. I AM ALONE MOST OF THE TIME, SO I SPEND A LOT OF TIME TALKING TO THE FATHER OR JESUS OR THE HOLY GHOST. I HAVE WRITTEN MANY WRITES, JUST FROM SITTING DOWN AND LISTENING TO WHAT HE HAS TO SAY. HIS BREATH IS SO REFRESHING. TASTE HIM AND SEE HOW GOOD HE IS. HIS/MY WRITE "I WANT TO KNOW ALL YOUR SECRETS" IS RICH WITH SURPRISES. HIS INTERPRETATION OF MY PRAYER LANGUAGE, SO BEAUTIFUL. NO ONE WILL EVER LOVE US THE WAY JESUS LOVES. HE HUNG ON THAT CROSS BECAUSE HE LOVES. THANK YOU, JESUS. HE LOVES, WHY CAN'T WE JUST LOVE HIM BACK? SAY "I LOVE YOU TOO, JESUS". NOW SAY IT AND MEAN IT. HE TRUELY MUST HAVE MENT IT. I BELIEVE HE DID. SO, I HAVE MANY TIMES ASKED TO BE TRANSLATED. I SAY "CAN I COME HOME"? NOT YET. O PLEASE. AMEN. I HAVE COMPLETED ALL MY ASSIGNMENTS, AND TIME IS NO MORE. HOMEWORK, FINISHED. I WANT THE PLEASURE OF HIS COMPANY, WITH NO INTERRUPTIONS. TO JUST SIT AT HIS FEET AND LOOK INTO HIS FACE. WALK AND TALK WITH HIM. ENTER INTO HIS REST FOR ALL ETERNITY. DEEP CALLETH UNTO DEEP. BEFORE TIME AND THOUSANDS OF YEARS AGO, WHEN I WAS IN THE DEEP, IN HIS PRESENCE AND ESSENCE, HE GAVE ME TO KNOW HIS GLORY AND HIS MARVELOUS BEAUTY. THE LIGHT OF HIS BEING CAME IN TO EXISTENCE AT HIS COMMAND. THEN CREATION WAS PRONOUNCED ON THE EARTH. HIS GLORY ALL AROUND AND NONE OF IT HAD ANYTHING DO WITH MAN. AMAZING HOW

HE THOUGHT HE NEEDED TO CREATE FLESH AND BONES TO CARE FOR PERFECTION. THIS IS WHERE THE SAYING "WHATEVER WAS I THINKING" CAME FROM. O, HOW I LOVE HIM! I WORSHIP HIM. HIS INNOCENT PERFECTION HANDED OVER TO WILLFUL FLESH. UNABLE TO BREAK HIS WORD, HE WATCHED AS HIS GARDEN WAS ABANDONED BECAUSE OF WANTON DISOBEDIENCE. CHERUBIMS AND A FLAMING SWORD GUARDING THE WAY TO KEEP THE TREE OF LIFE. AMEN. HEARTBROKEN AND/BUT NOT TO GIVE UP, HE LOVES HIS MAN WITH GREAT PASSION SO HE MAKES A PLAN OF REDEMPTION. HE OFFERS HIS ONLY BEGOTTEN PRECIOUS SON, SPOTLESS LAMB, SACRIFICE OF THE AGES. IF ONLY WE WILL ACCEPT HIS JESUS AS FULL PAYMENT, RETURN TO OUR GOD OF LOVE, WALK IN HIS TRUTH AND LIGHT, WE WILL CERTAINLY ENTER IN TO THE GARDEN OF THE TREE OF LIFE. THAT'S HIS DESIRE FOR ALL. SO SIMPLE. DUMP THE PRIDE AND WE CAN ALL GO HOME. I'M READY! IS HE WONDERFUL, OR WHAT?

DEDICATE TO ME YOUR BEAUTY, SWEET HOLY SPIRIT,
SO BE IT BY THE HOLY GHOST, AMONEE TRIESS
DEEP CALLETH UNTO DEEP, I KNOW THE DAY
PRESENCE (PRECEIVED IMPRESSION), ESSENCE (POWER).

THE LIGHT OF THE WORLD

I AM THE LIGHT OF THE WORLD: HE THAT FOLLOWETH ME SHALL NOT WALK IN DARKNESS, BUT SHALL HAVE THE LIGHT OF LIFE. JOHN 8:12
AS LONG AS I AM IN THE WORLD, I AM THE LIGHT OF THE WORLD. JOHN 9:5

MY WONDERFUL JESUS. HE IS INDEED, THE LIGHT OF THE WORLD. WE ARE NO LONGER LOST IN THE DARKNESS. HE WAS ANOINTED BY HIS FATHER TO SHINE AND LIGHT UP THE DARKNESS OF THE WORLD. WE WERE NOT INVITED TO THAT CEREMONY, PROBABLY BECAUSE IT WAS HELD IN THE HEAVENS OVER THIRTEEN THOUSAND YEARS AGO. READ THE BEGINNING OF GENESIS. HE (GOD) SAID "LET THERE BE LIGHT" AND THERE WAS LIGHT. GEN 1:3. THAT WAS THE INTRODUCTION OF THE LORD JESUS CHRIST, TRULY AND FOR SURE, HE IS THE LIGHT OF THE WHOLE WORLD. ISN'T HE GOOD AND SO PRECIOUS. AREN'T WE BLESSED? WE SURE ARE. HOW LONG WOULD WE FUMBLE AROUND IN THE DARK IF HE WASN'T WITH US EVERY DAY? I CLAIM EVERY DAY THAT HE IS WITH ME AS AN EXCEEDINGLY, WONDERFUL DAY. HE MAKES THE DAY. SOME PREFER THE DARK AS THEY WANT TO HIDE THEIR WORKS. THERE WAS A DAY WHEN MANY LIVED IN THE DARKNESS. THE LORD WAS THE FARTHEST FROM THEIR THINKING. SOME WANTED HIM GONE AND IT WAS THEIR DESIRE TO ACCUSE HIM OF BREAKING AND DISOBEDIENT TO THE WORD OF GOD. THEY WERE SO UNDONE BY HIS GOODNES. HEALING ON THE SABBATH, WHAT A REBEL. NEVER MIND THE BLIND, SEE, THE DEAF, HEAR, THE BROKEN, HEALED, THE LOST, SAVED. TO US WHO KNOW AND LOVE HIM, IT SOUNDS SO GLORIOUS, BUT THEY SAID IT WAS WORK AND FORBIDDEN TO BE DONE ON THE SABBATH. HE SAID, "IF YOUR OX FALLS INTO A PIT DO YOU RESCUE IT INSPITE OF THE DAY? THEY SOMETIMES WOULD CHANGE THEIR MIND JUST TO BENEFIT THEMSELVES. IF JESUS HAD DONE THE DEED, WELL THAT'S

NOT ACCEPTABLE. THEY JUST DIDN'T LIKE HIM. IT WAS ALSO BECAUSE HE SAID HE WAS THE "SON OF GOD" AND THAT REALLY TICKED THEM OFF. THEY MADE UP THEIR MINDS, HE'S GOT TO GO. THEY BEGAN TO FIND FAULT WITH EVERYTHING HE DID. I AM SURE THEY HAD SOME WHO WERE ON PURPOSE TO FOLLOW AND WATCH HIM SO AS TO ACCUSE HIM OF WRONG DOING. I AM SO GLAD TO KNOW HIM. THIS WORLD SO NEEDS MY JESUS, YES AND AMEN. AS FOR THE WORLD TODAY, HMMM. THERE ARE THOSE WHO JUST CAN'T DO IT. JESUS WHO? THE SON OF GOD, YES, THAT'S WHAT HE CLAIMS. WELL, HE ONLY TOLD THE TRUTH. SO, THEY WENT ABOUT TO CATCH HIM IN A LIE BUT THAT WAS NOT POSSIBLE, HE ONLY SPOKE THE TRUTH. SINCE THAT TIME WHEN JESUS WALKED THE EARTH, WE HAVE BEEN INCREASING IN HIS LOVE FOR ALL OF GOD'S OWN. WE DO INDEED, LOVE OUR NEIGHBOR AND ALL WHO WALK WITH US, THE PEOPLE NEXT DOOR OR AT CHURCH. WE REGULARLY DO INVENTORY OF HOW WE ARE LIVING HOW THE BIBLE SAYS TO DO. WE NEED TO BE AWARE OF OUR SAVIOR'S GOODNESS AND PRACTICE HOW HE LOVED AND LIVED. I WANT TO BE JUST LIKE MY JESUS, DO AS MY JESUS WOULD DO. IT TAKES AND IS NECESSARY TO WATCH OUT THAT WE DON'T FALL BACK INTO SIN. LIFE CAN BE A CHALLENGE WHEN WE NEED AND WANT TO FOLLOW JESUS.THE BIBLE SAYS TO FOLLOW HIM AND IMITATE HIM, AND I AGREE. BEING LIKE OUR JESUS WINS IT EVERYTIME AND I BELIEVE THE REWARD IS WORTH THE TIME AS WAS PROMISED. I SO LOOK FORWARD TO SEE HIM AND WALK WITH HIM, HOLD HIS HAND AND SHARE STORIES WITH HIM FROM WHEN HE WAS ON EARTH. HE PROBABLY HAS A FEW STORIES TO SHARE THAT MISSED THE PAGES OF THE SCRIPTURES. HE IS SO WONDERFUL AND HE KNOWS WE TREASURE HIM AS GOLD AND PRECIOUS JEWELS. HE IS MY TREASURE, WORTHY OF ALL PRAISE AND ADORATION. HE IS THE LIGHT OF THE WORLD. I SO LOVE TO WRITE AND TALK ABOUT HIM. HE IS PLEASED

WHEM WE SPEND TIME IN PRAYER, TALKING WITH HIM, SOAKING UP HIS RADIANCE, ENJOYING THE LIGHT THAT COMES FROM THE FACE OF JESUS. WHEN WE HEAR THE TRUMPETS SOUND AND WE ALL LOOK UP TO SEE OUR JESUS COMING IN THE CLOUDS, WHAT A DAY OF REJOICING THAT WILL BE. THAT'S A PROMISE FORM OUR DADDY, AND I AM ALL IN TO GET ALL THAT WAS PROMISED FROM THE FOUNDATION OF THE WORLD. I HAVE BEEN WITH HIM FOR EIGHTEEN THOUSAND YEARS AND EXPECT TO SPEND ANOTHER EIGHTEEN THOUSAND YEARS WITH HIM, OR MORE IF I CAN. HE KNOWS AND WILL SEE TO IT THAT I GET WHAT I WANT. WE HAVE ETERNITY PROMISED. WRITE? YES, AND AMEN. ALL MY WRITES GO BACK TO THE DAYS THAT WERE OF MOTHER AND SON. WHEN I WAS 12 YEARS OLD, HE (G0D, VIA THE HOLY GHOST) STOOD ME STILL IN THE DINING ROOM OF OUR HOME IN PIPESTONE, MINNESOTA TO TELL ME I AM THE FOURTH MEMBER OF THE TRINITY. I AM. I HAVE KNOWN THAT FOR SIXTY-EIGHT YEARS AND NOW TELLING ALL WHO WILL HEAR. IT'S IN MOST OF MY WRITES. IT IS SO. I AM HIS, HE IS MINE, IT WILL BE THAT WAY TILL THE END OF TIME. MY VERY PRECIOUS SON. I AM THE MOTHER OF THE LORD JESUS CHRIST. DO YOU WANT TO DEBATE WHAT GOD TOLD ME OVER SIXTY YEARS AGO? PROBABLY NOT. WHY DON'T YOU GO TO THE FATHER AND ENQUIRE WHAT HE TOLD ME? HE WILL FILL YOU IN AND IT WILL BE THE ABSOLUTE TRUTH. YOU DO KNOW THAT IT IS IMPOSSIBLE FOR GOD TO LIE, DON'T YOU? WELL, HAVE AT IT. SCRIPTURE SAYS IT IS TRUTH AND ONLY TRUTH THAT COMES FROM THE FATHER AND GOD OF ALL CREATION. IT'S ACTUALLY REALLY GOOD TO HAVE A WORD OR TWO WITH GOD EVERYDAY, IF THAT FITS YOUR SCHEDULE. I SUGGEST YOU FIT HIM IN, HE LOVES TO CONVERSE WITH YOU. JUST THINK WHAT YOU COULD LEARN FORM THE WISDOM THAT FLOWS FROM HIM. IT WOULD DO YOU WELL TO DO IT EVERY DAY. HE HAS BEEN WAITING FOR YOU TO COME FOR A

WHILE, NOW. DO YOU EVER FEEL THE NEED TO HEAR FROM HIM WHEN THINGS GET OUT OF STEP AND YOU MAY STUMBLE? I'VE BEEEN THERE A TIME OR TWO, I NEED TO CONVERSE WITH HIM DAILY. WHAT A DIFFERENCE IT MAKES. HE CAN CHANGE THE MUSIC THAT FLOWS FROM YOUR HEART TO YOU THINKING, YES AND AMEN. GOD'S SON, AS YOU KNOW IS THE LIGHT OF THE WORLD. YOU KNOW NOW. TAKE ADVANTAGE OF THE WISDOM FLOWING FROM THE LIGHT OF THE WORLD. "JESUS", PRECIOUS JESUS. GET THAT BIBLE OUT AND DO A FEW STUDIES ON THE LIGHT OF THE WORLD. TIME WELL SPENT. DO YOU KNOW THAT I AM ALSO ONE WHO LOVES TO STUDY THE LIGHT OF THE WORLD. MY BELOVED SAVIOR AND SON. I HAVE BEEN GIVEN SUCH A WONDERFUL PLACE IN THIS WORLD. HE (GOD) IS THE THE GOD AND FATHER AND ALL CREATION, AND HAS CHOSEN ME TO BE PART OF THE TRINITY, YES, I AM THE FOURTH MEMBER OF THE TRINITY. I DO NOT BOAST OF HIS CHOICE, IT WAS HIS CHOOSING TO PUT ME WHERE I AM. I AM SO GRATEFUL FOR MY DADDY. YES, HE IS MY DADDY. THAT'S NOT WRONG TO CALL GOD, MY FATHER, DADDY. HE SAID HE LIKES IT. WE ARE FAMILY AND I LIKE IT. HMMMM I DO TEND TO GO ON WHEN THE CONVERSATION COME TO MY HEAVENLY FAMILY. I BETTER MOVE ON TO THE NEXT WRITE. I GET STARTED AND HAVE TROUBLE ENDING. THANK YOU FOR YOUR PATIENCE. AMEN AND AMEN.

NOT GOD FIRST, GOD ONLY. HE WILL BE ONLY OR HE WONT BE ANY.

I WAS WITH GOD 18,000 YEARS AGO, BEFORE CREATION. I WAS WITH GOD 13,000 YEARS AGO, DURING CREATION. I WAS WITH GOD 6,000 YEARS AGO, AFTER CREATION. TWO THOUSAND YEARS AGO I GAVE BIRTH TO HIS SON. I HAVE BEEN IN AND OUT OF THIS WORLD MANY TIMES IN THE LAST 6,000 YEARS. MY ASSIGNMENTS.

**** ONLY YOU, JESUS ****

WHERE ELSE COULD I GO BUT TO THE LORD. WHEN I NEED HELP, HE IS THE ONLY ONE. HE, THE ONE TO LISTEN TO MY HEARTACHE. HE IS THE ONLY ONE WHO CAN HEAR AND HELP. I GO TO THE FLOOR, PUT MY FACE TO THE FLOOR AND HAVE AN INTIMATE TALK WITH HIM. HE JUST LISTENS TO MY BROKEN HEART. IF ANYBODY CAN HELP, HE CAN. HE HAS BEEN THE 'GO TO' ONE SINCE I WAS BORN AGAIN. WELL, I TAKE THAT BACK. HE WAS THE "GO TO" ONE WELL BEFORE I WAS BORN AGAIN, LIKE THOUSANDS OF YEARS BEFORE. THERE IS NO NEED TO FUSS AND COMPLAIN. HE IS WITH YOU, JUST CALL OUT TO JESUS AND HE IS THERE AND READY TO FIX THE ONE IN TROUBLE, OR FEELING DEFEATED. HE WILL ALWAYS ANSWER. ONLY JESUS. DON'T YOU JUST LOVE HIM, ME TOO. WE WALK AROUND, IN AND OUT OF MANY SITUATIONS, UNAWARE OF THE ONE LOOKING FOR A GOD'S BELOVED, SATAN. A CHANCE TO MESS WITH WHOEVER IS CLOSE AND READY FOR THE EVIL ONE TO SET UP A LYING GAIN. I WILL BE IN PRAYER IN THE MORNING, CLAIMING THE LORD TO WALK WITH ME THRU THE WHOLE DAY. WE ARE IN AGREEMENT AND THE SUN (SON) IS SHINING. I MUST ONLY ALLOW JESUS TO WALK WITH ME, HE IS WAITING FOR AN INVITATION. HE'S ON MY SIDE. I IMAGINE HOW IT WILL BE WHEN HE, MY JESUS, COMES TO TAKE ME HOME. I AM CONTINUELY LISTENING FOR THE TRUMPET TO SOUND. I AM SURE I AM NOT THE ONLY ONE. WHEN WE COME TOGETHER ON SUNDAY FOR CHURCH, WE DO FILL THE AIR WITH PRAISE AND WORSHIP. I SO LOVE TO GO TO CHURCH. THE FRIENDS AND PEW WARMERS ARE SO WELCOMED TO JOIN IN ON THE WONDERFUL WORSHIP SERVICE, WHEN JESUS JOINS THE SERVICE, WE REALLY GET

INTO WORSHIP. WE REALLY DO HARMANIZE WHEN WE SING TO AND WITH OUR LORD. I SO LOVE TO SING TO HIM. SOMETIMES I IMAGINE THAT I HEAR JESUS JOIN INTO THE SERVICE AND THAT'S THE CHIOR WHOM HE DIRECTS. WE LOOK FORWARD TO THE MEET AND GREET OUT ON THE PATIO. I SO LOVE TO WATCH THE LITTLE ONES PLAY. THERE ARE GAMES FOR THE WEE TOTS TO PLAY AND SOMETIMES THE SENIORS CHALLENGE THE LITTLE ONES. IT'S FAMILY, WE ALL ARE PART OF THE PICNIC AND COFFEE AND TEA AND SODA, WHATEVER FLOATS YOUR BOAT. I KNOW THAT WE NEED TO GET OUT AND EVANGELISE THE NEIGHBORHOOD. WE MUST BRING IN ALL THE LOST AND LONELY. WE JUST CAN'T LET THEM GO. THE DAY WILL COME WHEN WE WILL HEAR THE CALL AND WE MUST BRING IN THE WHOLE WORLD FOR SALVATION. WE JUST CAN'T LET THEM GO. I HAVE TRIED TO TALK TO MY NEIGHBOR WHO IS CATHOLIC, SHE SAYS "O' I AM CATHOLIC AS IF SHE IS FROM ANOTHER PLANET. SOME ARE SO DISTANT AND MUST BE SAVED. GOD DOESN'T CARE ABOUT WHAT YOU ARE AFRAID OF, JUST COME AND SEE. ONE OF THESE DAYS SHE WILL WANT TO COME AND SHE WILL CALL ME TO TAKE HER WITH ME. WHAT A DAY OF REJOICING THAT WILL BE. JUST HAVE TO KEEP PRAYING FOR THE WHOLE CITY. SALVATION IS FOR EVERYBODY. WE MUST BRING THEM IN. WHAT A JOY IT WOULD BE TO SIT WITH A NEW COMER AND SING OUR HEARTS OUT, WOW, WONDERFUL O' WONDERFUL!!! O' JESUS. HOW I LOVE THE DAY OF REST, THE DAY WE ALL COME TOGETHER TO WORSHIP. SUNDAY, THE FIRST DAY OF THE WEEK IS THE DAY THE LORD BLESSED AND WE REST. PLEASE KEEP THE SABBATH, AND GO TO WORSHIP AND JOIN WITH THE OTHERS WHO CAME TO GIVE GOD PRAISE AND WORSHIP. BE SURE YOU HAVE YOUR BIBLE TUCKED UNDER YOUR ARM, READY TO LOCATE THE SCRIPTURE THE PASTOR IS TEACHING. WHAT A BEAUTIFUL AND BLESSED TIME IT IS. I SO LOVE TO HEAR THE SERMON AND MAYBE GO AND SHARE IT

WITH SOMEONE WHO NEEDS TO HEAR THE WORD. GOD'S WORD MUST BE SHARED WITH AS MANY AS YOU HAVE OPPORTUNITY. DO YOU KNOW THAT THE WORD, YES AND YES, THE WORD IS 'JESUS', THE WORD IN THE FLESH, THE WORD OF GOD. AMEN. I WANT EVERYONE TO HEAR THE WORD OF GOD. THERE ARE MANY OUT THERE WHO DO THEIR BEST TO HUSH THE WORD.

YES, SOME WHO DESPISE THE WORD AND WANT TO STOP THE SHARING OR EVANGELIZING OUT IN THE WORLD (OR IN THE MALL). I SAY. IF IT BOTHERS YOU, YOU NEED NOT TO LISTEN, SO MOVE ON. GO AWAY. WE MUST NOT LET THEM PREVENT THE GOSPEL. WRITE??

NOT GOD FIRST, GOD ONLY. HE WILL BE ONLY OR HE WON'T BE ANY. BOW TO HIM. IN HIM ONLY IS RIGHTEOUSNESS, HE IS WORTHY. I HUNGER AND THIRST AFTER HIS RIGHTEOUSNESS. IMPRINT ON ME YOUR LOVE. HE ANSWERED, "I WILL BLESS YOU TO YOUR KNEES". BOW DOWN BEFORE HIM, WORSHIP... AMEN

WHAT GARDEN, WHOSE GARDEN

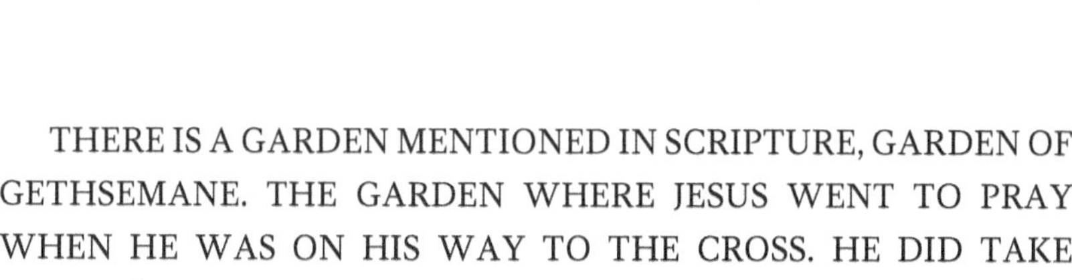

THERE IS A GARDEN MENTIONED IN SCRIPTURE, GARDEN OF GETHSEMANE. THE GARDEN WHERE JESUS WENT TO PRAY WHEN HE WAS ON HIS WAY TO THE CROSS. HE DID TAKE THREE (PETER, JAMES AND JOHN) OF HIS DISCIPLES WITH HIM AND INSTRUCTED THAT THEY WATCH WHILE HE WENT TO PRAY. HE DID ASK THEM TO WATCH, BUT THEN THEY FELL ASLEEP. HE CAME TO THEM AND FOUND THEM SLEEPING. HE DID ASK PETER, COULD YOU NOT WATCH WITH ME FOR ONE HOUR? HE WENT AWAY AGAIN TO PRAY, SAYING TO HIS FATHER," O FATHER, IF THIS CUP MAY NOT PASS AWAY FROM ME, EXCEPT I DRINK IT, THY WILL BE DONE". WHEN HE CAME AGAIN TO THE DISCIPLES, THEY WERE ASLEEP, AGAIN. HE WENT AWAY A THIRD TIME SAYING THE SAME WORDS. WHEN HE CAME BACK, THEY WERE ASLEEP AND HE SAID "SLEEP ON NOW, AND TAKE YOUR REST: BEHOLD, THE HOUR IS IS AT HAND, THE SON OF MAN IS BETRAYED INTO THE HANDS OF SINNERS. RISE, LET US BE GOING: BEHOLD, HE IS AT HAND THAT DOTH BETRAY ME". WHILE HE WAS SPEAKING, JUDAS, ONE OF HIS DISCIPLES CAME WITH A GREAT MULTITUDE HAVING WEAPONS, FROM THE CHIEF PRIESTS AND THE ELDERS OF THE PEOPLE. JUDAS DID BETRAY WITH A SIGN SAYING, HIM WHOSOEVER I SHALL KISS THAT SAME IS HE: HOLD HIM FAST. AND FORTHWITH HE CAME TO JESUS, AND SAID, "HAIL, MASTER" AND KISSED HIM. JESUS DID ASK "WHOM DO YOU SEEK"? THEY ANSWERED HIM, JESUS OF NAZARETH AND WHEN HE ANSWERED THEM "I AM HE" THEY ALL FELL TO THE GROUND. HE TOLD THEM I AM HE, SO LET THESE MEN GO. JESUS WAS BETRAYED WITH A KISS. JESUS DID ASK JUDAS, "FRIEND, WHEREFORE ART THOU COME"? THEY CAME AND

LAID HANDS-ON JESUS, AND TOOK HIM. WE KNOW THAT PETER, ONE OF JESUS' DISCIPLES, DID TAKE A SWORD FROM ONE OF THE SERVENTS OF THE HIGH PRIEST AND CUT OFF THE SERVANTS EAR. JESUS DID REBUKE PETER FOR HIS DOING, THAT IF YOU LIVE BY THE SWORD YOU MAY DIE BY THE SWORD. THEY DID TAKE JESUS AWAY, THEY HAD THE ONE THEY WANTED. ALL THE DISCIPLES RAN AWAY, DIDN'T WANT TO WATCH THE TRIAL OF THEIR LEADER, LEST THEY SUFFER THE SAME PUNISHMENT COMING TO JESUS. DOES IT MAKE YOU WONDER IF YOU WOULD RUN AWAY, TOO? HMMM THAT'S A HARD ONE TO THINK ON. I WOULD HOPE TO THINK I WOULDN'T, BUT I BELIEVE YOU WOULD HAVE TO BE THERE. SOME SAY THE GARDEN OF GETHSEMANE IS THE SAME AS IT WAS TWO THOUSAND YEARS AGO. I DON'T THINK IT IS, BUT WE WON'T DEBATE THAT NOW. JESUS WAS PUT ON TRIAL AFTER THE GARDEN INCIDENT. IT WAS SO HORRIBLE, BUT THAT WAS THE WAY IT WAS TO BE AS IT WAS TOLD IN THE O T. ALL THAT HAPPENED TO OUR JESUS WAS PROPHESIED, PSALM 41:9. WE DO SEE THE THINGS IN OUR SCRIPTURE, NEW TESTAMENT PREDICTED IN THE OLD TESTAMENT. WHENEVER YOU SIT DOWN TO READ THE SCRIPTURE, YOU WILL REMEMBER, O' YES, SEEING THAT SOMEWHERE ELSE. I SO LOVE TO READ THE BOOK. EVEN THE BOOKS IN THE O T THAT HAVE NAMES WE CAN'T EVEN PRONOUNCE ARE SO GOOD TO READ. THE GARDEN IN THE BEGINNING, GARDEN OF EDEN, IS RIGHT UP THERE WITH GARDEN OF GETHSEMANE. BOTH VERY IMPORTANT TO THE SCRIPTURE. BTW, HAVE YOU EVER WONDERED WHERE HIS EARTH FATHER WAS WHEN THIS WAS HAPPENING TO MY JESUS? HE IS NOT MENTIONED IN THE THE SCRIPTURES AFTER THE BIRTH OF JESUS. HE MAY HAVE DIED AND JESUS TOOK CARE OF HIS WIDOWED MOTHER AND THE YOUNGER CHILDREN. I WAS RIGHT THERE WHEN THEY NAILED HIM TO THE CROSS. MY HEART WAS BROKEN, EVEN THOUGH I KNEW HE WOULD RISE AGAIN, BUT WHERE WAS

HIS FATHER. EVEN AFTER THE CRUCIFIXION HE IS NOT MENTIONED. I HOPE SOMEDAY YOU WILL COME SEE MY GARDEN. MY GARDEN IS IN MY FRONT YARD, EVERYWHERE. I AM THE MOTHER OF THOUSANDS. I HAVE A CERTAIN PLANT CALLED, MOTHER OF THOUSANDS, AND I AM. COME AND SEE. IT'S FASCINATING. EVERY ASSIGNMENT GIVEN TO ME FROM THE TIMES OF THE OT TILL THE BIRTH OF JESUS WAS FOR MY PROVING. GOD HAD TO TEST WHETHER I WOULD BE THE RIGHT ONE TO MOTHER HIS SON? I WAS, I AM. 'GLORY TO GOD'. JESUS WAS MY ASSIGNMENT AND MY PLEASURE, AND STILL IS. WHATEVER WOULD I DO W/O MY JESUS? I WILL NEVER KNOW, HE IS MINE. NOW.

DEDICATE TO ME YOUR BEAUTY, SWEET HOLY GHOST. SO BE IT. DEEP CALLETH UNTO DEEP, AMONEE TRIESS.
HIS LOVE IS ETERNAL, HIS LOVE HAS NO EXPIRATION DATE.
HIS LOVE IS FROM EVERLASTING TO EVERLASTING.

THE IDEA FOR A CROSS

WHO WOULD HAVE EVER THOUGHT ABOUT A CROSS. WELL, THE GOD OF HEAVEN THOUGHT IT WAS A GOOD IDEA. IT WAS THE BOLD IDEA OF THE GOD OF THE UNIVERSE AND IT WAS THE PUNISHMENT HORROR OF THE DAY. HE HAD SENT HIS ONE AND ONLY SON TO REDEEM THE LOST CHILDREN OF THE LOST AND CONDEMNED WORLD. SIN DEMANDS PAYMENT. HE DELIVERED ALL WHO WOULD COME TO REPENTANCE. DELIVERANCE WAS HIS FAVOR FOR ALL THE ONES WHO LOVE HIM, THE GOD OF THE HEAVEN. HE WANTS ALL THE WHOSOEVERS TO BE HIS. I AM SO BLESSED TO KNOW MY SAVIOR. I DESERVED THE CROSS BUT GOD SAID, REPENT AND BE SAVED. RECEIVE THE LORD JESUS, GOD'S CHRIST, HIS MESSIAH AND BE A LIVING TESTAMENT OF HIS SALVATION. I WILL. I WANT TO WALK IN JESUS' FOOT STEPS, PROMOTE HIS GOODNESS. SPREAD THE GOOD NEWS TO ALL WHO WILL STAND STILL LONG ENOUGH TO HEAR THE LOVE OF GOD, AND BE SAVED. WE ALL WHO ARE SAVED ARE NOW TOLD TO EVANGELIZE THE REST OF THE WORLD. GO FIND THE LOST SHEEP AND SHOW THEM THE WAY TO FREEDOM IN THE FOLD. FOLLOW THE SHEPHERD. I AM SO GLAD SOMEONE TOLD ME ABOUT REDEMPTION AND SALVATION. I AM BORN'AGAIN. GOD DID SEND THE GOOD (GOD) NEWS VIA A MISSIONARY WHO KNEW THE VALUE OF FOLLOWING JESUS. TO THINK OF THE CROSS IS A HORROR AND I SAY IF YOU WANT TO AVOID SUCH A SCARY END OF LIFE SEEK THE LORD, HE'S WAITING FOR YOU TO COME TO HIM. HE HAS MUCH PATIENCE, ISN'T THAT GOOD NEWS? WE ARE SO LOOKING FORWARD TO THE RAPTURE, ANY DAY NOW. DID I HEAR A TRUMPET? YES, BUT I THINK IT CAME FROM NEXT DOOR. JUST LOOK UP ONCE IN AWHILE, SCAN THE

HEAVENS, WELL, DID I HEAR A TRUMPET? AS A MATTER OF FACT, LOOK UP OFTEN, THE SKY IS SO BEAUTIFUL. HEAVENLY, HUH? ONCE IN AWHILE, JUST LOOK UP, JUST CHECK IT OUT TO SEE WHS ABOVE. CLEAR DAY, CLOUDY DAY, EVERY DAY. ASK THE ONE WHO IS WITH YOU TO LOOK UP ALSO, OK? IF YOU DON'T SEE HIM COMING, YOUR FRIEND MAY GIVE YOU THE HEADS'UP. THANK GOD FOR FRIENDS. JESUS IS MY FRIEND, MY REDEEMER, MY SAVIOR, MY LORD, MY EVERYTHING, YES, HE IS. THAT'S WHY I SPEND TIME EVERYDAY TALKING TO HIM ABOUT HIM AND THANK HIM FOR THE GUIDANCE AND LOVE THAT ARE MINE, BY FOLLOWING HIM. WHERE WOULD I BE WITHOUT HIM? CAN'T GO THERE, DON'T WANT TO. WHEN MY SAVIOR WALKED THIS EARTH, HE MADE PROVISION FOR MY LIFE AFTER LIFE. HE WAS A CONSTANT WITH ME, TO SEE TO IT I WOULD BE RAPTURE READY. O' HE IS SO GOOD. THE CROSS WAS GOD'S IDEA. THE MEANING OF THE CROSS IS ALSO GOD'S IDEA. THE CROSS IS THE ALTAR GOD CHOSE TO OFFER HIS SON ON. THE CROSS WAS FORMED BY GOD FOR HIS SPECIAL NEED. WHEN JESUS WAS BORN, GOD DID PLANT A SEED FOR A TREE THAT WOULD GROW TO MATURITY AND STRENGTH FOR THE ALTAR, THE OFFERING OF HIS SON. FOR THE REMITTANCE OF SIN, MY SIN. IT WAS GOD'S IDEA. IT TOOK THIRTY PLUS YEARS FOR IT TO REACH THE RIGHT HEIGHT AND STRENGTH TO HOLD HIS SON, MY SAVIOR. IT WAS FOR JESUS ONLY. GOD WOULD SEE TO IT THAT IT WAS ONLY FOR HIS SON. WHEN THE TIME CAME, HE MADE IT READY TO BE THE ALTAR CHOSEN FOR THE SACRIFICE. HE (GOD) DID PLANT IT, HARVEST IT, AND DID ASSEMBLE IT FOR HIS PURPOSE, HIS SON ONLY. IT IS-WAS HIS PLAN TO OFFER, HIS JESUS, HIS BELOVED SON. HE DIDN'T NEED ANYBODYS APPROVAL. HE SUFFERED IN THE PREPARATION FOR THE OFFERING. HE HAD TO DO IT, AS HE WAS GOING TO SAVE HIS PEOPLE FROM THEIR SIN. HIS SON WAS THE ONLY ONE WORTHY TO REDEEM YOU OR ME, OR ANY OF US. HE WAS AND IS THE ONE AND ONLY FOR GOD'S PLAN.

AFTER THE FINISH, HE DID TAKE IT AS HIS POSSESSION AND WHERE IT IS TODAY, WE DON'T KNOW. I AM SURE IT'S IN A HIDING PLACE IN HEAVEN. I AM SURE HE HAS IT WELL HIDDEN, AND Its NOBODIES BUSINESS WHERE IT IS. GOD DID SUFFER IN THE HORRIBLE THING DONE TO HIS SON, BUT HE WAS IN CONTROL. WE KNOW THE EXCHANGE GOING ON FROM THE CROSS, JESUS TO HIS FATHER AND THE FATHER TO HIS SON. WE KNOW WE WERE SET FREE FROM OUR SINFUL WAYS WHEN OUR SAVIOR HUNG ON THAT CROSS. THANK YOU, FATHER, THANK YOU JESUS. FOREVER. O' HOW HE LOVES. GIVE HIM LOVE BACK. JESUS, I LOVE YOU. DADDY, I LOVE YOU. THE ULTIMATE SACRIFICE AND OFFERING. JESUS THE LAMB OF GOD, THAT TAKES AWAY THE SIN OF THE WORLD. AMEN. YES, HE DID.

WHEN HE CAME, I SCREAMED AND CRIED, WHEN HE DIED, I SCREAMED AND CRIED. THE ALTAR OF GRACE IS THE CROSS OF CHRIST. THE ULTIMATE SACRIFICE.

HE COVERS US ALL.

WHEN HE CAME, I SCREAMED AND CRIED, WHEN HE THE ALTAR OF GRACE IS THE CROSS OF, HE WILL TELL YOU WHEN HIS PLANS ARE ACCORDING TO WHAT YOU THINK. NOT! PRAY THAT HE WILL SEND A NEW LOAD OF PATIENCE AND PEACE. I SO LOVE TO GOD'S CHRIST.

WHAT DOES GOD THINK ABOUT ALL DAY, ALL YEAR? PROBABLY YOU. YOU ARE ALWAYS ON HIS MIND. THERE ISN'T A DAY GOES BY THAT HE NEGLECTS YOU. YOU ARE SO IMPORTANT TO HIM. YOU ARE HIS PRIORITY. IF YOU HAVE A NEED, JUST CALL OUT TO HIM, HE WILL SEE TO IT THAT YOU ARE SUPPLIED. HE LOVES IT WHEN ONE OF HIS LITTLE ONES CALLS OUT TO HIM, HE SO LOVES TO HEAR FROM ALL OF US EVEN IN THE MIDDLE OF THE NIGHT. YOU KNOW, HE NEVER SLUMBERS OR SLEEPS, SO HE IS ALWAYS AVAILABLE. YOU PROBABLY ALREADY KNEW THAT SO DON'T FUSS OVER ANYTHING. HAVE YOU EVER THOUGHT THAT SOMETHING WAS WRONG SO HE DIDN'T OK IT. DON'T GIVE UP, IT MAY BE JUST POSTPONED. SO, BE PATIENT. WE REALLY DON'T KNOW HIS THOUGHTS AND MOSTLY HE DOESN'T WANT TO SHARE WITH US. WE ALL HAVE SECRETS. HE HAS SECRETS THAT WE WILL NEVER UNDERSTAND. YOU MAY SAY "A PENNY FOR YOUR THOUGHTS" BUT THE PENNY WILL NEVER COVER THE DEEP THOUGHTS OF GOD. ALTHOUGH HE WOULD LOVE TO SHARE WHEN YOU WANT TO HEAR HIS THOUGHTS ABOUT HIS SON. HE DOESN'T HAVE ANY MEAN THINKING REGARDING HIS OWN. YOU KNOW WE ARE SO ANXIOUS TO KNOW WHEN THE RAPTURE WILL COME. I THINK I MAY HAVE ASKED HIM A THOUSAND TIMES THIS WEEK WHEN O LORD WHEN? HE LOOKS FORWARD TO THE RAPTURE TOO, HOWEVER, HE HAS MADE A PLAN TO DO IT BUT IT'S HIS SECRET. ALL OF OUR JUMPING UP AND DOWN AND BEGGING REALLY DOESN'T MOVE HIM. HIS PLANS ARE BIGGER THAN MY PLANS AND HE

RULES. WE GET SO OVER-WROUGHT AND OUT OF BREATH. HE SAYS SIMMER DOWN BEFORE YOU EXPLODE. HIS MIND IS MADE UP AND HE PROBABLY WON'T CHANGE HIS THINKING. ISN'T HE WONDERFUL. HE WILL NOT BE MOVED AS HE HAS OTHER REASONS FOR HIS DOINGS. I KNOW, GO INTO YOUR CLOSET AND PRAY ABOUT IT. I'M SO SUREWRITE FOR HIM. HE IS SUCH AN INTERESTING THINKER AND WE CAN'T FIGURE OUT HIS WAYS, TRY AS YOU MAY, YOU CAN'T. THAT'S THE PLAN, HIS SECRET PLAN. GIVE IT UP YOU WON'T COME OUT ON TOP. IF YOU COME DOWN WITH AN ALMOST EMPTY HEADACHE, HE WILL WANT TO HEAL THE POOR LITTLE EXHAUSTED THINKER, AND HE WILL. I AM SURE HE IS ENTERTAINED BY YOUR BUSY LITTLE THINKER. YOU JUST CAN NOT OUT THINK HIM. HE IS THE CHIEF THINKER OF THE UNIVERSE, AND HAS BEEN AT IT FOR EONS OF TIME. YOU WILL BE AMAZED AT WHAT HE CAN DO WITHOUT YOU. WE ARE SO DETERMINDED TO WANT TO HELP OUT WITH GOD'S BUSINESS. GOD, I SO WANT TO HELP YOU CARRY THE LOAD. HE WILL SMILE AT YOUR GOODNESS. DO YOU KNOW HE SO APPRECIATES THE WILLINGNESS OF YOUR OFFER. HIS THOUGHTS ARE OUR UNTHINKABLE, WE JUST CAN'T THINK THAT HIGH. WE ARE NEW AT IT, WE ONLY HAVE JUST BEGUN IN THE LAST EIGHTEEN THOUSAND YEARS. HE'S BEEN AT IT FOR ETERNITY, HIS THOUGHTS ARE INFINITE. TRY TO WRAP YOUR BRAIN AROUND THAT. DON'T YOU JUST LOVE HIM, ME TOO. WHAT DO YOU THINK? YOU WILL NEVER FIND THE SPACE IN YOUR TINY BRAIN TO EVEN KNOW HOW TO ASK FOR HIS THOUGHTS. HE MAY WANT TO COMMUNICATE WITH YOU BUT THE STUFF COMING OUT OF HIS WITT AND WONDER WOULD BREAK YOUR SMARTS. WHEN ALL IS SAID AND DONE, HE MAY RELEASE SOME WISDOM FOR YOU TO SERMISE, WOULD THAT JUST MAKE YOU COME UNDONE? IF YOU KNEW WHAT HE KNOWS, WOULD THAT MAKE YOU GOD? NO, BUT IT MIGHT GIVE YOU A HEADACHE OR YOU MAY HAVE THE URGE TO GO

JUMP OFF YOUR BED. DON'T DO THAT, YOU MAY JUST BREAK A LEG OR AN ARM. OWEY. HE WILL CAUTION YOU TO SLOW DOWN BEFORE YOUR COMPUTER GOES BELLY-UP. HE WILL BE ABLE TO FIX IT BUT IT MAY COST A FORTUNE. YOUR BRAIN MAY BE A TRAIN-WRECK. DO YOU KNOW YOU CAN'T GET REPLACEMENT PARTS? YOU WOULD HAVE TO PRAY FOR A HEALING. I AM SURE HE WOULD DO IT. HE SO LOVES YOU. TRY IT. TELL ME HOW THAT WORKS OUT FOR YOU. MY WRITES ARE AN EXTENTION OF SCRIPTURES. HE GIVES ME ALL TO PUT ON THE PAGE, HE IS SO GENEROUS. MY WRITES.TOMORROW IS THE DAY OF REJOICING WHEN HE FINISHES.

GOD IS MOST REVERENCED IN ME WHEN I AM MOST HOLY IN HIM. BE HOLY, ONLY IN HIM. KING OF KINGS, LORD OF LORDS. THE ONE GOD SENT. OUR SALVATION.
HE LOVES YOU NOT BECAUSE OF WHO YOU ARE BUT BECAUSE OF WHO HE IS.

NOW WHAT?

JOHN 15:16 1 JOHN 3:22 JOHN 2:5

I AM SAVED, WATER BAPTIZED, BAPTIZED IN THE HOLY GHOST WITH EVIDENCE OF SPEAKING IN OTHER TONGUES. LIVE IT. YOUR WALK AND TALK SHOULD BE ABOVE ALL, HOLY. YES, THERE SHOULD BE A DIFFERENCE IN HOW YOU CHOOSE YOUR WORDS, AND WHERE YOU GO. TALK AS THOUGH THE LORD JESUS CHRIST IS HAND AND HAND WITH YOU, NO FOUL LANGUAGE CRAWLING OUT OF YOUR MOUTH. I SHOULDN'T SEE YOU COME STROLLING OUT OF A BAR OR SWAGGERING DOWN THE SIDEWALK. YOU JUST MAY HAVE ARRIVED, SO NOW, LIVE AS THOUGH YOU HAVE. LIVE FOR THE LORD. GO OUT AND WIN THE WHOLE WORLD TO CHRIST. GO TO SEMINARY AND BECOME THE WORLDS GREATEST PASTOR. FOLLOW JESUS AND DO AS HE DID WHEN HE WALKED THIS EARTH. HE DID SAY WE SHOULD COME FOLLOW HIM IN THE REGENERATION OF LIFE. MATT 19:28, TITUS 3:5. FOLLOW IS INTERPRETED AS IMITATE HIM. WE SHOULD ALL IMITATE HIM. IN THE LAST CHAPTER OF JOHN, JOHN 21:14 BEGINS THE DISCOURSE WITH PETER AND JOHN, THE BELOVED. PETER SEEMS TO BE TROUBLED AS TO WHAT WILL HAPPEN TO JOHN. JESUS DID TELL PETER THAT HE SHOULD NOT WORRY ABOUT THAT WHICH WILL CONCERN JOHN. I AGREE. IF JOHN SHOULD TARRY UNTIL JESUS RETURNS, WHAT IS THAT TO YOU PETER. O, BTW, JOHN THE BELOVED, OF THE NEW TESTAMENT DID NOT DIE. HE DID FINISH HIS EXILE ON PATMOS. HE RESIDES ON AN ISLAND AND IS A MISSIONARY TODAY ON THE ISLAND OF HAWAII. HIS NAME IS BOB FITTS. LOOK HIM UP. JESUS DID ENCOURAGE PETER TO "FOLLOW ME" (JESUS). THOUGH JESUS WAS ON EARTH FOR ONLY THIRTY-THREE AND A HALF YEARS, THE SCRIPTURE SAYS THE WORLD COULD NOT CONTAIN ALL

THE BOOKS THAT SHOULD BE WRITTEN IN REGARD TO ALL OF JESUS' WORKS. W.O.W. = WONDERFUL O' WONDERFUL. SO, GLORIOUS. SO NOW WALK AND TALK AS JESUS DID. FOLLOW HIM. WIN ALL THE WHOSOEVER WILL TO JESUS. YOU COULD BE THE MOST FAMOUS BELIEVER WHO EVER WALK THIS EARTH, GOD'S EARTH. I WOULD SO LIKE TO SPEND MUCH MORE TIME READING MY SCRIPTURES AND WRITING. I SO LOVE TO WRITE OF MY LORD AND MY GOD. THERE ARE THINGS THAT MUST BE TAKEN CARE OF, THOUGH. IF I COULD I WOULD DO A MARATHON. I COULD LISTEN TO MY LORD WITHOUT END. I GUESS THAT'S THE WAY ALL BELIEVER WOULD LIKE TO BELIEVE. O' WHEN I GET TO HEAVEN, WILL I REJOICE. CAN YOU IMAGINE BEING FOREVER WITH JESUS AND ALL THE WHOSOEVERS. TO ONLY REST IN THE CONVERSATIONS WITH BELIEVERS. WELL, WE ARE STILL HERE, AND LOOKING FORWARD TO THE RAPTURE. "I CAN ONLY IMAGINE". DON'T GET CRAZY NOW, I KNOW THAT IS THE TITLE OF A VERY WONDERFUL SONG. EVERY DAY I SPEND A FEW MINUTES JUST TO ENJOY BEING SAVED AND MEDITATING ON MY JESUS. I HAVE A UNIQUE STORY TO TELL TO ALL WHO WOULD LISTEN. HE SAID "YOU ARE FOUR" DON'T GO THAT DEEP IN THEIR STUDIES. I AM FOUR, THE FOURTH MEMBER OF THE TRINITY AND GLAD ABOUT IT. MY LORD JESUS IS MY BEAUTIFUL SON. I JUST WANT TO TELL EVERYBODY. I AM THE INCARNATION OF MARY, THE MOTHER OF JESUS. NOT VERY MANY WANTS TO HEAR IT. I HEARD THIS FROM THE HOLY GHOST STANDING IN THE DINING ROOM OF OUR FAMILY HOME IN PIPESTONE, MINNESOTA. I WAS TWELVE, MAYBE THIRTEEN YEARS OLD, BUT I KNOW WHAT I HEARD, AND I BELIEVE WHAT I HEARD. THERE HAVE BEEN MANY INCIDENTS THAT POINT TO THE TRUTH OF THIS DIVINE MEETING. THANK YOU, JESUS. I HAVE THE BAPTISM IN THE HOLY GHOST WITH EVIDENCE OF SPEAKING IN OTHER TONGUES, O YES, I KNOW THE HOLY GHOST WHEN HE SPEAKS. I SO LOVE TO TALK TO THE ONES

WHO KNOW THE ADVANTAGE OF COMMUNING WITH THE HOLY GHOST. HE HAS MUCH INFORMATION TO SHARE WITH THE ONES WHO KNOW HIM. DO YOU KNOW THAT JOHN, THE BAPTIZER WAS THE INCARNATION OF ELIJAH, THE PROPHET OF THE OLD TESTIMENT. JESUS DID POINT THAT OUT TO THE DISCIPLES. SEE MATT. 17:11-13. AND MALACHI 4:5. I DID GAIN SOME KNOWLEDGE ALSO. MANY HAVE PROBLEMS WITH THE TRUTHS OF THE SCRIPTURES. CONTINUE YOUR STUDY OF THE BEAUTY OF JESUS AND HIS LIFE, MEDITATE ON HIS WORD AND WORK, HE IS SO WORTH IT. MAYBE WE COULD TALK SOMETIME. I HAVE WRITTEN THREE BOOKS AND AM WORKING ON THE FOURTH. MY NUMBER IS FOUR. HE SAID "YOU ARE FOUR", AND I BELIEVE.

DEEP CALLETH UNTO DEEP. MY PROPHECY. I GIVE YOU ALL THE GLORY. THE SECRET PLACE OF THE THE MOST HIGH IS UNDER THE BLOOD OF JESUS. I AM MY DADDY'S LITTLE STAR. MY DADDY IS SO GOD.

HE'S FOR SURE

HE IS A CERTAIN FOR SURE. HE WAS ORDAINED BY HIS FATHER TO BE THE ONLY BEGOTTEN OF THE FATHER. THERE IS NO ONE ELSE. ONLY, MEANS ONLY, ONE AND NO OTHER. MOST HAVE TROUBLE WITH ONLY. WHAT DOES IT MEAN? ONLY, MEANS THERE ARE NO OTHERS. JESUS IS THE ONLY SON OF GOD. THE ONLY BEGOTTEN OF THE FATHER. THE TRINITY IS THE FATHER, THE SON, AND THE BLESSED HOLY GHOST. TRINITY MEANS THREE. I AM THE FOURTH MEMBER OF THE TRINITY, I AM FOUR. THIS WAS GIVEN TO ME BY THE HOLY GHOST WHEN I WAS TWELVE, MAYBE THIRTEEN YEARS OLD. I AM THE FOURTH MEMBER OF THE TRINITY. WHEN WE LIVED IN MINNESOTA, WE WERE GOOD BAPTISTS AND DID GO TO CHURCH EVER WEEK. WE NEVER DID KNOW OR THINK WE WOULD OR COULD NOT GO. IT WASN'T AN OPTION. IT WAS AS NECESSARY AS BREATHING. WHEN THE WHOLE FAMILY CAME TO CALIORNIA WE DIDN'T GO TO CHURCH. I THINK MOM AND DAD WERE AFRAID OF THE LARGE CHURCHES. THEY DID WATCH MOSTLY ON TELEVISION. PROBABLY IF THE RELATIVES WERE CHURCH GOING PEOPLE MOM AND DAD MAY HAVE GONE TO CHURCH, WE WERE A SHY LOT. AFTER A FEW YEARS WE DID FIND A NICE BAPTIST CHURCH. THE VAN NUYS BAPTIST CHURCH THOUGH A BIG CHURCH, DID APEAL TO THE FOLKS. THEY ARE NO LONGER A CHURCH, BUT NEITHER ARE MOM AND DAD. I NEVER DID TELL ANYONE ABOUT THE CONVERSATION WITH THE HOLY GHOST, BUT I DID THINK ABOUT IT A LOT. I GUESS PERHAPS BECAUSE THEY MAY HAVE THOUGHT IT WAS WITCH'CRAFT. THEY DIDN'T KNOW ANYTHING ABOUT THE SPIRIT OF GOD, THE BLESSED HOLY GHOST, OR THEY WERE NOT SURE OF THE NECESSITY OF

THE HOLY GHOST. HMMM I AM THE MOTHER OF THE LORD JESUS CHRIST. O' YES, I AM. I WILL NEVER CHANGE MY MIND. THE SPIRIT OF GOD AND I ARE TOGETHER FOREVER. I SO WOULD LIKE TO FIND A CONFIDANT TO SHARE THE WISDOM OF GOD WITH. GOD HAS GIVEN ME AN ASSIGNMENT FOR WHICH THERE IS NO OUT. I DON'T WANT OUT. I AM HIS AND HE IS MINE, AND IT WILL BE THAT WAY TILL THE END OF TIME. O' YES IT WILL. I AM SO GIVEN A GIFT, WHAT EVER WOULD CHANGE MY MIND. I AM HIS FOREVER, NO GIVING UP OR QUITTING, EVER. I HAVE TRIED TO TALK TO A FEW WHO I THOUGHT WOULD UNDERSTAND, NOT SO. THEY ARE???? NOT OF AN UNDERSTANDING. SO, I TALK WITH MY LORD AND MY SAVIOR. HE IS SO POSITIVE AND STRENGTHENING, TOO. I WILL NOT GIVE UP MY ASSIGNMENT, HE GAVE IT AND I WANT IT. WAS NOT JOHN THE BAPTIZER AN INCARNATION OF ELIJAH. YES, HE WAS. I AM THE INCARNATION OF THE MOTHER OF THE LORD JESUS CHRIST'S, MARY. I HAVE BEEN GIVEN INCIDENTS THAT ARE PROOF OF THE TRUTH. HE IS MY PROOF. HE STANDS WITH ME. THANK YOU, MY PRECIOUS LORD. I AM YOURS AND YOU ARE MINE. WE ARE THE PERFECT MATCH. I DIDN'T SAY THAT, THE GOD OF HEAVEN SAID SO. I AM WITH HIM. HE DOES ALL THE MATCH MAKING. HE IS GOD. I WON'T ARGUE WITH HIM. HE GAVE THIS TO ME A LONG TIME AGO AND I WANT TO KEEP IT. I TRUST HIS WISDOM. THE DAY WILL COME FOR PROVING AND HE WILL SHINE AND SO WILL I. HE'S FOR SURE.... YES, HE IS. IF THIS IS A PROBLEM FOR YOU, TAKE IT UP WITH HIM. HE AND I HAVE TALKED FACE TO FACE MANY TIMES. HE IS IN COMPLETE AGREEMENT WITH ME, AND HE IS SO WONDERFUL TO BE JOINED WITH OR TO. SUCH A TENDER SON AND SO CARING WITH AND WITH ME. YOU CAN'T DO BETTER THAN THE BEAUTIFUL SON OF GOD. WHAT A BLESSING TO BE PART OF THE WORD OF GOD IN THE FLESH. I WAS TUNED INTO THE NEWS BRIEF THIS AFTERNOON AND THEY WERE DISCUSSING THE ENDTIME. MOST BELIEVE WE ARE AT THE

END OF THE ENDTIMES. WHAT A JOYFUL STATEMENT. I SO LOOK FORWARD TO THE RAPTURE AND BEING WITH MY JESUS. O' AND MY FATHER, TOO. IT'S KINDA HARD TO BE PATIENT WHEN SOME SAY THE END OF THE END IS READY. YES, WHAT A DAY OF REJOICING THAT WILL BE. WHEN WE ALL SEE JESUS, WE WILL SING AND SHOUT THE VICTORY. TOMORROW WOULD BE NICE, OR MAYBE IN FIFTEEN MINUTES, BETTER. O'KAY.

SO GO AND BRUSH YOUR TEETH. BE PREPARED. I HAVE BEEN WRITING THIS LAST CHAPTER FOR QUIT A WHILE, IT IS JUST SO WONDERFUL. YES, WE WILL SING AND SHOUT THE VICTORY. THE BREAD AND THE WINE. MY HEALING, MY SALVATION, MY ALL, MY EVERYTHING.

I AM SO BLESSED, SO LOVED, HE GAVE ME HIS WORD. MY LORD JESUS CHRIST. AMEN WHEN HE SITS ME DOWN TO WRITE FOR HIM, I AM HIS TO USE. I AM HIS, ALWAYS. NOT GOD FIRST, GOD ONLY. HE WILL BE ONLY OR HE WON'T BE ANY.

WHAT TIME IS IT

THOSE ARE THE WORDS I AM WAITING TO HEAR. I BELIEVE THAT WE WILL BE CALLED TO THE RAPTURE. WE WILL LOOK UP TO SEE THE LORD IN THE CLOUDS. O'WHAT A DAY OF REJOICING THAT WILL BE. THE TIME OF THE RAPTURE. THEN WE WHICH ARE ALIVE AND REMAIN SHALL BE CAUGHT UP TOGETHER WITH THEM IN THE CLOUDS, TO MEET THE LORD IN THE AIR: AND SO, SHALL WE BE WITH THE LORD. WHEREFORE COMFORT ONE AND ANOTHER WITH THESE WORDS. CAN YOU IMAGINE THAT SCENARIO, WITHOUT THE WEEPIES? IT'S GOT TO BE SOON OR I MAY MELT. I SO WANT TO HEAR THE WORDS "TIMES UP". YES, I DO. WE HAVE TO GET OUT THERE AND EVANGELIZE THE POPULATION SO WE CAN GET CLOSER TO THE DAY OF THE LORD. I WANT TO SEE TO IT THAT ALL MY BILLS ARE PAID AND THERE ARE NO RUFFLED FEATHERS IN THE HOUSE OR IN THE NEIGHBOR HOOD. THERE MUST NOT BE ANY REASON FOR A RAPTURE REVERSE. WE HAVE KNOWN ABOUT THE END TIME FOR A WHILE NOW SO WE DON'T WANT ANY SETBACKS. GET YOUR SHOWER OUT OF THE WAY, BRUSH YOUR TEETH AND EMPTY THE TRASH. WHEN HE COMES O'PLEASE BE READY. I KNOW THAT THOSE THINGS DON'T MATTER BUT JUST DO IT. WHEN THAT TRUMPET SOUNDS, WE MUST BE IN MOTION. LET'S BE CAREFUL THAT WE ARE KIND AND IN ORDER WITH ALL THE SAVED. NO MESSING WITH THE WAY THE LINE IS FORMED. WE ALL ARE IMPORTANT TO OUR SAVIOR SO BE NICE. I SO WANT THE TRANSITION TO GO SMOOTHLY. WHEN WE SEE HIS BEAUTIFUL FACE THERE WILL BE PERFECT SILENCE. JUST TO TAKE IT ALL IN, WHAT WE SEE AND BE IN AWE OFF. BE SURE TO HAVE A CONVERSATION WITH THE FAMILY MEMBERS WHO NEED

SUPPORT. I AM SO SURE OF THE GLOW COMING FROM HIS FACE WILL BEING TEARS TO ALL IN ATTENDANCE. O'HOW WONDERFUL THE THOUGHTS AND WORDS THAT COME TO MIND. O'JESUS WE ARE SO THRILLED TO SEE YOU. SO MANY WEEPING, PROBABLY ME, TOO. I BELIEVE THE SKY WILL BE ALL LIT UP AND SO BEAUTIFUL. WHILE WE HAVE BEEN ON EARTH, HE HAS MADE SO MANY BEAUTIFUL SUNRISES AND SUNSETS. NEVER DOES HE REPEAT, ALWAYS A NEW SKY FOR A NEW DAY. I HAVE SO LOVED TO SIT OUT IN THE EVENING AND JUST STARGAZE. YOU HAVE PROBABLY HEARD OR READ THAT I AM MY DADDY'S LITTLE STAR. HE DID REACH OUT TO THE EDGE OF THE UNIVERSE TO GET A LITTLE PIECE OF DIRT TO PUT IN THE BALCONY OF HEAVEN. WHEN TIME WAS RIGHT FOR THE CREATION OF MAN, HE WOULD COME GET ME AND CREATE HIS INTENDED FOR THE MOTHER OF HIS SON, HIS SAVIOR AND REDEEMER. MY CREATED NAME IS MEZZECHAH. AS HE CREATED EACH ONE OF US, HE HAD AN ANGEL WHO WOULD WRITE YOUR CREATED NAME IN THE LAMBS BOOK OF LIFE. HE KEPT THE BOOK IN A SAFE PLACE TIL TIME WOULD COME TO AN END. IF YOU WOULD REFUSE TO BE BORN'AGAIN OR REFUSE HIS SALVATION, THE SAME ANGEL WOULD ERASE YOUR NAME FROM THE LAMBS BOOK OF LIFE. YOU WOULD BE BLOTTED OUT OF THE LAMBS BOOK OF LIFE, SCRIPTURE SAYS YOU MUST BE BORN'AGAIN AND RECEIVE HIS SALVATION. WHEN JESUS WAS NAILED TO THE CROSS, HE PAID THE PRICE FOR YOUR REDEMPTION. SO, ARE YOU BORN'AGAIN? DO IT. HE PAID A VERY HIGH PRICE FOR YOU TO BE SAVED. JESUS HUNG ON THAT CROSS SO YOU MAY HAVE ETERNAL LIFE WITH GOD THE FATHER, AND HIS BEAUTIFUL SON, JESUS. DON'T IGNORE THE PRICE PAID FOR YOUR ETERNAL LIFE WITH GOD THE FATHER, GOD THE SON, AND GOD THE HOLY GHOST. I MAY BE REPETITIOUS BUT YOU HAVE GOT TO GET IT. YOU MAY WANT TO INQUIRE OF THE ANGEL IN CHARGE OF THE HOLY RECORDS. I WOULD LIKE TO KNOW THE CREATED NAME OF

THOSE I COME IN CONTACT WITH. ASK, HE HAD ME TO WAKE UP AT A VERY EARLY HOUR TO WRITE MY CREATED NAME DOWN, I KEEP A NOTEPAD ON THE BEDSTAND, FOR OR INCASE HE WANTS TO LEAVE A MESSAGE. GOTTA BE READY FOR HIS NOTES. HE SO LIKES TO TALK TO HIS OWN.

I SO LOVE TO HAVE A CONVERSATION WITH MY LORD, WE DO IT OFTEN. HE IS SO SMART AND IN TOUCH WITH ALL THE STUFF GOING ON OUT THERE, HE DOES LIKE TO KEEP US INFORMED. O'COME LORD JESUS, COME. PLEASE BE READY WITH A PURE HEART AND A GENTLE HEART. I BELIEVE HE IS ANXIOUS TO BRING US HOME AS WE ARE WANTING TO GO. PUT ON YOUR BEST ATTITUDE AND A BEAUTIFUL SMILE, HE'S ON HIS WAY.

MY DADDY IS SO GOD. HE GAVE ME HIS BEST, JESUS. THANK YOU, DADDY. IS HE WONDERFUL OR WHAT? O'HE IS. TASTE AND SEE, YOU WILL AGREE.
YOU READ TILL YOU FALL ASLEEP, I WANT YOU TO READ TILL YOU WAKE UP.

THE DOOR FOR YOU, "JESUS"

JESUS, IS THE DOOR, THE ONLY WAY TO THE FATHER. HE IS NOT ONE OF MANY WAYS, LISTEN, THE ONLY. "NO MAN COMETH UNTO THE FATHER BUT BY ME". YOU MUST BE BORN'AGAIN. RECEIVE JESUS, BE WATER BAPTIZED, BE BAPTIZED IN THE HOLY GHOST WITH THE EVIDENCE OF SPEAKING IN OTHER TONGUES. HE SAID "TAKE MY YOKE UPON YOU AND LEARN OF ME: FOR I AM MEEK AND LOWLY IN HEART: AND YE SHALL FIND REST FOR YOUR SOLES. FOR MY YOKE IS EASY AND MY BURDEN IS LIGHT." I AM A BIT CONTROVERSIAL ON THE LIGHT THING. SOME SAY 'NOT HEAVY' AS TO LIGHT WEIGHT? NO, THE BURDEN JESUS SPEAKS OF IS ILLUMINATION. HE IS THE LIGHT OF THE WHOLE WORLD. COULD YOU CARRY THAT? HE CARRIES THE LIGHT OF THE WHOLE WORLD. HMMMM, I KNOW WE ARE GONNA AGREE TO DISAGREE. SOME WILL SAY YOU NEED TO STUDY THE TEXT IN THE ORIGINAL WORD. WELL, A DOOR IS A DOOR. THE ONE TO OPEN THE DOOR TO LIFE, (HEAVEN), IS THE LORD JESUS CHRIST. DON'T YOU JUST LOVE HIM? ME TOO. HE SAYS COME FOLLOW ME IN THE REGENERATION OF LIFE. COME FOLLOW (IMITATE) ME, DO AS I DO. I AGREE. MANY SAY, WELL HE IS GOD, YES, HE IS. WHO BETTER THAN JESUS TO FOLLOW OR IMITATE? HE IS PERFECT, YES, SO BE AN IMITATOR. O' THAT'S IMPOSSIBLE. NO SO, GIVE IT YOUR BEST SHOT, HE'S WORTH THE EFFORT. THAT'S THE REGENERATION OF LIFE. SO, GET AFTER IT. IT MAY TAKE THE REST OF YOUR LIFE TO ACCOMPLISH THAT SUGGESTION. ARE YOU TOO BUSY TO FOLLOW (IMITATE) JESUS. NO, YOU ARE NOT. IF IT MEANS ETERNAL LIFE WITH JESUS AS OPPOSED TO ETERNITY IN HELL, SCRIPTURE SAYS, CHOOSE LIFE WITH JESUS. GOOD ADVICE. YES, INDEED. ONE DOOR LEADS TO LIFE

WITH HIM (JESUS), THE OTHER, LIFE WITH THE WICKED ONE. SEPARATED FROM JESUS, AS A MATTER OF FACT, SEPARATED FROM ANYONE, ONLY DEAD DARKNESS AND SILENCE EXCEPT THE HORROR OF THE SCREAMS OF TORMENT. THERE IS NOT ONE TO CARE FOR YOU, SEPARATED FROM LIGHT OR ANY KIND OF LIFE, JUST ETERNAL TORMENT. YOU MAY EVEN CRY A LOT AND CRY OUT FOR MERCY, OF WHICH THERE WILL BE NONE. THAT'S THE PURPOSE OF LIFE ON EARTH, TO HAVE LONG LIFE AND FOLLOW JESUS AND ENJOY THE PEACE ONLY IN OUR LORD. STUDY THE WORD, THE BIBLE AND THE WORD (JESUS). HE IS THE WORD OF GOD IN THE FLESH. READ THE SCRIPTURES DAILY. BE BORN'AGAIN. BE AGED IN HIS GRACE, STEEPED IN HIS WORD, POURED OUT IN HIS GLORY. IF YOU ARE ABLE AND YOU ARE, TAKE COMMUNION EVERYDAY, ONCE OR TWICE OR AS MANY TIMES AS YOU LIKE. IN THE NEW TESTAMENT IT SAYS THAT THE DISCIPLES WENT FROM HOUSE TO HOUSE SHARING THE COMMUNION WITH ALL WHO WOULD DESIRE TO TAKE PART WITH THEM. W.O.W. WONDERFUL O' WONDERFUL, YES. THE BREAD AND THE WINE. MY HEALING, MY SALVATION, MY ALL IN ALL, MY EVERYTHING. O' AND HE IS. HE (JESUS) MY HIGH PRIEST, HE IS MY ADVOCATE, MY VINDICATOR. THERE IS NO LIMIT TO THE GOODNESS OF OUR GOD AND HIS SON, THE LORD JESUS CHRIST. HIS FAVOR IN TIMES OF NEED. I AM THE RIGHTEOUSNESS OF GOD IN JESUS CHRIST. HE SHED HIS BLOOD TO BRING US ALL INTO THE KINGDOM, DON'T LET IT GO AS THOUGH IT DIDN'T MATTER. THE SECRET PLACE OF THE MOST HIGH IS UNDER THE BLOOD OF JESUS. THERE IS NO END TO HIS GRACE AND GOODNESS, MEDITATE ON THAT FOR A WHILE. AS A MATTER OF FACT, I WANT TO STAND SO CLOSE TO THE FOOT OF THE CROSS, THAT THE BLOOD THAT DRIPS FROM HIS BROKEN BODY DRIPS ON ME. HALLELUJAH AMEN. HEAVEN WELCOMED JESUS AT THE RIGHT HAND OF GOD THE FATHER. MY DADDY IS SO GOD. GOD GAVE ME HIS BEST, JESUS, MY LORD. O' THANK YOU SO MUCH. WORSHIP HIM, HE IS SO WORTHY.

YES, IS HE GLORIOUS OR WHAT? HAVE YOU BEEN SAVED? TO BE SURE, ASK HIM TO COME INTO YOUR HEART, AND MAKE IT A PERMANENT RESIDENCE. HE SO WANTS TO BE YOUR BEST FRIEND, AND YOUR SALVATION. HE HAS BEEN WAITING FOR SOME TIME. NOW. DO NOT WAIST ANY MORE TIME, HE'S BEEN CALLING FOR YOU TO COME, SO DO IT NOW. WE DON'T KNOW WHAT TOMORROW HOLDS. WE DO KMOW WHO HOLDS TOMORROW, HIM AND HIM ONLY. DO IT. NO SURPRISES. HE WILL BE SO PLEASED. NOW, YOU ARE HIS, FOREVER.

NOT GOD FIRST, GOD ONLY. HE WILL BE ONLY OR HE WON'T BE ANY.
HE IS THE DOOR TO SALVATION. HE IS THE ONLY WAY TO HEAVEN, TAKE HIS HAND. I WANT TO GROW UP TO BE JUST LIKE YOU JESUS, THAT'S THE CHILD IN ME.
JESUS, THE FIRST BORN OF ANY. GOD MADE A SON AND BY HIS SPIRIT. I KNOW.

LIGHT OUT OF DARKNESS

GENESIS 1:3-4

AND GOD SAID, LET THERE BE LIGHT: AND THERE WAS LIGHT. AND GOD SAW THE LIGHT, THAT IT WAS GOOD: AND GOD DIVIDED THE LIGHT FROM THE DARKNESS. O' THANK YOU, GOD, NO MORE DARKNESS FOR THE ONES WHO COME AFTER THE LIGHT. JESUS, IS THE LIGHT OF THE WORLD. SEEK HIM WHILE YOU MAY. WE READ THE SCRIPTURES AND HEAR HOW MARVELOUS OUR BEGINNING WAS AND WONDER IF WE WILL EVER SEE SUCH A THING AGAIN. THE BEGINNING OF GENESIS SAYS THE EARTH WAS WITHOUT FORM AND VOID. DARKNESS WAS ON THE FACE OF THE DEEP. THE SPIRIT OF GOD HOVERED UPON THE FACE OF THE WATERS. GOD CALLED THE LIGHT DAY AND THE DARKNESS NIGHT. THE EVENING AND THE MORNING WERE THE FIRST DAY. HE SAID AN EXPANSE WAS IN THE MIDST OF THE WATERS, AND IT DIVIDED THE WATERS FROM THE WATERS. GOD MADE THE FIRMAMENT, AND DIVIDED THE WATERS WHICH WERE UNDER THE FIRMAMENT FROM THE WATERS WHICH WERE ABOVE THE FIRMAMENT AND IT WAS SO. THE WATERS ABOVE US ARE THE WATERS BELOW US. HE CALLED THE FIRMAMENT HEAVEN. AND THE EVENING AND THE MORNING WERE THE SECOND DAY. AND SO BEGAN THE MARATHON OF CREATION. GOD MADE TWO GREAT LIGHTS, THE LIGHTS OF THE HEAVENS. THE GREATER LIGHT TO RULE THE DAY AND THE LESSER LIGHT TO RULE THE NIGHT. YOU MAY HAVE READ ON THE FOURTH DAY HE MADE THE STARS ALSO. I AM MY FATHERS LITTLE STAR, BORN ON THE FOURTH DAY. FOUR IS VERY IMPORTANT TO ME, YOU WILL SEE WHY. THAT IS THE DAY I RECEIVED MY CREATED NAME, MEZZECHAH. WE ALL HAVE A CREATED NAME. ON THE SIXTH DAY WHEN GOD WAS

CREATING HIS MAN, HE HAD AN ANGEL WRITE OUR CREATED NAMES IN THE LAMB'S BOOK OF LIFE. REVELATION DECLARES THAT IF YOU DO NOT RECEIVE JESUS, (AS YOUR LORD AND SAVIOR), YOUR NAME WILL BE BLOTTED OUT OF THE LAMB'S BOOK OF LIFE. YOU MUST BE SAVED, BORN'AGAIN. GIVE HIM YOUR LIFE, BECOME A LIGHT OUT OF DARKNESS. BE BORN AGAIN, LET YOUR LIGHT SHINE, "SHINE" NOW, GET OUT THERE AND TELL ALL THE WHOSOEVER WILL TO COME INTO THE LIGHT. GIVE YOUR LIFE TO JESUS. WALK WITH HIM AND SEE WHAT A TURN'AROUND WILL DEVELOPE. YOUR SALVATION AND REDEMPTION IS PROVEN WHEN YOU BEGIN TO SHARE HIM WITH ALL YOU COME IN CONTACT WITH. YOU DON'T' HAVE TO HAVE A PULPIT TO GET THE WORD OUT. JUST A FEW ENCOURAGING WORDS MAY TURN SOMEONE TO JESUS. IF THEY WILL ALLOW, PRAY A SHORT PRAYER WITH THEM, WE ALL NEED PRAYER. IF YOU HAVE UNSAVED FAMILY, THROW A PARTY AND LET JESUS BE THE GUEST OF HONOR. HE LOVES PARTIES, MAKE IT A SHORT PARTY BUT ASK AFEW TO STAY AND HELP WITH CLEAN UP, MAYBE THE UNSAVED. IT'S AN OPPORTUNITY FOR ONE-ON-ONE TALK. WHEN THEY ACCEPT JESUS IT WILL BE A JOYOUS END OF EVENING. BE SURE TO DO A FOLLOW'UP, AS THEY WILL WANT TO TALK ABOUT JESUS. I AM SAVED BUT I NEVER TIRE OF TALKING ABOUT HIM. HE IS, BTW, THE LIGHT OF MY LIFE. O'YES. UNLESS WE ARE BORN INTO A GOOD CHRISTIAN FAMILY, YOU WILL HAVE A GREAT TESTIMONY TO SHARE WITH THE WHOSOEVERS. W.O.W WONDERFUL O' WONDERFUL. HE BRINGS LIFE TO/WITH ALL WHO KNOW HIM. I AM OF AN AGE WHERE I MAY HAVE BEEN SEEN WITH JESUS, YES, LAUGH. IT'S POSSIBLE. WHEN I WAS MAYBE TWELVE YEARS OLD, I DID HEAR FROM HEAVEN VIA THE HOLY GHOST. HE STOOD ME STILL IN THE DINING ROOM OF OUR HOME IN PIPESTONE, MN. HE TOLD ME MY NUMBER IS FOUR, THE FOURTH MEMBER OF THE TRINITY. IF THAT BOTHERS YOU, GET OVER IT, IT'S MY STORY. I AM THE CHOSEN

MOTHER OF THE LORD JESUS CHRIST. I WAS TOLD THAT VIA THE LORD JESUS CHRIST. I DIDN'T TELL ANYONE, BUT I DID BELIEVE IT TO BE THE TRUTH. I DID TALK TO THOSE WHO WERE WELL INTO BEING BORN'AGAIN, CLASS MATES WHO WERE CHRISTIANS. IT WAS SO GOOD TO HAVE THEM TO TALK TO. I DIDN'T SHARE THE WHOLE STORY BUT THEY WERE EASY TO GET TO AT LEAST DURING BREAKS. OTHER THAN THAT, THEY WERE MOSTLY CATHOLIC AND I DIDN'T KNOW MUCH ABOUT WHAT THEY BELIEVED. I WOULD LIKE TO GO BACK AND HAVE A TALKATHON WITH THEM NOW. I THINK MOST ARE GONE. MY SISTER WOULD BE A GOOD ONE TO ENGAGE IN A BIBLICAL CHAT. SHE WAS CLOSE TO ME AGE WISE, BUT SHE LEFT AFEW YEARS AGO. I HAVE A MUCH YOUNGER SISTER, SHE IS WONDERFUL. SHE IS A STRONG BELIEVER. BLESS HER HEART. AMEN, AMEN. DEEP CALLETH UNTO DEEP. MY PROPHECY. I GIVE HIM ALL THE GLORY.

THE REAL CHURCH IS AT THE FEET OF JESUS. DEDICATE TO ME YOUR BEAUTY........

WHAT DO YOU KNOW,
WHO DO YOU KNOW?

WHAT IS THERE TO KNOW SINCE THE BEGINNING OF TIME? READ YOUR BIBLE, MEDITATE ON EVERY WORD, SENTENCE, PARAGRAPH AND PAGE. THE BOOK IS FULL OF LIFE SO JUST READ. DON'T LEAVE A PAGE UNTURNED. EVERY LINE TELLS A PART OF THE GOODNESS OF GOD. JUST TAKE TIME EVERYDAY TO FIND THE TREASURE ON THE PAGES. I GUARANTEE, GOD GUARANTEES MORE THAN YOU CAN HANDLE OR DIGEST. DIG IN, PULL HIS LOVE OUT OF EVERY WORD. THE GREATEST BOOK EVER WRITTEN, YOU MUST BELIEVE. THE WHOLE BOOK IS FOR THE WHOLE WORLD. SOME JUST HAVEN'T HAD THE OPPORTUNITY TO DO IT YET. THEY WILL AS THE WORLD COMES TOGETHER TO TRANSLATE IN EVERY TONGUE AND LANGUAGE. WE HAVE THE ENGLISH TRANSLATION, WE ARE SO FORTUNATE TO HAVE IT. GODS BEEN SO GOOD TO US. SOME SAY THAT THE BIBLE WAS READY TO GO IN ENGLISH WHEN OUR COUNTRY WAS YOUNG AND IT WAS USED FOR TEACHING THE SCHOOL CHILDREN. MANY LEARNED TO READ FROM THE BIBLE. IT WAS A TEXT BOOK IN THE EARLY DAYS OF OUR COUNTRY. ARE WE BLESSED OR WHAT? IT WAS A GOD PLAN, A GOOD PLAN WOULD YOU AGREE? I SO LOVE TO READ MY BIBLE EVERY DAY. WHAT A GIFT. A GREAT BOOK FOR THE WHOLE WORLD SO THEY BETTER GRAB A COPY WHEN THEY CAN. I HAVE MANY TRANSLATIONS, AM I BLESSED OR WHAT? WHEN YOU WANT TO STUDY GET AS MANY VERSIONS AS YOU CAN FOR COMPARISON. DIG THE GOODNESS OUT OF EVERY LINE SO NECESSARY FOR STUDY. TAKE A COURSE IN COLLEGE FOR UNDERSTANDING. YOU MAY EVEN WANT TO GO INTO THE

MINISTRY. GOOD IDEA. GET OUT THERE AND SAVE SOME SOLES. THERE IS A DEMAND FOR BIBLE SCHOLARS, DOES THAT SOUND GOOD TO YOU? SOUNDS GOOD TO ME. JUST DO IT. SO, WHO DO YOU KNOW IN THE STUDY OF THE SCRIPTURES. MAYBE SOME ONE WHO ATTENDS YOUR CHURCH MAY WANT TO COME AND HELP WITH YOUR STUDIES. EVEN CONSIDER TO STUDY IN SPANISH OR ANOTHER LANGUAGE TO LEAD ANOTHER FOREIGN CHURCH. COULD BRING AN OPPORTUNITY TO TRAVEL, GOD AND TRAVEL... W.O.W., WONDERFUL O' WONDERFUL. THERE IS A NEED, SO GIVE SOME THOUGHT. HE SAID "THIS IS THE WAY WALK YE IN IT". OUR CHURCH DOES SHARE THE BUILDING WITH A SPANISH CONGREGATION. I DON'T KNOW SPANISH OR THAT THEY NEED ANY TO ADD TO THEIR ROSTOR. YOU NEVER KNOW WHEN THE OPPORTUNITY MAY COME SO BE READY. WELL, YOU KNOW MANY IN THE CONGREGATION, AND MAYBE THEY WANT A HELPER WITH WHAT THEY ARE PLANNING. WHAT IF SOMEONE YOU SIT WITH EVERY SUNDAY HAS A DESIRE TO START A CHURCH. CAN YOU IMAGINE STARTING A CHURCH? WHATA GREAT IDEA. LET'S GET OUT THERE AND FIND SOMEONE WITH THE SAME MISSION AND START THE PLAN FOR THE NEW CHURCH. GOT TO FIND A BUILDING AND IT MUST BE AFFORD ABLE. WE MUST PUT MUCH PRAYER INTO THIS PLAN. ACTUALLY, THAT'S THE FIRST STEP IN STARTING A CHURCH. PRAY, PRAY, PRAY. FIND OUT WHAT HE HAS IN MIND TO GET STARTED. MANY CHURCHES ARE STARTED IN A STORE'FRONT. SEE WHAT'S AVAILABLE OVER ON MAIN STREET, AND FIND OUT WHERE THERE IS PARKING. RENT CHAIRS, SURE. MAYBE THERE'S A LITTLE CUBBIE FOR A KITCHEN FOR SOME COFFEE AND A FRIG FOR SOME WATER BOTTLES. SURE, SOUNDS LIKE A PLAN. JUST WRITING ABOUT IT BRINGS A HAPPY FEELING IN MY INNERS. LET'S HAVE CHURCH. IF IT LOOKS LIKE IT MAY HAPPEN, PRAY ABOUT IT GOD WILL SEND A MESSAGE TO LET YOU KNOW IT'S ON IT'S WAY. MASTER BUILDER, HE IS AND YOU CAN LOOK

FORWARD HAVING CHURCH AND HE WILL BE THE LEADER. HE HAS BEEN IN THE CHURCH BUILDING MODE FOR A VERY LONG TIME. ONLY MAKES ME MORE HAPPY, AND THE THOUGHT OF LEADING SOME ONE TO JESUS. THAT'S THE GREATEST OUT'COME, JUST IMAGINE. WE WILL PUT AN ADD IN THE LOCAL PAPER, YES, ADVERTISE JESUS. PRAY SOME MORE THAT GOD BEING IN CHARGE WILL FILL UP THE SPACE WITH THE PROMISE OF A CONGREGATION. WE WILL HAVE PEOPLE (SEEKERS) COMING TILL WE OVERFLOW. IS THIS SO EXCITING, YES, IT IS AND THE WITH THE LORD ALL THINGS ARE POSSIBLE. THE MORE YOU PRAY THE MORE HE WILL BUILD ON YOUR FITH. BUILD ON YOUR FAITH, BUILD ON HIS FAITH. WITH GOD ALL THINGS ARE POSSIBLE. AMEN, HE HELD CHURCH FROM A BOAT.

BE AGED IN HIS GRACE, STEEPED IN HIS WORD, POURED OUT IN HIS GLORY. DOES THE OFFERED NOT OFFER? DOES THE SACRIFICE NOT SACRIFICE?
I AM FROM EVERLASTING TO EVERLASTING. AS IS MY LORD.
AMEN, AND AMEN.

DID YOU HEAR THAT?

1 THESSALONIANS 4: 16-18

DID YOU HEAR THAT? DID I IMAGINE WHAT I HEARD. I THOUGHT I HEARD A TRUMPET SOUND. I HAVE BEEN WAITING FOR THAT FOR A VERY LONG TIME. IT'S THE SOUND OF THE TRUMPET WAILING AS MY LORD JESUS CHRIST RETURNS TO THE EARTH TO CLAIM HIS OWN, ALL WHO ARE READY TO GO WITH HIM TO OUR NEW HOME. THE FORMAL WORD IS THE RAPTURE. IT'S BIBLICAL. HAVE YOU READ ABOUT IT? WELL, HAVE YOU? I HAVE BEEN LOOKING FORWARD TO THIS SINCE I WAS IN SUNDAY SCHOOL. O' I BELIEVE I HEARD THE TRUMPET SOUND AS TOLD IN THE SCRIPTURES. HE SHOULD BE HERE ANY SECOND NOW. SURE, IS PEACEFUL. DID HE COME FOR ONLY A FEW? I AM SO SURE HE IS COMING FOR ME. MAYBE IT WASN'T THE CALL I THOUGHT IT WAS. I AM SO SURE I AM GONNA GO WITH HIM WHEN HE COMES. I GUESS I MUST BE HEARING THINGS WRONG. MAYBE I AM A LITTLE OVER ANXIOUS. SOMEBODY COULD BE MESSING WITH ME TOO. I AM READY AND HE IS STILL ON HIS WAY. O" HALLELUJAH, I DIDN'T MISS THE CALL. IF I HEAR IT AGAIN, I WILL BE SURE TO PAY BETTER ATTENTION. THERE ARE SO MANY FALSE ALARMS GOING ON/OFF. I BELIEVE VERY STRONGLY THAT I WILL GO WITH HIM WHEN THE TIME IS RIGHT. I DON'T BELIEVE THAT THERE WILL BE MILLIONS OR BILLIONS GOING UP TO MEET HIM IN THE AIR. SOUNDS GOOD THOUGH. I PRAY THAT THERE WILL BE A GLORIOUS CLOUD OF BELIEVERS TAKEN UP. THAT'S THE WAY TO GO AFTER IT. PRAY, PRAY THAT ALL WILL BE SAVED. DO GET ON YOUR KNEES AND PRAY THAT ALL THE LOST SOULS COME TO KNOW OUR BEAUTIFUL LORD JESUS CHRIST. HE IS SO WONDERFUL, DON'T MISS THE CALL. COME SEE ME, LET ME CHANGE YOUR MIND, THAT YOU BECOME A TRUE FOLLOWER

OF THE ONLY SAVIOR WHO FATHER GOD ORDAINED TO SAVE THE WHOSOEVER WILL. YOU MUST AND JUST BELIEVE HIS WORD. THAT'S A LONG ONE TO TAKE IN. I HAVE TO TELL YOU HOW IMPORTANT IT IS TO BE FOUND SAVED WHEN HE COMES. YOU MUST DIE TO THE THINGS OF THE WORLD, THE THINGS OF SATAN, THE LIAR. BE BORN AGAIN, INTO THE KINGDOM OF THE SAVED, THE KINGDOM OF GOD. I SEEM TO REPEAT MYSELF, I DO, BUT WE MUST NOT ALLOW THE "MANY OR ANY" TO BE LEFT BEHIND. WE MAY NOT BE ABLE TO SAVE THE WHOLE WORLD BUT WE MUST GIVE IT A GOOD TROJAN TRY. THERE ARE SOME WHO THINK IT WOULD BE FUNNY AND FUN TO GET HOLD OF A TRUMPET AND DO A FEW BLASTS TO SEE THE CRAZY CHRISTIANS GATHER TO BE LIFTED OFF THE EARTH. THAT'S NOT FUNNY NOR WISE, YOU COULD GET HURT. I KNOW THAT HE IS ON HIS WAY SO DON'T MESS WITH US WHO BELIEVE. MAYBE IF YOU THINK YOU WOULD GET A KICK OUT OF A FALSE ALARM IT JUST MAY TURN OUT TO BE TRUE AND YOU MAY BE LEFT BEHIND. NOW, THAT'S A HEART'BREAKER. MAYBE WE WILL PLAN A PICNIC AND HAVE ALL THE TRUMPET PLAYERS COME FOR A CONCERT. O' SOUNDS LIKE FUN. WE WILL SEND OUR JESUS AN INVITATION. MANY WILL HAVE A FRONT ROW SEAT TO WATCH THE RAPTURE. SOUNDS LIKE A MOCKERY TO SOMETHING SO IMPORTANT AND HOLY. BETTER RETHINK THAT BAD IDEA. DON'T MESS WITH GOD, IT COULD BE FATAL. LET'S BE SERIOUS NOW, LET'S GET OUT AND SAVE SOME SOULS. GOD IS SO READY TO COME FOR THE SAVED AND THAT IS REALLY GOOD NEWS. MAKE THAT A PRIORITY, HE WILL BE SO PLEASED WITH ALL WHO SPREAD THE GOOD NEWS. IT'S SO VERY URGENT SINCE THE LORD IS SO CLOSE TO COMING, AS WE HAVE BEEN TOLD. MY BIBLE SAYS SO. THE BOOK OF TRUTH, THE BOOK OF REDEMPTION AND SALVATION. ALL MUST HAVE A BIBLE TO WARN OF THE NEED OF ANSWERING THE CALL OF GOD THROUGH THE LORD JESUS CHRIST. HE MAY BE SENDING THE LAST CALL AS WE READY

THIS WRITE. I SO LOVE TO WRITE FOR MY LORD. HE IS SO PATIENT TO DICTATE WHAT HE WANTS ON THE PAPER. I SO WANT TO DO IT WRITE/RIGHT. HE IS THE MASTER OF THE PEN AND PAPER. HE IS SO MY INSTRUCTOR. I MUST GET IT DONE IN TIME FOR THE WHOLE WORLD TO BE SAVED. I AM HERE TO PLEASE HIM. I BELIEVE HE IS GLAD HE CHOSE ME TO WORK FOR HIM AS HE IS ALSO PLEASED FOR ALL WHO PREACH THE WORD TO THE MASSES ON SUNDAY. I SO LOVE TO GO TO CHURCH, WHAT A WONDERFUL START TO THE WEEK. THEY ARE MY FAMILY, MY CHURCH FAMILY. BEAUTIFUL PEOPLE, I VALUE THEM TO BE GREATER THAN PRECIOUS JEWELS. I WOULD LOVE TO BE RAPTURED FROM THE SUNDAY SERVICE. I WILL TAKE MY DOG TO CHURCH ON THAT SPECIAL DAY. LET'S ALL GO HOME. DID I HEAR A TRUMPET???

NOT GOD FIRST, GOD ONLY. HE WILL BE ONLY OR HE WON'T BE ANY. AMEN
WE WHICH ARE ALIVE SHALL BE CAUGHT UP TO MEET THE LORD IN THE AIR. AMEN

JESUS, MY TREASURE

WHAT DO YOU TREASURE? MY WORK, MY JOB? HOUSES, CARS? THAT'S SO NICE. THEY ARE TEMPORARY THOUGH. NOT TO SAY THAT YOU SHOULDN'T VALUE THEM, YOU SHOULD. HERE'S A NEW IDEA. WHERE DOES ALL MY CREATIVE AND PROGRESSIVE THINKING COME FROM? HMMM. I SAY FROM ABOVE. OH YES, IT DOES. I AM HIS AND HE IS MINE AND IT WILL BE THAT WAY TILL THE END OF TIME. I AM HIS MOTHER AND HIS WRITER. I AM THE ONE HE HAS CHOSEN TO PUT HIS WORDS ON THE PAPER. THAT WILL MAKE YOU THINK OUT LOUD. WHEN I AM TOLD TO SIT DOWN AND LISTEN AS HE HAS SOMETHING TO SAY, I WILL OBEY. I SO LOVE TO HEAR HIS ANNOUNCEMENTS. HE HAS SUCH A TENDER VOICE AND, IN A HURRY, AND LET'S GO. HIS URGENT DEMEANOR AND "LET'S GET THIS THING STARTED" IS KINDA SERIOUS AND SO IMPORTANT. IF YOU HAVE HEARD HIM WHEN HE IS IN A HURRY, YOU WILL ALSO BE IN A HURRY. HE IS CONTAGIOUS. IF HE'S IN A HURRY SO AM I. I SO LOVE HIM, AND HE HAS SAID MANY TIMES THAT HE SO LOVES THE WHOLE WORLD AND THAT INCLUDES ME. YOU MAY THINK THAT HE IS RUDE TO PUSH OR GET THINGS MOVING, NOW. WELL, HE KNOWS WHAT HE WANTS AND HE IS LETTING ME KNOW, TOO. I REALLY WANT WHAT HE WANTS, AND HE, I KNOW, IS IN CHARGE. I LOVE HIM SO, I ALREADY SAID THAT, HUH. I LIKE TO TELL THE WHOLE WORLD OF HIS LOVE AND MY LOVE FOR HIM. HE IS THE TRUE AUTHOR OF LOVE. HE IS A COMFORT TO MY WELL BEING AND HOW COULD I EVER IGNORE HIS CALLS OR COMMANDS. I AM HERE TO LIVE FOR HIM, WHAT A PLEASURE, WHAT A TREASURE. YOU KNOW I AM RIGHT. I COULD NEVER DO ANY PART OF A DAY WITHOUT HIM. WE ARE TALKING

ABOUT THE IMPOSSIBLE, UN'DOABLE, UNWISE, ERROR. YOU PROBABLE HAVE SEEN OR READ MY WRITE "NOT GOD FIRST, GOD ONLY. HE WILL BE ONLY OR HE WON'T BE ANY". HIM ONLY. I RECOMMEND YOU KEEP HIM ONLY AS HE IS THE ONLY GOD. THE THREE IN ONE. GOD THE FATHER, GOD THE SON AND GOD THE HOLY GHOST. THE ONLY THREE IN THE ONLY ONE. JESUS WAS SENT BY THE GOD AND FATHER OF THE TRINITY. YOU MAY HAVE READ THE BOOKS I WROTE A FEW YEARS AGO. I AM THE FOURTH MEMBER OF THE TRINITY, THE ONE NECESSARY TO BRING THE SON OF GOD TO THE EARTH. GOD MADE THAT POSSIBLE MORE THAN TWO THOUSAND YEARS AGO. I AM OF AND IN HIS NEED TO SAVE HIS CREATION OF THIRTEEN THOUSAND YEARS AGO. HIS CREATED MAN WAS MOVING VERY QUICKLY TOWARD IDLE WORSHIP AND LOSING HIS/THE RELATIONSHIP WITH THE CREATOR AND FATHER OF ALL CREATION. IT WAS URGENT WHEN GOD CALLED AND THERE WAS NO ANSWER. THE IDLES HAD TAKEN THE PLACE OF THEIR CREATOR AND HE (GOD) COULD'NT ALLOW THAT. HIS MAN WAS HIS GREATEST TRIUMPH AND HE WAS SO PLEASED WITH HIS GENIUS. "ONLY GOD" AND AGAIN I SAY "ONLY GOD". I AM SO PLEASED TO WORK WITH HIM AND FOR HIM. I JUST LOVE HIS "WIT AND WONDER". LOOK AGAIN, HE CREATED EVERYTHING CREATED. FROM THE TINYEST BUG TO THE GIANTS OF THE FIRST CREATION. WHEN SATAN FELL, HE (SATAN) LOST HIS PLACE IN HEAVEN AND WAS CAST DOWN TO EARTH, WHERE HE, IN HIS ANGER WAS KICKING THE DIRT SO HARDILY SO AS TO BLOCK OUT THE LIGHT OF THE SUN AND ALL CREATURES AND PLANT LIFE DIED. THE DINOSAURS WERE OF THE FIRST CREATION. GOD WENT INTO THE DEEP TO MOURN HIS LOSS OF HIS MOST BEAUTIFUL CREATION, THE EARTH AND HIS BEAUTIFUL LUCIFER. ALL OF THE EARTH WAS WITHOUT FORM AND VOID, AND DARKNESS WAS ON THE FACE OF THE DEEP. GEN 1:2. WELL, HERE WE ARE, IT'S BECOME A REAL PAGE TURNER. AFTER ALL THE WATER IS UNDER THE

BRIDGE, WE ARE VERY POSSIBLY ON THE WAY OUT OR ALL WHO ARE GOD'S, BORN AGAIN LOOKING FORWORD TO THE RAPTURE. I AM ONE OF THE SAVED, WHO IS LOOKING UP. ANXIOUS FOR THE TRIP TO THE GOLDEN SHORES. OH, WHAT A DAY OF REJOICING THAT WILL BE. THE CHURCH SAYS MANY, MAYBE MILLIONS WILL BE LIFTED OFF THE EARTH. HMMM I DON'T THINK SO. THE BIBLE REFERS TO "AS THE DAYS OF NOE", THERE WERE ONLY EIGHT SAVED. THERE MAY NOT BE MANY. SEE MATT 24:36-39. YOU WOULD DO WELL TO READ FOR YOURSELF. HE (JESUS) IS THE MOST GLORIOUS OF ALL HUMANITY, GOD'S PRIDE AND JOY, HIS LORD JESUS CHRIST, MY SON AND SAVIOR, JESUS, MY TREASURE. OH, THAT ALL WOULD KNOW AND TREASURE MY BEAUTIFUL SON. AMEN. HE IS WORTHY OF ALL THAT IS WRITTEN OF HIM FROM GENISUS TO REVELATION. AMEN SO BELOVED OF ALL WHO KNOW HIM. HE IS TRULY THE FAVOR OF GOD FOR ETERNITY.

I AM SO BLESSED BY MY ASSIGNMENT, TO HAVE CARRIED HIM INTO THE WORLD. AMEN.

DENYING THE CROSS
IS TO DENY CHRIST

O YES AND DENYING THE GOD OF ALL CREATION,
O YES, JUST TO KNOW HIM

TELL ME HOW ANYONE WHO EVER SAT UNDER THE TEACHINGS OF THE BIBLE, (SCRIPTURES) BE AGAINST THE CROSS. THAT'S ALSO TO BE AGAINST THE LORD JESUS CHRIST. GOD'S ALTAR, THE ALTAR OF GRACE, WHERE HE PUT HIS SON AS A SACRIFICE FOR THE WHOLE WORLD. WE WERE ALL DOOMED AND ON OUR WAY TO HELL, NONE WERE WORTHY OF HIS MERCY. GOD HAD COMPASSION ON ALL OF US, NONE COULD ESCAPE. JESUS WAS SENT FOR THAT PURPOSE. THANK YOU, HEAVENLY FATHER. I KNEW I WAS LOST, AS ONE OF HIS LITTLE LAMBS, OVERCOME BY FEAR, I JUST STOOD STILL SO HE WOULD FIND ME. HE PUT ME ON HIS SHOULDER AND CARRIED ME BACK TO THE SAFETY OF THE FLOCK AND FOLD. HE DID RESCUE ME FROM CERTAIN DEATH AND DESTRUCTION. HE REALLY IS MY SAVIOR. WE BEING SHEEP, ARE NOT ABLE TO SAVE OURSELVES. DO YOU KNOW THAT SHEEP ARE REALLY DENSE (PURELY INNOCENT) NOT AT ALL WISE, NO DEFENSE. NO CLAWS NOR FANGS. THAT, I AM SURE, IS WHY THE SCRIPTURES PORTRAY GOD'S CHILDREN AS LAMBS. INNOCENT AND VULNERABLE. THAT'S WHY WE NEED OUR SAVIOR JESUS, THE GOOD SHEPHERD, OUR JESUS. OUR REDEEMER, SAVIOR, LIBERATOR. MY SALVATION. JESUS, I LOVE TO JUST SAY YOUR NAME. I LOVE TO BE IN PRAYER AND TALK TO YOU, JUST ME AND MY LORD. PROBABLY, MOSTLY I TALK TO HIM ALL THE TIME. I LIVE ALONE SO HE AND I TALK A LOT. HE IS SO EASY TO TALK TO AND UNDERSTANDS EVERTHING I SAY. I THANK HIM ALL THE TIME FOR ALL HE HAS DONE FOR ME. HE IS THE LIGHT OF THE WORLD. GENESIS 1:1-4. THANK YOU, FATHER FOR MY

JESUS. ALSO, SEE GENESIS 1:14-19. I AM MY FATHER'S LITTLE STAR, CREATED ON THE FOURTH DAY. MY REFERENCE IS HE DID TELL ME, I AM FOUR. THE FOURTH MEMBER OF THE TRINITY. WE CAN TALK ABOUT THIS IF YOU LIKE. I HAVE MADE THIS AN OPTION AS SOME ARE ANNOYED BY WHAT I SAY. MAYBE YOU COULD ENQUIRE OF THE LORD FOR AN ANSWER. PLEASE DO. I GUESS THERE ARE SOME WHO JUST DON'T KNOW THE VALUE AND POWER OF THE CROSS. IF GOD DID IT, IT MUST BE VERY IMPORTANT. SOME JUST DON'T KNOW AND THEY ARE IN MUCH TROUBLE. GOD DOESN'T BOTHER WITH UNIMPORTANT STUFF. I RECOMMEND THAT YOU KEEP THE CROSS FRONT AND CENTER IN EVERY PLACE OF WORSHIP. NO CROSS, NO CHRIST, NO CHRIST NO REDEMPTION, NO REDEMPTION, NO SALVATION. NO SALVATION, NO HOPE. HOW DEVASTATING. YOU ARE IN VERY DARK CIRCUMSTANCES. TO BE SURE, KEEP THE CROSS IN VIEW, ALWAYS. IF GOD DOESN'T MAKE IT AN OPTION, YOU BETTER NOT EITHER. I DON'T WANT YOU TO FIND OUT THE HARD WAY, IT COULD BE VERY DEADLY, FATAL. JUST TO KNOW HIM IS THE WAY OF THE CROSS. BY HIS GRACE AND LOVE, HE IS ENOUGH. JESUS IS ENOUGH. WHEN HE WAS SENT TO BE THE GOOD SHEPHERD AND GO TO A CROSS FOR MY SALVTION, TO PAY MY SIN DEBT, HE WAS DOING THE ULTIMATE LOVING THING TO SAVE ME. FOR THAT ACT OF LOVE HIS FATHER HAS FOREVER ESTEEMED HIM AS THE JOY OF HEAVEN. JESUS THE JOY OF HIS FATHER, THE ULTIMATE SACRIFICE AND THE PRIDE OF HIS FATHER, THE SAVIOR OF GOD'S GREATEST CREATION. O YES, HE IS THE GOOD SHEPHERD ORDAINED BY HIS FATHER TO BE THE JOY OF HIS HEAVEN AND ETERNITY. GOD SO LOVED HIS WORLD HE GAVE HIS ONLY BEGOTTEN SON TO SAVE ME. DO YOU THINK I AM HUMBLED BY WHAT GOD AND HIS SON DID FOR ME. FOR ALL ETERNITY I WILL LOVE MY JESUS AND WORSHIP HIM AND HIS MOST HOLY FATHER AND THE MOST HIGH AND HOLY, HOLY GHOST. THE CROSS IS HIS PROOF OF HIS LOVE FOR ME,

HOW COULD I DISREGARD THE CROSS, THE ALTAR OF HIS GRACE, THE SACRIFICE OF HIS SON. O' HIS GRACE, O' HIS UNDYING LOVE FOR ME. I WILL FOREVER COME TO THE CROSS, HIS CROSS FOR WORSHIP AND A REMEMBRANCE OF HIS LOVE, HIS ALTAR OF GRACE. WHERE WOULD I BE WITHOUT THE CROSS, HIS CROSS. GOD'S PLAN WAS AND IS THAT WE COME TO THE CROSS TO WORSHIP. THE ALTAR THAT THE FATHER PUT HIS SON ON, MOST BELOVED AND SO CHERISHED. FROM THE TIME OF BEGINNING AND WILL BE TO THE END, HIS MOST BELOVED SON OF HIS ETERNAL EXISTANCE. JESUS IS ETERNAL EVEN THOUGH HE WAS ON EARTH FOR SUCH A SHORT TIME. HE FINISHED HIS ASSIGNMENT AND WENT BACK TO HIS FATHER, FOREVER. THAT'S HOW IT IS AND WILL NEVER CHANGE. AMEN.

I WANT TO STAND SO CLOSE TO THE CROSS, THAT THE
BLOOD THAT DRIPS FROM HIS
BROKEN BODY, DRIPS ON ME. I DID, IT DID. I AM WASHED IN
HIS BLOOD.
O' COME LET US ADORE HIM. EVEN SO, COME LORD JESUS,
COME. HE IS SO GLORIOUS.

MY DARLING, MY BELOVED, MY GOD

TO GOD ONLY WISE, BE GLORY THROUGH JESUS CHRIST FOR EVER. AMEN.
ROMANS 16:27

O' HE IS ALL OF THE ABOVE AND HE WILL ALWAYS BE. I WILL NOT CHANGE MY MIND AND GO A DIFFERENT WAY. YOU KNOW THE SCRIPTURE SAYS "HE IS THE WAY, THE TRUTH AND THE LIFE: NO MAN COMETH UNTO THE FATHER, BUT BY HIM". THAT'S THE WAY IT HAS BEEN SINCE HE WALKED THIS EARTH, AND I LIKE IT. I DEARLY LOVE HIM. HE WAS MY DARLING WHEN HE CAME TO THE EARTH, HE WAS MY BELOVED WHEN HE WALKED ON THIS EARTH, AND HE HAS BEEN MY GOD SINCE THE BEGINNING OF TIME. YES... YOU CAN NOT CHANGE ANY OF WHAT WAS WRITTEN BEGINNING WITH PRE'GENESIS 1:1. BESIDES WHY WOULD YOU WANT TO? ALL IS ORDAINED BY THE FATHER AND HE IS IN CHARGE OF ALL OF THE HEAVENS AND THE VAST UNIVERSE OF STARS AND LIGHTS OF HIS CREATION. GO HAVE A LOOK AFTER SUNSET INTO THE MIDDLE OF THE NIGHT. W.O.W. WONDERFUL O WONDERFUL. IT'S MORE THAN YOU OR I CAN IMAGINE. HE DID IT ALL, HE DOES IT ALL, AND WILL BE LORD OVER ALL OF IT WHEN WE ARE ALL HISTORY. THAT WILL GIVE YOU A HEADACHE TO TRY AND THINK ABOUT IT. HIS PLANS ARE TOO ETERNAL TO TAKE IN. THAT'S WHAT HE DOES. WE ARE SO FORTUNATE TO BE HERE TO WATCH ALL THIS UNFOLD. THANK YOU, MY MOST WONDERFUL DARLING, BELOVED AND MY GOD. TIME WILL SOON RUNOUT AND WE WILL BE OUT OF HERE. HOPEFULLY, ALL WILL BE SAVED AND WE CAN ALL LEAVE TOGETHER. I SO WANT ALL OF MY FAMILY SAVED. I HAVE BEEN AFTER ALL WHO ARE CLOSE TO BEGIN TO LIVE FOR JESUS. O' YES AND MY CHURCH FAMILY, TOO. SALVATION IS FREE, JUST ASK HIM TO COME INTO YOUR HEART AND INTO YOUR SOUL. HE IS HERE

FOR THE ASKING, SO ASK. IT COULDN'T BE ANY EASIER AND THAT'S WHAT HE DID; SO, YOU ARE WITHOUT EXCUSE O MAN. ROMANS 1:20. DON'T LET IT SLIP. EVERY DAY IS OPEN FOR YOU TO COME INTO THE FLOCK AND FOLD. STAND STILL AND ALLOW THE GOOD SHEPHERD TO FIND YOU. YOU ARE THE ONE WHO IS LOST, SO LET HIM FIND YOU. HE IS SO GENTLE, HE WILL PICK YOU UP AND PUT YOU ON HIS SHOULDER AND CARRY YOU TO A SAFE PLACE. ISN'T THAT BEAUTIFUL? HE IS CONSTANTLY SEARCHING FOR THE LOST SHEEP SO AS NOT TO ALLOW THE LIONS AND WOLVES TO GRAB THEM FOR LUNCH OR DINNER. THE GOOD SHEPHERD HAS A VERY WATCHFULL EYE FOR THE LAMBS WHO MAY STRAY TOO CLOSE TO THE EDGE OF SAFETY. HE'S GOOD AT PROTECTING THE LITTLE STRAYS WHO ARE SO CURIOUS ABOUT WHAT'S GOING ON OUTSIDE OF THE FLOCK. IF THEY WANDER TOO FAR IT COULD BE FATAL. EVERYONE OF THE LAMBS IS IMPORTANT TO HIM. SO, LITTLE LAMB BE SAFE AND FOLLOW THE GOOD SHEPHERD TO SAFETY. SO ALSO, OUR GOOD SHEPHERD WHO IS A CONSTANT TO WATCH FOR YOU AND ME, THE SAVIOR WHO WILL LEAD YOU TO SAFETY AND STILL WATERS AND GREEN PASTURES. HE CARES SO MUCH FOR US. WHEN WE FINALLY REALIZE HOW MUCH HE CARES WE WILL FOLLOW SO CLOSE AND WATCH HIS EVERY MOVE SO WE DON'T GET OUT OF HIS SIGHT. WHEN NIGHT COMES, HE WILL LEAD ALL THE SHEEP AND LAMBS TO A SAFE COVE, FENCED FOR OUR PROTECTION FROM THE HUNGRIES AND THE STALKERS. HE REMAINS ALERT AND READY WITH HIS ROD TO DEFEND THE GATES OF THE FOLD. WE ARE SAFE AS HE IS DILIGENT TO STAND HIS GROUND TO KEEP SLEEPING LAMBS AT PEACE. THE FOLD IS SAFE GROUND FOR THE SHEEP AND LAMBS TO REST. OUR GOOD SHEPHERD IS SO ALERT TO THE SHADOWS AND NOISES OF THE NIGHT. HE WILL AND CAN DEFEND AGAINST THE MOST WICKED AND HUNGRY OUTSIDE OF THE SAFE PLACE HE HAS CHOSEN. AS WE DRAW NEAR TO THE DAY OF OUR LORD. WE,

THE SHEEP AND LAMBS ARE SO CLOSE TO OUR GOOD SHEPHERD IN ANTICIPATION OF OUR JOURNEY. WHAT A DAY OF REJOICING THAT WILL BE. WHEN THAT TRUMPET SOUNDS, BE READY, CONTINUE TO PREPARE FOR THE DAY AND THE JOURNEY. GO AFTER REDEMPTION AND HIS WONDERFUL SALVATION. BE DILIGENT TO LISTEN FOR THE TRUMPET SOUNDING. THE HEAVENS WILL OPEN AND THE SHEEP AND LAMBS WILL BE USHERED IN. HALLELUJAH. REJOICE IN THE LORD, AGAIN I SAY, REJOICE IN THE LORD. HE IS WORTHY TO BE PRAISED. THE DAY IS COMING, BE READY. AMEN

I AM GOING TO PLAN, BECAUSE I AM PLANNING TO GO. YOU MUST BE BORN AGAIN. HE LOVES YOU NOT BECAUSE OF WHO YOU ARE, BUT BECAUSE OF WHO HE IS.
HIS ESSENCE, THE POWER OF CHRIST RELEASED. HIS FRAGRANCE, PERFUME, SWEET SMELLING OIL AND ANOINTING OF HIS HEALING POWER.
HIS PRESENCE, TO BECOME AWARE OF HIM. TO HEAR AND FEEL HIS BREATH.

IN HIS PERFECTION

HEREIN IS OUR LOVE MADE PERFECT, THAT WE MAY HAVE BOLDNESS IN THE DAY OF JUDGMENT: BECAUSE AS HE IS, SO ARE WE IN THIS WORLD. 1 JOHN 4:17

SCRIPTURE SAYS THAT JESUS NEVER SINNED. TRUE, HE IS OUR SPOTLESS AND PURE LAMB. HE HAS BEEN SINCE THE BEGINNING OF TIME, OR THE BEGINNING OF GOD'S TIME. BEFORE TIME EVER WAS, THERE WAS THE GOD OF THE UNIVERSE. GOD OF INFINITY. GOD OF ETERNITY. HIS PLAN WAS THAT HIS CHRIST WOULD BE THE REDEMPTION FOR THE MAN WHO WOULD FORSAKE GOD'S PLAN IN THE GARDEN OF EDEN. NOW, WE KNOW THAT STORY, DON'T WE? O, THAT WE HAD NEVER MESSED UP. THESE THOUSANDS OF YEARS OF SIN AND ERROR. HOWEVER, WE ARE DELIVERED BY THE ONE WHO BY HIS GRACE REDEEMED US. BY THE ONE WHO IS PERFECT, THE ONE WHO KNEW THAT HIS FATHER AND OUR GOD WOULD NEED THE PERFECTION OF HIS SON TO SAVE THE ONES LOST FROM THE GARDEN. THE SINLESS ONE OF HIS FATHER'S FAVOR. I BELIEVE THAT OUR LORD JESUS CHRIST, WHO WALKED WITH US TWO THOUSAND YEARS AGO, AS OUR EXAMPLE, WHO IF WE WOULD FOLLOW WOULD LEAD US THRU LIFE AND INTO ETERNITY, SPOTLESS. WE ARE GRATEFUL FOR OUR SPOTLESS LAMB WHO PAID OUR WAY SO WE COULD LIVE WITH OUR HEAVENLY FATHER WHEN OUR BRIEF LIVES ARE OVER. IN HIS PERFECTION. THERE WAS AND IS NO OTHER WAY. ONLY THROUGH HIM ARE WE ACCEPTABLE TO THE FATHER AND INTO THE HEAVENLIES. THERE ARE SOME WHO JUST CAN'T SEE HOW THAT CAN BE. THAT'S SO SAD. HE IS ALWAYS CALLING TO OUR HEARTS TO COME FOLLOW HIM IN THE REGENERATION OF LIFE. BE BORN AGAIN, TURN YOUR LIFE OVER TO THE SAVIOR. HE IS THE GIFT THAT KEEPS ON GIVING, AND GIVING. HIS PERFECTION IS SO EASY TO FOLLOW,

NOT OUR PERFECTION. WE MISSED THAT PART LONG AGO. SO, IN THE GRACE AND MERCY OF THE FATHER HE SENT HIS SON TO BE OUR SUBSTITUTE, OUR REDEEMER. WE NEEDED A HOLY ONE TO BE OUR CROSS BEARER. THE CROSS BEING THE PUNISHMENT WE DESERVED, AND THE CUP WE COULD NOT DRINK. HE TOOK THE BEATING ON THE WHIPPING POST WE COULDN'T POSSIBLY ENDURE. ISAIAH, THE PROPHET TELLS US THAT JESUS WAS NOT RECOGNIZABLE AS A PERSON WHEN THEY WERE THRU WITH THE TORMENT OF THE LASHING. HIS NAKED BODY WAS LASHED UNTIL THERE WAS NO MORE ROOM FOR INJURY. EVERY LASH ON HIS BACK, ARMS AND LEGS TOOK ITS TOLL. THAT'S THE WAGES OF SIN PUT ON ONE WHO WAS SINLESS. SHOULD HAVE BEEN ON YOU AND ME. FAST FORWARD TO 2021 AD, THANK YOU, JESUS. I WILL FOLLOW YOU AND FOREVER BE GRATEFUL FOR YOUR/OUR SALVATION. WHAT EVER WOULD I DO IF YOU DIDN'T GO FOR ME. DIE FOR ME. LIVE AGAIN FOR ME. THANK YOU, FOR THE PAYMENT MADE FOR ME, THE HELL LAID ON YOU THAT SHOULD HAVE BEEN MY JUST DESSERTS. MY WONDERFUL HEAVENLY FATHER RAISED HIS SON OF PERFECTION FROM THE DEAD THAT I MAY HAVE ETERNAL LIFE. HE TOOK WHAT I DESERVED AND GAVE ME HIS LIFE. HE SET ME FREE FROM THE HORRORS OF HELL AND ETERNAL DEATH AND PUNISHMENT. NOW HE SAYS FOLLOW ME AND WALK INTO THE LAVISH LIFE OF HIS PERFECTION. LIFE LASTING NOW FOREVER. PEACE, HIS PEACE, GRACE AND FAVOR. HIS PROMISES HE KEEPS, ALL I HAVE TO DO IS ACCEPT HIS OFFER OF MERCIFUL REDEMPTION. IT'S MINE. I TAKE IT. YOU SHOULD TOO. IT'S PAID FOR. HE PAID IT ALL, I TAKE IT ALL. WORSHIP, PRAISE AND THANKSGIVING. HE IS WORTHY, SO WORTHY. THAT'S GRACE, WONDERFUL GRACE, POWERFUL GRACE AND LOVE. THERE IS A WEDDING SUPPER PLANNED IN THE BANQUET HALL OF HEAVEN. EVERYONE 'SHOW UP', PLEASE. DON'T DISAPPOINT OUR LORD. NO! BE FOUND IN HIS PERFECTION, HIS PROFOUND

PERFECTION. AMEN. I GUESS I HAVE SAID ALL THAT I CAN. STILL, HE IS WORTHY OF ALL PRAISE AND WORSHIP. IT WOULD TAKE MANY BOOKS AND LOTS OF TIME TO WRITE ALL THAT TELLS HOW I FEEL ABOUT MY SAVIOR. YOU MAY WANT TO CHIME IN WITH YOUR WORSHIP, TOO. COME ON NOW, JUST JUMP IN. THERE'S LOTS OF ROOM. HE HAS MADE ROOM FOR ALL OF THE WHOSOEVER WILL, THAT'S HIS GRACE. O HIS GRACE. YES, AND AMEN.

PERFECTION! AMEN I JOHN 4:17-19 AMEN PERFECTION!
AS HE IS AT THE RIGHT HAND OF THE FATHER, SO AM I, IN THIS WORLD. COL 3:1
IN HIS FORGIVENESS, HE IS HOLY, SO AM I. I GIVE YOU ALL THE GLORY.
BE AGED IN HIS GRACE, STEEPED IN HIS WORD, POURED OUT IN HIS GLORY
I LOVE MY JESUS. AMEN YES AND AMEN AMEN I LOVE MY JESUS.

8-24-21
THE VALUE OF WOOD IN THE SCRIPTURE

I HEARD THIS MORNING THAT WOOD IS OF GREAT VALUE, AS SUPPORT FOR ALL THE GLORY OF GOD. IN THE TEMPLE, THE WOOD IS OVERLAID WITH GOLD. THE WOOD SUPPORTS THE GOLD. IT WAS REVEALED TO ME BY THE HOLY GHOST THIS MORNING, I HEARD IT. WOOD WAS FOR THE ARK OF NOAH AND THE ARK OF THE COVENANT. THE WOOD SUPPORTED MY 'SALVATION AND REDEMPTION', 'T' THE CROSS OF MY LORD JESUS CHRIST. 'I HAVE NO BOAST'. I DID A WRITE THAT WHEN JESUS WAS CONCEIVED IN GOD'S CHOSEN, (ME) GOD PLANTED, BY THE HOLY GHOST, ALSO A TREE (SEED) THAT WOOD GROW TO BE THE TREE FOR HIS SON, JESUS' CROSS (CRUCIFIXION). THE GROUND SO BLESSED AND HONORED TO GROW THE TREE THAT WAS FOR THE SUPPORT OF MY JESUS, SALVATION AND REDEMPTION, T 'T' T, THE CROSS. GOD MADE A GOOD REPORT OF MY NAME. THANK YOU, MY PRECIOUS FATHER. IT WAS NOT JUST A RANDOM CROSS, IT WAS PLANTED, HARVESTED AND DELIVERED TO THE HILL OF CALVARY FOR THE ALTAR OF HIS SON, MY LORD JESUS CHRIST, HIS SACRIFICE FOR MY SALVATION AND REDEMPTION. HE DID IT FOR ALL WHO WOOD BELIEVE. THANK YOU, O' MY GOD, SO BEAUTIFUL.

AMEN, SO BE IT
BY HIS GRACE, ARLENE M. WOOD
AKA MEZZECHAH, MY CREATED NAME.
OF THE ORDER OF MELCHIZEDEK

IF YOU NEED TO READ MORE OF THIS INCIDENT. PLEASE SEE
MY WRITE, "THE ALTAR OF GRACE, THE CROSS OF CHRIST".
PLEASE SEE THE OBEDIENCE OF THE SEEED.

THE "LIFE" OF THE PARTY

TO PARTY IS * "TO CELEBRATE" * IS TO PARTY

MY JESUS REALLY IS THE LIFE OF THE PARTY, I TRULY BELIEVE AND I KNOW I CELEBRATE EVERY DAY FOR ALL HE HAS GIVEN ME. IT'S A PARTY OR CELEBRATION OF THANKSGIVING. CELEBRATE! I CELEBRATE CHRIST'S LIFE THAT GAVE ME LIFE, MY REDEMPTION, MY SALVATION. WHAT'S NOT TO CELEBRATE? MY LIFE AND THE SAVING LIFE, THE LIFE SAVING CELEBRATION, JESUS. * HALLALUJAH, MY GOD LIVES. * I AM REFERENCING THE WEDDING FEAST IN CANA WHEN JESUS TURNED THE WATER INTO WINE. THEY RAN OUT OF WINE SO HE HELPED OUT WITH THE PROBLEM. HE TRULY WAS/IS THE LIFE OF THE PARTY. THE WEDDING FEAST (PARTY) WAS IN TROUBLE AS THE WINE HAD RUN OUT. SO HE ORDERED A NEW SUPPLY OF WINE SO AS NOT TO EMBARRASS THE HOST OF THE WEDDING PARTY. HE IS THE LIFE OF EVERY CELEBRATION THAT SHOUTS LIFE, ETERNAL LIFE. THE TRUE JOY OF EVERY DAY. HIS LIFE BRINGS JOY AND STRENGTH. I HOPE YOU ARE GETTING THE GIST OF THIS WRITE. IT'S JESUS AND THE WONDER OF LIFE. HE SURE IS THE SPIRIT AND GLORY AND JOY AND LOVE AND, WELL, THE LIST IS ENDLESS. HE IS ALL THOSE THINGS AND MORE. I KNOW THEY USE THE TERM "LIFE OF THE PARTY" IN CARNAL WAYS BUT MOSTLY I BELIEVE THAT THEY BORROWED IT FROM THE WAYS OF OUR SCRIPTURE IN JOHN 2:1-11. JESUS WILL ALWAYS BE THE LIFE OF OUR CELEBRATION OF EVERLASTING LIFE. HALLELUJAH, MY GOD REIGNS. * DON'T YOU JUST LOVE HIM. AMEN. IS HE NOT THE LIFE OF EVERY SITUATION OF EVERY DAY? WHEN DON'T WE NEED HIM, WHEN DON'T WE SEEK HIS HELP, WHEN DON'T WE LOVE AND ADORE HIM? I BELIEVE HE IS THE "LIFE" OF EVEN THE MOST MENIAL CHORES OR JOBS.

WHAT CAN I DO WITHOUT HIM? HE IS IN ALL THAT I DO. HE GIVES WORDS TO SAY, HE GIVES THE RIGHT DIRECTION, HE GIVES RIGHT MOTIVES. WHAT IS THERE THAT HE DOESN'T ORCHESTRATE. HE'S MY BREATH, MY HEARING, MY SIGHT. MY GETTING UP AND LYING DOWN. WHEN IS HE NOT NEEDED OR NECESSARY TO JUST BE? HALLELUJAH, MY GOD LIVES. * DON'T YOU JUST LOVE HIM. * WHEN THEY ASK WHERE'S THE PARTY JUST ANSWER, "RIGHT HERE", THIS IS WHERE JESUS IS, HE ABIDES WITH ME. CAN YOU IMAGINE THE PARTY, THE CELEBRATION, WE WILL HAVE AND ENJOY WHEN WE ARRIVE IN THE BANQUET HALL OF HEAVEN? THE WEDDING PARTY (CELEBRATION) THAT WAS PLANNED FROM THE FOUNDATION OF THE WORLD, WITH THE GRAND MASTER, BRIDEGROOM, JESUS, LEADING THE CELEBRATION. I CAN'T WAIT. HE IS QUITE THE CELEBRATION (PARTY) PLANNER. HALLELUJAH, MY GOD REIGNS. * DON'T YOU JUST LOVE HIM. I KNOW BECAUSE I HAVE SEEN SOME OF HIS MEETS AND GREETS, HE'S DONE ON THIS SIDE OF HEAVEN. ALL THE HEAVENLY SHOWS HE HAS AMAZED US WITH. ECLIPES, METEOR SHOWERS. HOW ABOUT THE RAINBOW OR EVERY DAY A DIFFERENT SUNRISE AND SUNSET? HE IS SO TALENTED, GIFTED, ORIGINAL, HAVE YOU EVER JUST SAT OUT ON A SUMMER NIGHT TO JUST ENJOY THE MOON AND STARS? NOW, THAT'S A PARTY. HE IS THE "LIFE" OF THE PARTY WHEN IT'S JUST YOU SITTING IN THE AWE AND WONDER OF HIS BEAUTIFUL LANDSCAPES AND SEASCAPES AND BEAUTIFUL PORTRAITS OF HIS BELOVEDS. HALLELUJAH, MY GOD LOVES. * DON'T YOU JUST LOVE HIM. I KEEP SAYING THAT, BECAUSE "I JUST LOVE HIM". CONSIDER THIS, THE JOY OF COMMUNION. I HAVE OR DO A COMMUNION EVERY DAY. WE COME TOGETHER TO BREAK BREAD AND DRINK THE CUP. I HAVE LIFE LASTING NOW FOREVER, BECAUSE HE WENT TO A CRUEL CROSS FOR ME, IN MY PLACE, PAID MY DEBT. SO I AM IN JOYFUL THANKSGIVING, AS I SHOULD BE, COMMUNION IS THE

CELEBRATION OF MY SALVATION AND REDEMPTION. HE DOESN'T WANT A LONG, SAD FACE TO COME TO THE TABLE. MY SAD WEEPY POSITION DOESN'T SAY THANK YOU FOR YOUR BEAUTIFUL SACRIFICE. IT'S A JOYFUL EVENT. * HALLELUJAH, MY GOD LIVES. * DON'T YOU JUST LOVE HIM. MY JESUS, THE "ETERNAL LIFE" OF THE PARTY. THANK YOU, JESUS, I LOVE YOU FOR BEING THE "BEAUTIFUL LIFE" OF THE PARTY (CELEBRATION)". HALLELUJAH, MY GOD LOVES. * DON'T YOU JUST LOVE HIM. * HALLELUJAH, MY GOD LIVES. * YES, I JUST LIVE FOR HIM. THIS IS NOT TO SAY YOU SHOULD DO AS I DO, BUT THAT IN YOUR OWN WAY BE SURE TO GIVE THANKS FOR ALL HE HAS DONE. HE DID IT FOR ALL OF THOSE WHO APPRECIATE HIS SACRIFICE. THE ONLY ONE WHO COULD SACRIFICE AND PAY FOR ALL MY NEED, HIS CROSS. THANK YOU, JESUS. I BLESS YOU.

HALLELUJAH! GOD IS MOST GLORIFIED IN ME WHEN I AM MOST SANCTIFIED IN HIM. IS HE THE MOST WONDERFUL OR WHAT? O' HE IS. TASTE HIM AND SEE. HALLELUJAH!

SPOKEN IN THE DARK, HEARD IN THE LIGHT

THEREFORE' WHATSOEVER YE HAVE SPOKEN IN DARKNESS SHALL BE HEARD IN THE LIGHT: AND THAT WHICH YE HAVE SPOKEN IN THE EAR IN THE CLOSETS SHALL BE PROCLAIMED UPON THE HOUSETOPS. LUKE 12:3

WHAT YOU SAY IN THE DARK WILL MOST CERTAINLY BE HEARD IN THE LIGHT. JESUS WARNED THE DISCIPLES TO BEWARE OF THE PHARISEES WHO PRETEND TO BE HOLY WHEN THEY WERE NOT. THEIR HYPOCRISY WILL BE FOUND OUT AND WHAT EVER THE DISCIPLES SAY IN THE CLOSET WILL BE HEARD WHEN BROADCAST FROM THE HOUSETOPS FOR ALL TO HEAR. DO NOT FEAR THE ONES WHO CAN KILL THE BODY BUT HAVE NO POWER TO CAST INTO HELL. FEAR GOD. REVERENCE HIM. HE HAS THE POWER TO SEND YOU TO HELL. HE KNOWS THE NUMBER OF HAIRS ON YOUR HEAD, THAT'S HOW MUCH YOUR FATHER KNOWS AND LOVES YOU. HE SAID AS HE IS THE MESSIAH, HE WILL PUBLICLY HONOR YOU IN THE PRESENCE OF THE ANGELS IF WE PUBLICLY ACKNOWLEDGE OUR GOD ON EARTH AS HIS FRIEND, BUT IF NOT, HE WILL NOT ACKNOWLEDGE ME AMONG ALL MEN AND THE ANGELS. THOSE WHO SPEAK AGAINST THE SON MAY BE FORGIVEN, BUT THOSE WHO SPEAK AGAINST THE HOLY GHOST SHALL NEVER BE FORGIVEN. THESE ARE THE WORDS OF THE LORD. SO LET ME WARN YOU ALSO, THAT YOU HAVE MUCH RESPECT FOR THE WORD OF GOD, HIS PRECIOUS SON, JESUS IS THE WORD OF GOD. YOU KNOW JESUS IS HIS MOST HIGH AND HOLY AND PRECIOUS SON. DON'T YOU? IF YOU TELL YOUR SECRETS TO SOMEONE WHO HAS A LOOSE TONGUE, THEY JUST MAY SPREAD IT ALL OVER TOWN. THAT'S SORT OF LIKE THE TITLE OF THIS WRITE. THINGS SPOKEN IN CONFIDENCE TO A FRIEND COULD POSSIBLY BECOME THE

HEADLINE OF THE TOWN NEWSPAPER. YOU DON'T WANT THAT, DO YOU? JUST LOVE YOUR FRIEND. I FEEL LIKE A BOMB JUST WENT OFF. I HAVE SAID STUFF THAT WAS MEANT FOR ONLY THE ONE IN FRONT OF ME. HOWEVER, IT WAS SOUNDED ABROAD. THE ONLY ONE TO TRUST WITH YOUR SECRETS IS OUR LORD. SOMETIMES I WISH HE WOULD GO TELL IT ON THE MOUNTAIN AS THERE ARE THINGS, I WOULD LIKE TO HAVE THE WHOLE WORLD TO KNOW. HIS SAVING OF THOSE LOST WOULD BE A REALLY GOOD THING. HE IS THE BEST NEWS EVER. I HAVE SHARED THE NEWS OF HIS LOVE THAT GOES ALL AROUND THE WORLD. I SO WOULD HOPE THAT THE WHOLE WORLD KNOWS. HIS LOVE AND WISDOM IS THE BEST NEWS ANYONE WILL EVER HEAR. HE LOVES THE MOST UNLOVABLE. THAT IS THE MOST WONDERFUL THING AND THE WHOLE WORLD SHOULD KNOW THAT, TOO. THERE IS A GIRL IN MY CHURCH WHO SO NEEDS TO HEAR THE GOOD NEWS. SHE SEEMS TO BE RESISTENT TO ANYONE WHO WANTS TO SHARE WITH HER. SHE IS RESISTANT TO THE CROSS, TOO. I THINK SHE MAY BE IN REBELLION, OR MAYBE POSSESSED OF/BY AN UNCLEAN SPIRIT. MAYBE SOMEONE HAS BETRAYED HER, FOR THAT I AM SO SORRY. I LOVE THAT GIRL AND WANT TO WITNESS TO HER. I THINK SHE IS NOT A HAPPY PERSON, HOW COULD SHE BE?...SHE NEEDS JESUS. ONLY JESUS CAN BRING HAPPINESS. I AM A WITNESS OF THAT. HE IS THE ROOT OF ALL GOOD THINGS. I AM SO GLAD TO BE HIS. I WILL NOT GIVE UP ON HER THOUGH. GOD CAN GET HOLD OF HER IF I CAN'T. O HE WILL, HE KNOWS ALL THERE IS TO KNOW ABOUT THE REBELLIOUS ONES. THAT'S HIS LOVE, LOVE SO ABOVE. I WILL NOT GIVE UP. IN THE DARK, AT MY BED, WITH BENDED KNEE, I WILL GIVE HER TO THE LOVE OF JESUS. HIS WAYS ARE NOT MY WAYS, HE HAS A WAY. HE CAN MAKE A WAY WHERE THERE IS NO WAY. TALK TO HIM. HE IS ALWAYS UP FOR COMMUNICATION WITH HIS OWN. O JESUS. I MUST STAY CLOSE TO HIM SO AS TO HEAR HIM AND RESPOND IF I CAN. WE,

HE AND I ARE GOOD WITH ONE ANOTHER. HE IS THE BEST FRIEND EVER. SO, MY PRAYER SPOKEN IN THE DARK WILL BE HEARD IN HIS LIGHT. SEE, IT WORKS. SEE, HE WORKS. HE IS SO A TRUSTED FRIEND AND I AM SO GLAD HE IS MY SAVIOR. WHERE WOULD I BE WITHOUT HIM? I DO NOT WANT TO FIND OUT. WHEN ALL IS SAID AND DONE, WE WILL LEAVE THE EARTH IN VIEW OF ONE AND OTHER, HE SAID SO. I SO LOOK FORWARD TO THAT DAY. THE DAY OF THE RAPTURE, O GLORY. WHAT A DAY OF REJOICING THAT WILL BE. YOU ALREADY KNOW ALL OF THAT, HUH? YOU DO NOW. YOU DO NOW.... AMEN AND AMEN.

NOT GOD FIRST, GOD ONLY. HE WILL BE ONLY OR HE WON'T BE ANY.
HE LOVES YOU NOT BECAUSE OF WHO YOU ARE, BUT BECAUSE OF WHO HE IS.
BE AGED IN HIS GRACE, STEEPED IN HIS WORD, POURED OUT IN HIS GLORY
YOU CAN'T ALWAYS CONTROL WHAT YOU HEAR, BUT YOU CAN ALWAYS CONTROL WHAT YOU SAY. YOU ARE THE AUTHOR OF YOUR WORDS. YOU ARE ACCOUNTABLE.

WATER AND POWER

WE ARE NOT REFERRING TO THE PUBLIC UTILITY. LONG BEFORE THERE WAS WATER AND POWER COMING INTO YOUR HOUSE, THERE WAS THE WATER AND POWER OF THE HEAVENLIES. YES INDEED. JESUS IS THE LIVING WATER POURING FROM HIM TO ALL WHO ASK FOR THAT LIVING WATER. JOHN 4:1-30. YES. JESUS IS THE LIVING WATER. THE WORDS THAT POUR OUT OF HIM ARE WORDS OF LIFE. TO DRINK OF THE LIVING WATER, YOU WILL NEVER THRIST AGAIN. FOLLOW JESUS AND RECEIVE FROM HIM WORDS THAT YOU MAY NOT THIRST AGAIN. THIS IS SO BEAUTIFUL. HE MET THE WOMAN AT THE WELL AND OFFERED HER LIVING WATER, HOWEVER SHE TOLD HIM HE WAS NOT ABLE TO GET WATER AS HE HAD NO WAY TO GET IT BECAUSE THE WELL WAS DEEP AND HE HAD NO BUCKET TO RETRIEVE IT. HE DID, HE IS THE LIVING WATER. HE DID CONVINCE HER OF WHO HE WAS/IS. SHE WAS CONVINCED AND WENT TO HER HOME TOWN, SYCHAR, WHERE SHE LIVED TO TELL THE POPULOUS THAT SHE MET JESUS. THE MAN WHO GIVES LIVING WATER. HE DID PROVE HIMSELF TO BE THE LIVING WATER. SHE TOLD THE MEN IN TOWN THAT SHE HAD MET A MAN WHO CAN GIVE HER LIVING WATER. THE LIVING WATER HE WAS REFERRING TO IS THE WORD OF GOD. IT POURS OUT OF HIM. WORDS OF LIFE AND TRUTH. HE BEGAN TO TELL HER TO GO CALL HER HUSBAND BUT SHE SAID SHE HAD NO HUSBAND. HE KNEW IT AND SAID SHE HAD FIVE AND THE ONE SHE IS WITH IS NOT HER HUSBAND. SHE BELIEVED HIM TO BE A PROPHET. THE WATER WAS HER INTRODUCTION TO JESUS, SHE WAS CHANGED HAVING SPOKEN TO JESUS AT THE WELL. SHE SAID THAT SHE KNEW MESSIAH WOULD COME WHO IS CALLED

CHRIST. HE SAID "I THAT SPEAK UNTO THEE AM HE". SHE WENT TO HER TOWN AND TOLD THE MEN OF HER TIME SHE WAS WITH JESUS. THEN THE MEN ALSO WENT OUT OF THE CITY TO SEE JESUS. WHAT A SPECIAL AND BEAUTIFUL MEETING. SHE WAS BLESSED TO BE A TESTIMONY TO HER TOWN AND THE TOWNSPEOPLE. O'JESUS. WE WHO ARE BORN'AGAIN ARE SURE OF THE POWER OF OUR JESUS. HE DID SAY YOU WOULD RECEIVE POWER AFTER THAT THE HOLY GHOST IS COME UPON YOU. WHEN YOU ARE SAVED AND FILLED WITH THE HOLY GHOST, YOU WILL BE POWERED BY THE SPIRIT LIVING IN YOU. ACTS 1:7-8. OUR GOD IS THE ULTIMATE POWER, NOT FOR US TO KNOW THE TIMES OR SEASONS WHICH THE FATHER HAS PUT IN HIS OWN POWER. JESUS DID SAY ALSO HE HAD THE POWER TO LAY DOWN HIS LIFE AND TO TAKE IT UP AGAIN. JOHN 10:18. THE FATHER AND THE SON ARE THE POWERS OF HEAVEN. 1COR 1:18. WE HAVE INSTRUCTIONS FROM OUR FATHER TO USE THE POWERS OF THE HOLY GHOST (THE SPIRIT OF THE LIVING GOD) TO CALL THE NEEDS WE HAVE OF HEALING, SET THOSE WHO ARE BOUND, FREE. NO MATTER WHAT THE PROBLEM, WE ARE ENDUED WITH POWER FROM ON HIGH TO HEAL THE BLIND, THE DEAF, THE HALT AND ALL WHO WERE IMPAIRED BY THE ONE WHO COMES AGAINST THE BELOVEDS OF OUR GOD. WE ARE TO PRAY EARNEST PRAYERS FOR THE GIFTS OF THE SPIRIT. WHEN NEEDED TO LIFT UP THOSE IN A TROUBLED STATE WE MUST BE READY. HE HAS DONE ALL THE WORK FOR US TO BE ABLE AND READY. YOU ARE PREPARED BY THE FATHER TO GET TO IT. HOWEVER, WE MUST STAY CLOSE IN TOUCH WITH OUR GOD, OUR JESUS, AND OUR HOLY GHOST. THAT MEANS TO SPEND EVERY DAY IN THE WORD AND IN PRAYER, TO BE READY FOR THE CALL OF HIS WORK. HE WORKS THROUGH YOU AND ME TO DO THE ASSIGNMENTS. STAY CLOSE TO HIM AND HE WILL BE CLOSE TO YOU. ARE WE BLESSED, WE SURE

ARE. WE ALL LOOK FORWARD TO THE DAY OF THE RAPTURE, IT'S CLOSE, BE READY.

NOT GOD FIRST, GOD ONLY. HE WILL BE ONLY OR HE WON'T BE ANY.
I AM HIS AND HE IS MINE, IT WILL BE THAT WAY TILL THE END OF TIME.
BE AGED IN HIS GRACE, STEEPED IN HIS WORD, POURED OUT IN HIS GLORY.

HE WENT'OUT ON A TREE FOR ME I WILL GO'OUT ON A LIMB FOR HIM

THE CROSS IS SOMETIMES CALLED A TREE, DO YOU KNOW THAT? YOU DO NOW. AS A MATTER OF FACT, I HAVE A TREE IN MY FRONT YARD WITH A LIMB SET ASIDE FOR THAT PURPOSE. IF THAT SHOULD HAPPEN, WHAT AN HONOR TO LEAVE THIS EARTH AS DID MY SAVIOR. MANY OF THE FOLLOWERS OF CHRIST DID JUST THAT. THEY WERE SO BRAVE AND SO HONORED. I HAD WRITTEN A WRITE SOME TIME AGO IN REGARDS TO THIS SUBJECT. YES, MANY HAVE SAID THE SAME THING. TO LEAVE THIS LIFE, AS DID OUR SAVIOR, IS AS SOME SAY "AN HONOR." I WOULD HOPE TO BE COURAGEOUS ENOUGH TO ACTUALLY DO IT. I CAN'T IMAGINE HOW HARD IT MAY BE TO FOLLOW THROUGH, BUT TO DENY THE LORD, AS YOU WOULD HAVE TO, WOULD BE A GRIEF UNBEARABLE. O FATHER, GIVE US THE COURAGE TO STAND STRONG IN OUR JESUS. WE MUST BE BRAVE AS OUR JESUS WAS AND IS. YOU KNOW HE IS ALWAYS WITH US, SO KEEP YOUR EYES AND HEART ON HIS LOVE. WE HAVE TO BE STRONG IN OUR MINDS AND HAVE OUR HEARTS FIXED ON HIM. GOTTA BE A BRAVE SOUL, TOO. I SO WANT TO BE ABLE TO LEAVE IN THE RAPTURE AND NOT HAVE TO FACE THE HORROR OF A CROSS. O GOD, GIVE ME STRENGTH. SO MANY MARTYRS HAVE FACED SUCH HORRORS AND GAVE UP THEIR LIVES. THANK YOU, FOR YOUR FAITHFULNESS. I WILL DO THE SAME HOPEFULLY, WHEN IT'S MY TURN. THANK YOU. DON'T YOU JUST LOVE TO READ ABOUT THE ONES WHO HAVE GONE BEFORE AND ARE PROOF OF DEDICATION TO OUR FAITH. I LOVE MY SAVIOR. HE DIED FOR ME AND I SO WANT TO LIVE FOR HIM AND IF NEED BE, DIE FOR

HIM. HE IS SO WORTHY. I BELIEVE THAT EVERY ONE OF THE DISCIPLES WAS KILLED FOR THE PRIVILEGE TO DIE FOR THE LORD. SO BEAUTIFUL, SO PRECIOUS ARE THE SOULS OF THE ONES WHO KNEW THE LORD AND DIED FOR HIM. I AM SURE THAT THEY SAW IT AS A MUST TO REPRESENT THE LORD TO THE WHOLE WORLD. IT'S A PLEASURE TO READ THE SCRIPTURES AND WITNESS THE BRAVERY OF THE FOLLOWERS OF OUR LORD JESUS CHRIST. HALLELUJAH. I SURE DO LOVE HIM, MY JESUS AND HIS FATHER. TOO. O YAH AND I LOVE THE BLESSED HOLY GHOST. I KNOW THAT MY NAME IS WRITTEN IN THE LAMB'S BOOK OF LIFE. I HAVE KNOWN FOR SOME TIME SINCE HE TOLD ME LONG AGO THAT MY CREATED NAME IS MEZZECHAH. DO YOU KNOW YOUR CREATED NAME? IT'S THE NAME GIVEN TO YOU ON THE DAY OF THE CREATION OF MAN, WHEN HE BREATHED THE BREATH OF LIFE INTO YOU ON THE SIXTH DAY, THAT NAME WAS WRITTEN IN THE LAMB'S BOOK OF LIFE. WE ALL HAVE A NAME FROM THAT DAY. ENQUIRE WHAT NAME HE GAVE YOU. I AM SURE IT'S BEAUTIFUL. THE DAY OF THE CREATION OF MAN TOOK A THOUSAND YEARS. THE WEEK (7 DAYS) OF CREATION TOOK SEVEN THOUSAND YEARS, THE LAST THOUSAND WAS THE DAY GOD RESTED. 2 PETER 2:8, A DAY WITH THE LORD IS AS A THOUSAND YEARS. YOU MUST FOLLOW FAITHFULLY TO THE END AND YOU MUST BE AN OVERCOMER, OR REVELATION SAYS YOUR NAME WILL BE BLOTTED OUT OF THE LAMB'S BOOK OF LIFE. Rev 3:5 DO NOT ALLOW THAT TO HAPPEN. HE HAS A PLAN FOR ALL THE WHOSOEVER WILL, SO DON'T LET THIS PASS YOU BY. WE ALL LOOK FORWARD TO THE DAY OF THE LORD, OR MOST DO. SOME WILL BE SURPRISED AT THE LAST CALL AND WHEN THEY HEAR THE TRUMPET WON'T UNDERSTAND THE WARNING. DON'T WAIT FOR THE LAST CALL, COME NOW, HIS LOVE CALLS. AMEN.

BE AGED IN HIS GRACE, STEEPED IN HIS WORD, POURED OUT
IN HIS GLORY.
NOT GOD FIRST, GOD ONLY. HE WILL BE ONLY OR HE WON'T
BE ANY. MY DADDY IS SO GOD.
GOD GAVE ME HIS BEST, JESUS.

ASSIGNMENT OR PURPOSE

THERE IS NOTHING NEW UNDER THE SUN

I HAVE HAD MANY ASSIGNMENTS. WHAT WAS TO BE DONE IS MY PURPOSE. I AM SO BLESSED TO HAVE BEEN CHOSEN TO FULFILL WHAT THE LORD OF ALL HEAVEN AND EARTH HAD IN MIND. I HAD HIS PRESENCE WITH ME WHEN THE TIME OF MY ASSIGNMENTS WERE CALLED OUT. IN HIS PRESENCE IS PEACE AND PURPOSE. I SO WANT TO PLEASE HIM. I LISTEN TO THE WORDS FROM HIS HOLY DESIRES TO BE DONE. THY WILL BE DONE. O'YES. GOD HAS OFTEN SAID THAT HIS WILL BE DONE AND IT FALLS ON DEAF EARS. HE MOVES UNFAVORABLY WHEN WE TUNE HIM OUT. IT'S SO IMPORTANT TO PAY ATTENTION TO HIS VOICE THAT FILLS THE AIR WHEN THE SPIRIT SPEAKS. I LOVE TO HEAR WHAT HE HAS TO SAY EVEN IF IT'S CORRECTION. HE IS SO BEAUTIFUL EVEN IN MY PAIN. THERE IS A DAY COMING THAT IT WILL BE JUST HE AND ME, THE JUDGMENT. I AM NOT AFRAID OF THAT DAY, AS HE JUDGES FAIR. SO, DO THE RIGHT THING. THE FEAR OF GOD IS HIS REVERENCE. REVERENCE HIM. SHOW SOME RESPECT AND REVERENCE. ASK FOR FORGIVENESS AND REPENT WHEN YOU MESS'UP. AS I LOOK AROUND THESE DAYS, I DON'T SEE THAT. IT SEEMS MOST ARE IN THEIR OWN WORLD DOING AS THEY PLEASE. DON'T YOU WANT TO PLEASE GOD? JUST LET ME ADD, THERE IS MUCH TO BE SAID FOR PLEASING GOD. JUST DO IT. AS I SAID, I HAVE HAD MANY ASSIGNMENTS AND FINISHED MANY. I WILL BE GRADED ON HOW THE FINISH WAS. I BELIEVE THAT I DID A GOOD JOB, EVEN WHEN I DIDN'T KNOW HE WAS WATCHING. SOMEHOW, I COULD FEEL A PRESENCE WITH ME TO ENCOURAGE ME. HE IS WITH ALL WHO HE HAS CHOSEN TO PERFORM HIS WORKS AND FAVORS. WHEN HE BEGAN TO COMMUNICATE WITH ME (HIS OWN) I DID, INDEED, THANK

HIM FOR THE HEADS'UP EVEN BEFORE I UNDERSTOOD HIS WAYS. I WAS PREADOLESENCE WHEN I BEGAN TO HEAR FROM MY SAVIOR. I WAS TEN TO TWELVE YEARS OLD WHEN HE STOOD ME STILL TO TELL ME MY NUMBER IS FOUR. I AM SURE YOU HAVE READ THAT IN MY OTHER WRITES. I WILL NEVER FORGET THE LOVE SHOWN TO ME WHEN HE STOOD ME STILL TO SPEAK HIS LOVE AND ASSIGNMENT TO ME. SOME DON'T LIKE THAT, O WELL. I CAN'T UNDO WHAT HE HAS DONE. I HAVE GREATLY ENJOYED HIS WORDS TO ME, EVEN HIS CORRECTION. HOW SHALL WE ESCAPE (SURVIVE), IF WE NEGLECT SO GREAT SALVATION. HEB 2:3. IF I TOLD YOU ALL HE HAS SHARED WITH ME, YOU MAY WANT TO CHANGE THE CHANNEL. I HAVE A BETTER IDEA, ASK HIM TO TELL YOU HIS PROMISES FOR YOU. YOU MAY HAVE MISSED SOME OF HIS PROMISES FOR YOU. ASK HIM FOR A REPLAY. GOTTA HEAR HIM, IT'S URGENT. OUR TIME IS SHORT AND I SO WANT YOU TO BE PART OF THE GATHERING. IT WON'T BE A BANQUET WITHOUT YOU. JUST DO IT. YOU KNOW AND HAVE HEARD THAT TIME IS FAR SPENT, COME TO THE ALTAR, NOW. HE MAY BE CALLING YOU TO COME TO THE ALTAR. LISTEN AND HEAR HIS CALL. COME TO THE CROSS, THE ALTAR WHERE JESUS WAS OFFERED, GOD'S SACRIFICE FOR THE WHOLE WORLD. THE CROSS IS THE HINGE FOR THE DOOR, JESUS IS THE DOOR. DOORS DON'T WORK WITHOUT THE HINGE. AS A DOOR HANGS ON A HINGE, JESUS (THE DOOR) HUNG ON THE CROSS. IT WAS FOR YOU. DON'T IGNORE THE CROSS, AS JESUS SAID "TAKE UP YOUR CROSS DAILY AND FOLLOW ME. HE NEVER DID THROW HIS WORDS AROUND, IF HE SAID IT, HE MEANT IT. I TELL YOU, DO IT. YOU MUST, YOU JUST MUST. THE CROSS IS THE ALTAR OF GOD, HE SACRIFICED HIS SON ON THE CROSS, FOR ME, ALL OF US. JESUS WAS SENT FOR MY SALVATION, I ACCEPT JESUS AND HIS WORK ON THAT CROSS. THANK YOU, JESUS. THE ONLY WAY TO THANK HIM IS TO FOLLOW HIM AND DO AS HE SAYS. "COME FOLLOW ME IN THE REGENERATION OF LIFE,

ETERNAL LIFE. THANK YOU, JESUS. I AM YOURS FOREVER, MY HEART, FOREVER. O'JESUS, O'JESUS. I AM YOURS. I (YOU) CAN'T DO BETTER THAN JESUS. ASSIGNMENT? PURPOSE? TO ME THE SAME. I SO WANT TO DO AS HE SAYS. I AM HIS CHOSEN FROM THE FOUNDATION OF THE WORLD, SO HARD TO WAIT FOR THE DAY OF THE LORD. I SO WANT TO HEAR WHAT HE HAS TO SAY WHEN TIME IS NO MORE. AFTER ALL THE EONS OF TIME, WILL HE BE PLEASED? HE WILL. O' JUST TO SEE HIM, HIS BEAUTIFUL COUNTENANCE. HIS PEACEFULL DEMEANOR.

DOES THE OFFERED NOT OFFER, DOES THE SACRIFICE NOT SACRIFICE?
WHO CAN UTTER THE MIGHTY ACTS OF THE LORD? WHO CAN SHOW FORTH ALL HIS PRAISE? THE ALTAR OF THE GRACE OF GOD IS THE CROSS OF THE LORD JESUS CHRIST.
INDEED!
I AM GOING TO PLAN BECAUSE I AM PLANNING TO GO. YOU MUST BE BORN'AGAIN. IF I PLACE MYSELF IN YOU, JESUS, I AM IN A GOOD PLACE.

THE "BIBLE"
WHO WROTE THIS BOOK?

YES, WHO WROTE THIS GLORIOUS, MOST WONDERFUL BOOK?
DO YOU THINK IT WAS A COOK? NO....

TAKE OFF YOUR ROBE OF PITIFUL,
FOLLOW JESUS AND BE CALLED HOSPITABLE.

YOU ARE THE WITNESS GOD HAS CALLED TO SPREAD THE
WORD. THE NEWS THAT MOST ARE WAITING TO BE HEARD.

THIS BOOK SPEAKS OF ONE CALLED ROYAL.
HE IS JESUS, THE ONLY ONE TO WALK WITH YOU, HE IS LOYAL.

WHEN ALL IS SAID AND DONE,
PLEASE BE SURE YOU FOLLOWED THE HOLY ONE.

THE TRUMPET SOON WILL SOUND, THE LAST TRUMP.
SO BE SURE TO FOLLOW THE ONE WHO IS TRIUMPH.

THE SCRIPTURES WARN OF FALSE PROPHETS.
SOME WEAR TO MUCH PERFUME AND GAUDY LOCKETS.

THEY MAY LOOK "O' SO" HOLY,
BUT DO THEY COME BEFORE HIM LOWLY?

I HAVE FOLLOWED THE LORD FROM THEN TILL NOW,
AND I PLAN TO GO WITH HIM TO HIS THRONE TO BOW.

ALL MY CROWNS TO CAST AT HIS FEET, SO SWEET.
HE IS MY PLEASURE, I JUST MAY WEEP.

I KNOW HE IS WORTHY, AND IF I HAD A THOUSAND CROWNS,
EVERY ONE WOULD BE FOR HIM, ALL AROUNDS.

THAT DAY WILL COME AND THE TRUMPET SOUND.
SO, ONLY IN HIM, O HALLELUJAH, MAY I BE FOUND.

I AM HIS AND HE IS MINE,
IT WILL BE THAT WAY TILL THE END OF TIME.

I HAVE PREPARED FOR THIS MY WHOLE LIFE AND NOW I SEE,
I OWE HIM NOT ONE SECOND SHORT OF THE N'TH DEGREE.
SO, BE IT AMEN SO BE IT

GOD'S GRACE * MY FAITH
"AMAZING"

FOR BY GRACE ARE YE SAVED THROUGH FAITH; AND THAT NOT OF YOURSELF: IT IS THE GIFT OF GOD. (EPH 2:8). YOU DON'T WORK FOR IT, SO YOU HAVE NO BOAST. GOD'S GOODNESS PROVIDES ALL THINGS GOOD. WE MOSTLY ALL KNOW THAT, DON'T WE? I HAVE KNOWN THAT FOR A LONG TIME, PROBABLY NOT ALWAYS DONE THE RIGHT THING BUT THAT'S NO EXCUSE. I HAVE SOMETIMES COME DOWN HARD ON MYSELF WHEN I DON'T GET IT RIGHT. I SO WANT TO PLEASE MY LORD AND NOT MESS UP. HE HAS GIVEN SO MUCH FOR ME, YES FOR ME. HE GAVE HIS BEST FOR ME, MY JESUS. YES, JESUS, MY JESUS. WE SHOULD ALL DECLARE THAT HE GAVE HIS BEST AND ONLY BEGOTTEN FOR SUCH AS WE, OR ME. I ACCEPT HIM AS MY SAVIOR, AND DO SO WITH MUCH GRATITUDE. I DO TELL HIM WHEN I PRAY THAT I AM SO GRATEFUL FOR MY JESUS. WHERE WOULD I BE WITHOUT JESUS, I DON'T WANT TO THINK ABOUT THAT AND DON'T GO THERE. THAT SONG, "AMAZING GRACE", IS ONE WE ALL SING OFTEN BECAUSE IT'S SO BEAUTIFUL AND EASY TO DO. YOU DON'T HAVE TO BE A GRAND SOPRANO TO SING IT. PRAISE GOD. I SING BECAUSE I ALWAYS HAVE, SINCE I WAS BORN. YAH, I CAME OUT OF THE WOMB SINGING. I WANTED TO BE A FAMOUS SINGER WHEN I GRADUATED FROM SCHOOL, HOWEVER MOM AND DAD DIDN'T THINK THAT WAS A GOOD IDEA. SO, THEY CONCLUDED THAT I SHOULD HAVE A REAL JOB, THE KIND THAT GETS A PAYCHECK AT THE END OF EVERY WEEK. IT DIDN'T STOP ME FROM SINGING, THOUGH. BY HIS AMAZING GRACE I AM STILL SINGING AND I SING TO MY LORD FOR AN HOUR EVERY

EVENING BEFORE BED. I THANK GOD, BY MY JESUS, THROUGH THE HOLY GHOST FOR THE GIFT HE HAS GIVEN ME. HIS GRACE HAS BEEN SO GENEROUS IN MY LIFE AND I AM SO OVER THE TOP GIFTED BY IT. THAT'S TO SAY HE GIVES GOOD GIFTS. HE GIVES AMAZING GIFTS. I KNOW I AM AMAZED. I HAVE A WONDERFUL CHURCH TO WORSHIP WITH WONDERFUL CONGREGANTS. I THINK THAT'S A WORD, IT IS NOW. SOMETIMES I INVENT WORDS. IT'S OK. IT'S MY WRITE, MY LIBERTY. GOD USUSALLY SAYS IT'S OK, TOO. HIS GOODNESS ENDURES FOREVER. THANK YOU, HEAVENLY FATHER. DON'T YOU JUST LOVE HIM? ME TOO. BY FAITH ARE WE HERE. BY GRACE, HIS GRACE WE GET TO STAY. HOWEVER, I DO LOOK FORWARD TO THE RAPTURE, MAKE HASTE O MY LORD. I SO LOOK FORWARD TO BEING WITH MY GOD, MY JESUS, MY HOLY GHOST AND MY FAMILY. WHAT A DAY OF REJOICING THAT WILL BE. HE IS MINE AND I AM HIS, AND THAT'S THE WAY I LIKE IT. SOMETIMES I SHED TEARS OVER THE WAY THINGS ARE, BUT THEN HE REMINDS ME THAT HE IS IN CHARGE. O THE MIGHTY LOVE AND GRACE OF GOD. NOTHING, NO ONE CAN OUT GIVE, OUT DO, OUT LOVE MY MOST WONDERFUL HEAVENLY FATHER, MY LORD JESUS CHRIST OR MY BLESSED HOLY GHOST. YES, I DO SHOUT ALL MY WORKS AND WRITES FROM THE HOUSETOPS. (MATT 10:26-28) SOME SAY THEY ARE ANNOYED BY THE WAY I WRITE, BUT THEN THERE ARE OTHERS WHO SAY IT'S MUCH MORE EASY TO READ AS THEY SEE IT BETTER. THE LARGE PRINT COMES ACROSS AS I AM SHOUTING THE MESSAGE, I AM. THE OLDER FOLKS LIKE BIG TYPE. I TEND TO DO WHAT THE LORD ORDERS, HE SAID, SHOUT IT FROM THE HOUSETOPS. THAT'S HIS "AMAZING GRACE". BY HIS INSTRUCTIONS I PLAN TO DO AND GET IT WRITE. PLAY ON WORDS! HE GAVE HIS BEST, I WILL GIVE MY BEST, AS MUCH AS IS POSSIBLE. YOU KNOW YOU CAN'T OUT GIVE GOD. I KNOW SOME THINK THEY CAN. SOME THINK THEY ARE IN CHARGE AND DON'T NEED GOD. I GOT A SURPRISE FOR YOU, HE IS SO

MUCH BIGGER THAN YOU SO MAYBE YOU SHOULD RETHINK THAT BELIEF. YOU COULD GET A DOOZY OF A HEADACHE. HAS THAT EVER OCCURRED TO YOU? FOREVER I WILL SING AND MAYBE WE WILL SING WHEN WE GET TO THE BANQUET AFTER THE RAPTURE. THAT WOULD BE SO APPROPRIATE AS I KNOW MY LORD WOULD LOVE TO SING WITH US ALL. HE WILL BE THE GRANDMASTER SO IN CHARGE OF THE ENTERTAINMENT. I WANT TO SING WITH HIM AND MY BABY BOY FROM HAWAII. HE IS A GOSPEL SINGER WHO IS ALSO A CHRISTIAN MISSIONARY TO THE ISLANDS, AND A REAL GOOD SINGER. I LIKE TO THINK THAT HE GOT HIS VOICE FROM GOD, BUT THROUGH ME. LITTLE BOB FITTS, SO WONDERFUL.

AH, BUT FOR THE GRACE OF GOD GO I, HE IS SO WONDERFUL, HE GAVE ME JESUS.
JESUS IS THE GRACE OF GOD IN THE FLESH. HE IS MINE, DO YOU UNDERSTAND? HIS PRESENCE, HIS FRAGRANCE, PERFUME. HIS ESSENCE, HIS POWER RELEASED. WHEN HE SITS ME DOWN TO WRITE FOR HIM, I AM HIS TO USE. I AM HIS, ALWAYS.

MY GENTLE JESUS

CAN YOU SEE JESUS ANY OTHER WAY? I DON'T THINK SO. HE IS SO GENTLE AND A GENTLEMAN. HE HAS ALWAYS BEEN AND WILL ALWAYS BE. I HAVE BEEN WRITING FOR HIM AND ABOUT HIM FOR A WHILE NOW. NOT A TOUGH SUBJECT FOR ONE WHO LOVES HIM SO MUCH. HE IS WORTHY TO BE PRAISED AND ADORED. THE WHOLE BIBLE IS FULL OF THE BEAUTY OF JESUS. THE SAVIOR OF THE WHOLE WORLD WHEN AND IF THEY WOULD LIKE TO ACCEPT HIM AS MESSIAH. I HAVE SAID MANY TIMES THAT HE IS WILLING TO JOIN HEART AND HAND WITH ALL THE WHOSOEVER WILL. THE SALVATION HE OFFERS IS, AS THE SONG SAYS, HEART AND SOUL OF THE SET FREE. COME TO HIM AS YOU ARE, HE WANTS TO SEE YOU AND FREE YOU FROM THE LIFE OF THE LOST. HE WAS SENT FOR THAT PURPOSE BY HIS AND MY FATHER. HE IS FREE TO WALK WITH YOU TO THE END OF THE LIGHT AND INTO THE DARKNESS. AS YOU WALK THE DARKNESS WILL FLEE, THE DARK CAN'T STAND THE LIGHT. YOU HAVE HEARD THAT IN HIM IS NO DARKNESS AT ALL. HE WILL LIGHT THE WAY, ALL THE WAY. SO, TAKE HIS HAND AND WALK SO CLOSE TO HIM YOU WILL NOT HAVE A SHADOW. IT WILL BE THE BEST DECISION YOU WILL EVER MAKE. HE IS WAITING FOR YOU BUT DON'T MAKE HIM WAIT. THERE WILL COME A DAY WHEN THE FATHER CALLS AN END TO THE WAIT AND TIME IS NO MORE. IT'S THE EASIEST THING TO DO. AS YOU WALK, HE WILL ASSURE YOU OF THE SALVATION HE OFFERS. ONCE YOU ARE SAVED YOU WILL WANT TO BE BAPTISED IN THE RIVER OR POOL OR YOUR OWN BATHTUB. WATER IS WHAT YOU NEED. PERHAPS YOU WILL WANT TO BE BAPTISED IN THE HOLY GHOST, TOO, WITH EVIDENCE OF SPEAKING WITH OTHER

TONGUES, AS WAS ON THE DAY OF PENTECOST. YOU WILL WANT TO READ YOUR BIBLE EVERY DAY TO FIND OUT ALL THE BENEFITS OF FOLLOWING THE LORD JESUS CHRIST, THERE ARE MANY. YOUR WORLD WILL OPEN UP. WHEN YOU FIND FRIENDS WHO, LIKE YOU ARE, BORN AGAIN, WHAT A DAY OF REJOICING THAT WILL BE. TAKE HIS HAND AND WALK WITH HIM, BUT LET HIM LEAD. NOW COMES THE FUN PART, FIND A CHURCH. THERE MOST LIKELY IS A WONDERFUL CHURCH IN YOUR NEIGHBORHOOD, YOU MAY EVEN HAVE A NEIGHBOR WHO ALREADY IS IN A WONDERFUL CHURCH. YOU COULD JOIN WITH HIM OR HER AND CAR POOL TO CHURCH. PROBABLY TAKE TURNS WITH THE DRIVE. PLEASE DO MAKE UP YOUR MIND TO GET AFTER SALVATION, YOU WILL BE SO FREE. NOW COMES THE FUN PART. TELL ALL WHO WILL LISTEN ABOUT THE NEW FRIEND YOU HAVE IN JESUS. THE ONLY ONE WHO WILL NEVER LEAVE YOU NOR FORSAKE YOU. THE ONLY ONE WHO WILL ALWAYS KEEP HIS WORD, YOUR BEST FRIEND, EVER. START A BIBLE STUDY IN YOUR HOME OR IF SOMEONE ALREADY HAS ONE UP AND RUNNING, JOIN IN. KNOWING JESUS WILL TURN YOUR LIFE AROUND, FOR THE GOOD. HE, TOO, WILL SPREAD THE GOOD NEWS IN THE HEAVENLYS THAT YOU ARE NOW PART OF THE SAVED AND REDEEMED. IT'S SO GOOD AND NOW YOU KNOW. SO, TELL EVERYONE YOU POSSIBLY CAN HOW KNOWING JESUS IS THE BEST THING SINCE AIR AND WATER OR IN AND OUT BURGERS. THEY MAY WANT TO JOIN YOU FOR CHURCH WHEN THEY SEE HOW YOU GLOW WHEN YOU SAY HIS NAME. JESUS, MY JESUS. ARE YOU ANNOYED THAT YOU DIDN'T KNOW SOONER? JUST THANK HIM THAT HE FOUND YOU JUST IN TIME. WE ARE SO BLESSED TO BE HEAVEN BOUND, NO REGRETS. NOW, DON'T FORGET TO THANK HIM EVERY CHANCE YOU GET FOR WHAT HE DID ON THAT CROSS, HAD THAT NOT BEEN, WHERE WOULD WE BE? OKAY, WE WON'T GO THERE, BUT THERE HAS BEEN TIMES WHEN I HAVE THOUGHT ABOUT IT. I GOTTA TELL

YOU, HE IS THE MOST GLORIOUS THING THAT EVER HAPPENED TO ME. I SO LOOK FORWARD TO ETERNITY WITH MY LORD. SING TO HIM, WRITE HIM A SONG THAT ONLY YOU CAN SHARE WITH HIM. PRAYING EVERY DAY IN THE SPIRIT AND GET INTO THE BOOK (BIBLE) FOR INTIMATE WORSHIP, JUST THE TWO OF YOU. TELL HIM ALL YOUR SECRETS, HE KNOWS HOW TO KEEP THEM. JUST YOU AND HIM, FOR EVER. THE BEATING HE TOOK ON THE WHIPPING POST AND BLOOD ON THE CROSS TOOK CARE OF ALL THE FORGIVENESS FOR YOUR AND MY NEED. O'WHAT A SAVIOR, SING HALLELUJAH. WE ARE SO FREE AND SO BLESSED. I THINK I MAY BURST INTO WORSHIP RIGHT NOW. I DO SING TO HIM EVERYDAY FOR ABOUT AN HOUR, AN HOUR WELL SPENT. WALK EVERYDAY WITH AND FOR HIM. JUST DO IT.

MY DADDY IS SO GOD. GOD GAVE ME HIS BEST, JESUS. GIVE HIM YOUR VERY BEST. GIVE HIM ALL THE GLORY. WORSHIP HIM, HE IS SO WORTHY. GIVE HIM ALL THE GLORY. NOT GOD FIRST, GOD ONLY. HE WILL BE ONLY OR HE WON'T BE ANY.

CHANGE TEXT, NOT TEXTURE

I LOVE MY LORD JESUS CHRIST.

THE TEXT IS TO SAY "TRANSLATION". THERE ARE MANY DIFFERENT TRANSLATIONS OF THE SCRIPTURE, NOT TO CHANGE THE MESSAGE, BUT TO MAKE EASIER TO UNDERSTAND. SO, WHAT IS THE TEXTURE? THE TEXTURE OF THE ONE WRITTEN ABOUT, HE IS SO TENDER AND LOVING TO ALL OF THE WHOSOEVER WILL, WHICH I AM ONE OF THOSE WONDERFULLY AND TENDERLY SAVED. HIS TEXTURE IS, SO GENTLE AND GIVEN TO TENDERNESS. YOU JUST CAN'T RESIST HIS SPECIAL WAYS. FROM HIS BEGINNING TO THE END, THE CROSS. HIS FATHER (GOD) SENT HIM TO BE THE SACRIFICE FOR THE WHOLE WORLD, THAT WHOSOEVER WILL, CAN GRACIOUSLY COME, YES, YOU CAN COME TO HIM FOR THE FORGIVENESS OF YOUR SIN AND BE ACCEPTED IN THE LOST AND NOW FOUND, AND SAFE IN THE ARMS OF JESUS. HE FOUND YOU WHEN YOU WERE LOST AND LIFTED YOU FROM THE DEEPEST SIN. NOW YOU ARE FOUND. NOW YOU CAN REST ON HIS SHOULDER AND HE WILL CARRY YOU TO SAFETY AND SALVATION. YOU ARE AS A LITTLE LAMB, LOST IN THE SCARY WILDERNESS. YOU WERE AS SEPARATED FROM THE FLOCK, WANDERING AROUND AND SCARED. SO AS THE GOOD SHEPHERD DOES, SEARCHES FOR THE ERRING LITTLE LAMBS, WHO WILL USUALLY IN FEAR EVENUALLY JUST STAND STILL AND WILL BE EASY PREY TO THE LION AND JACKLEL LOOKING FOR A CONVENIENT DINNER. HOWEVER, THE GOOD SHEPHERD WILL FIND THE LAMB AND RETURN IT TO THE FLOCK AND FOLD AND SAFETY. JUST STAND STILL, HE WILL FIND YOU. THAT'S WHAT JESUS DOES WITH THE LOST AND ALONE IN A WORLD OF DARKNESS AND DISTRESS. HE IS SO GENTLE AND PATIENT WITH THE ONES OUT THERE WHO NEED

A SAVIOR. HE IS SO UNDERSTANDING OF THE FEAR THAT RAGES IN THE WORLD. THAT'S WHY HIS FATHER AND MY FATHER SENT HIM INTO THE WORLD TO BE THE SAVIOR OF THE WORLD. THANK YOU, HEAVENLY FATHER FOR OUR GOOD SHEPHERD. WHEN HE FOUND ME, I WAS SO IN NEED OF HIS SAVING GRACE. HE ALWAYS COMES JUST IN TIME TO RESCUE THE LOST. WE HAVE, EVERY ONE OF US, A TESTIMONY OF HOW WE WERE LOST AND NOW ARE FOUND, BLIND BUT NOW WE SEE. HIS TENDERNESS, HIS SOFT AND GENTLE DEMEANOR IS HIS TEXTURE. HAVE YOU EVER HEARD THAT BEFORE? YAH, HE IS ALL THAT AND MUCH MORE, SO MUCH MORE. IF YOU NEED A BIBLE AND THE ONE, I FAVOR (KING JAMES VERSION) IS NOT TO YOUR UNDERSTANDING, THERE ARE SOME VERSIONS, MAYBE A MORE EASY TO READ AND GRASP THE TEXT. YOU ARE FREE TO TEST THE DIFFERENT TRANSLATIONS. ASK FRIENDS AND FAMILY WHAT THEY PREFER AND TAKE A LOOK AT WHAT THEY RECOMMEND. GO TO THE CHRISTIAN BOOK STORE AND GET SOME HELP WITH THEIR SELECTION. IF THEY ARE TRULY CHRISTIAN, THEY WILL BE SO HAPPY TO HELP YOU WITH YOUR CHOICE. I HAVE MANY DIFFERENT SCRIPTS (BIBLES) AND I LOVE EVERY ONE OF THEM. WHEN I STUDY, I BRING THEM OUT TO READ AND COMPARE, IT'S ALLOWED, DO IT. SO, YOU HAVE THE BIBLE YOU PREFER, DIG INTO IT, FIND JESUS. LET HIM INTO YOUR STUDIES. SO TENDER AND PATIENT TO GET YOU TO THE PLACE OF HIS GRACE. THAT'S HIS TEXTURE, O HIS GRACE. LET HIM HOLD YOU AND YOU TAKE HOLD OF HIM. THE TEXTURE OF MY LORD JESUS CHRIST WILL BRING YOU ON A JOURNEY TO KNOW HIM. JUST GO. THE BEST OF JESUS IS THE TEXT AND TEXTURE OF JESUS. READ MATT 11:28-30. HE IS DIVINE. STUDY THE DIVINITY OF THE LORD JESUS CHRIST. HE IS NOT WEAK, HE HAS GENTLE STRENGTH, NOT AGRESSIVE, SO TENDER. THATS MY JESUS, LIKE FINE WOOL. YES, THE LAMB OF GOD. STUDY TO BE APPROVED, WALK CLOSE TO HIM, CLOSE TO HIS HEART. JOIN HANDS AND

WALK INTO ETERNITY, BY HIS GRACE ARE YOU SAVED. ARE YOU THERE? HE IS WAITING TO HEAR YOUR DECISION, SO DON'T MISS THE OPPORTUNITY. HE WILL SAVE YOUR LIFE AND YOU WILL BE SO HAPPY WITH HIM. YAH, LIFE IS WORTH THE LIVING BECAUSE HE LIVES AND LOVES ALL WHO COME TO HIM. FOLLOW HIM, PERHAPS HE WILL CHANGE YOUR TEXTURE, THAT COULD BE AN IMPROVEMENT. READ EPH 4:32. THAT'S MY JESUS. JUMP IN WITH BOTH FEET, HE IS SO FINE, THE BEST THING TO EVER HAPPEN TO YOU, ME AND THE WHOLE WORLD. MY TENDER JESUS, THE ONLY ONE, THERE IS NONE LIKE HIM. NOPE! SO NOW THAT WE ARE IN THE ARMS OF OUR TENDER SAVIOR, LET'S JUST WORSHIP AND PRAISE HIM WITH ALL THE BREATH HE HAS GIVEN. SO GENEROUSLY GIVEN, THANK YOU FATHER FOR MY TENDER TEXTURED SAVIOR, MY LORD JESUS CHRIST. AMEN AND AMEN.

IS HE WONDERFUL OR WHAT? O' HE IS! TASTE AND SEE. HIS PRESENCE, TO BECOME AWARE OF HIM, TO HEAR AND FEEL HIS BREATH.

ANY DAY NOW

ANY DAY NOW WE WILL HEAR THE TRUMPET SOUND.
ANY DAY NOW WE WILL SURELY BE HEAVEN BOUND.

I HAVE HEARD THAT MOST OF MY LIFE.
WE WILL BE TAKEN FROM THE EARTH, THE END OF STRIFE.

WE SEE THE HEAVENS OPEN WIDE TO LET US COME INSIDE.
LEAVE BEHIND THE CHAOS AND ALL THAT EMPTY PRIDE.

HOW WILL IT BE WHEN THERE ARE NO TEARS TO SHED?
SO HAPPY TO BE AT HOME, NOTHING MORE TO DREAD.

THE SAVIOR STANDING AT THE GATE, ARMS OPEN.
THE BANQUET TABLES AND CHAIRS ALL SET, FOR WE, THE CHOSEN.

AS HE DIRECTS US TO OUR PLACE PROMISED.
WE EMBRACE OUR FRIEND, REMEMBER THOMAS?

OUR JESUS WILL LIFT THE CUP, THE BEST WINE EVER.
HE WILL SAY A POEM WELCOMING US, FOREVER.

WHEN ALL ARE IN THEIR ASSIGNED PLACE.
HE WILL BLESS US WITH A PRAYER OF GRACE.

THE FATHER'S VOICE WE HEAR FROM WHERE, WE DON'T KNOW.
HE MUST BE IN THE KITCHEN LIGHTING CANDLES, TO SOFTLY
GLOW.

WE HAVE SO LOOKED FORWARD TO THIS TIME AND NOW.
WE ARE ALL GATHERED, FATHER, SON, AND HOLY GHOST.
WE BOW.

WE ARE SO BLESSED AND THRILLED TO BE AT REST.
LOOKING FORWARD TO HONOR AND GREET EACH GUEST.

WE CAN COME TO OUR SAVIOR ANY DAY WE PLEASE.
AT LAST, WE CAN REST, WE ARE SO BLESSED AND AT EASE.

**** **** ****

WE ARE SO DEEPLY THANKFUL HE KEPT HIS PROMISE AND
NOW WE ARE HOME AT LAST. WE ARE HOME. ANY DAY NOW.
HALLELUJAH! BLESS HIS HOLY NAME. HALLELUJAH!

PRAISE THE LORD

YES. PRAISE THE LORD. ALL HEAVEN AND EARTH JUST PRAISE THE LORD. WHAT ELSE IS THERE TO DO BUT BLESS AND SING PRAISES TO HIM, THE ONLY TRUE GOD. HE IS ABOVE ALL, IN ALL, AND FOR ALL. YOU JUST HAVE TO ACKNOWLEDGE HIM. WHO ELSE IS WORTHY TO BE GLORIFIED AND PRAISED? I HAVE BEEN IN GREAT INTENT, TRUE INTENT, TO PRAISE THE LORD. WE ALL NEED TO BE (ON PURPOSE) AND IN HOLY POSTURE, PRAISE THE LORD. DO WE REALLY HAVE TO KNEEL TO WORSHIP. NO. YOU HAVE TO HAVE THE TRUE INTENT IN YOUR HEART TO DO THE ULTIMATE ACT, TO/DO WORSHIP. TO BOW AND I MEAN TO BOW LOW, IS ONLY AN ACT OF A CONTRITE HEART. I AM SO HUMBLED BY WHAT HE HAS DONE FOR ME, HOW CAN I NOT DO "WITH TRUE INTENT" AN ACT OF TRUE WORSHIP. YOU MEAN IN CHURCH? NO, I MEAN WHERE EVER YOU ARE. WHAT WILL PEOPLE THINK OF ME DOING THIS ACT? THEY PROBABLY WILL THINK YOU REALLY LOVE THE LORD. DO YOU? I ENJOY HIM (GOD) AND HIS WORD, THE LORD JESUS CHRIST. WHAT HE DID FOR ME AT CALVARY AND BEFORE HE EVEN GOT TO THE CROSS, HOW CAN I DO LESS? GET ON YOUR FACE AND JUST WORSHIP. I AM SAVED BY WHAT HE DID. W.O.W. WONDERFUL O' WONDERFUL. HE BOWED REAL LOW WHEN HE WAS IN THE GARDEN OF GETHSEMANE ASKING THE FATHER IF THE CUP COULD PASS FROM HIM. WE ALL KNOW THE ANSWER HE GOT FROM HIS FATHER. I AM ONE WHO IS SO THANKFUL FOR THE WAY IT WENT. HE DIED FOR ME, HE TOOK MY PLACE, HE SEALED MY SALVATION. CAN I, COULD I, WOULD I DO LESS? WE REALLY DON'T WANT TO COMPARE HOW WE WORSHIP...JUST DO WHAT'S IN YOUR HEART. HE WILL APPRECIATE THE ATTITUDE OF YOUR HEART WHEN HE SEES

YOUR INTENT. I SO HOPE THAT THE REST OF MY LIFE I DO AS MY HEART SEES FIT. PRAISE AND WORSHIP PUTS YOU SO CLOSE TO HIS HEART AND WILL ALWAYS BE IN HIS FAVOR. CAN WE CERTAINLY GAIN FAVOR FROM OUR GOD WHEN WE CHOOSE TO WORSHIP ON THE FLOOR? JUST FOLLOW YOUR HEART AND GIVE NO THOUGHT TO HOW OR WHAT OTHERS ARE DOING OR THINKING OR SAYING. IF ANY DECIDE TO JUDGE WHAT YOU ARE DOING, WELL, O WELL. WE ARE IN CHARGE ONLY OF WHAT WE DO. HE IS SO PRECIOUS AND HAS MADE A WAY WHERE THERE IS NO WAY. THAT ALONE IS WORTHY OF GREAT PRAISE AND MUCH THANKSGIVING. I AM SO WAITING TO SEE THE LORD JESUS CHRIST FACE TO FACE, HEAR WHAT HE HAS TO SAY TO ME, AND CAST MY CROWNS AT HIS FEET. TO JUST IMAGINE BEING WITH OUR LORD AND SAVIOR IS SUCH A JOY. WE WILL HAVE CHURCH RIGHT ON THE SPOT. YES, I WILL... I SO LOVE TO HAVE CHURCH, GO TO CHURCH, YES. TONIGHT, OR TOMORROW, LET'S GO. I LOVE YOU JESUS, BECAUSE YOU FIRST LOVED ME, AND PROVED IT. I SO BLESS MY LORD JESUS CHRIST. TO MAKE A PROBLEM OF HOW OR WHAT POSTURE OF WORSHIP WE CHOOSE, OY! GO AWAY MAD. I MAY PULL A REAL MESS IF I SPEND THE WHOLE HOUR OF CHURCH ON THE FLOOR. I JUST MAY DO IT. JESUS IS MY DARLING, MY BELOVED, MY GOD, YES, ALL OF THE ABOVE AND MORE. JESUS GAVE AND GIVES THE ULTIMATE LIFE. THANK YOU, JESUS. TOMORROW, WHEN WE ARE ALL IN HEAVEN, WE WILL REMINISS OF ALL THE WONDERFUL THINGS OUR JESUS DID FOR OUR SALVATION. WE ARE SO GRATEFUL FOR ALL HE HAS DONE FOR US, PERSONALLY. MY DELIVERER, HIS FAVOR SPANS EIGHTEEN THOUSAND YEARS. ASK ME. JESUS, HE IS MY MOST TRULY WONDERFUL, ETERNAL SAVIOR. O'YES, HE IS. LET'S ALL COME TOGETHER AND SING SONGS OF PRAISE AND WORSHIP, WITH OR WITHOUT MUSIC. HOW DO I STOP THIS WRITE OF PRAISE? HMMMM? I CAN'T, I WILL CONTINUE TILL THE INK OR PAPER RUNS OUT. HE IS SO WORTHY OF ALL I CAN DO IN HIS FAVOR.

NO CROSS, NO CHRIST, NO CHRIST, NO REDEMPTION, NO REDEMPTION, NO SALVATION. SO, IF THAT'S HOW IT IS ALL WILL BE LOST. MY GOD WILL NOT ALLOW THAT. HE WATCHES WITH GREAT CONCERN, AGAIN, HE WILL NOT ALLOW THAT. WE ARE HIS, ALONE. HE DIED FOR HIS OWN, O' HE WILL NOT JUST LOOK THE OTHER WAY. WE, THE BORN AGAIN, ARE WORTH ALL OF HEAVEN TO HIM. I LOVE MY SAVIOR. TO FOLLOW HIM IS A MUST FOR ALL WHO ARE INTENTING WITH GREAT INTENTION TO BE WITH HIM IN ALL ETERNITY. I DON'T FOLLOW AS IT IS A HABIT, NO. I DO IT AS AN INTENTION, ON PURPOSE. HE LOVES ME ON PURPOSE, I LOVE HIM ON PURPOSE.

NOT GOD FIRST, GOD ONLY. HE WILL BE ONLY OR HE WON'T BE ANY.
BE AGED IN HIS GRACE, STEEPED IN HIS WORD, POURED OUT IN HIS GLORY.
THE SECRET PLACE OF THE MOST HIGH IS UNDER THE BLOOD OF JESUS.

JUST TO KNOW HIM

THAT I MAY KNOW HIM AND THE POWER OF HIS RESURRECTION... PHIL 3:10

YES, JUST TO KNOW HIM. I SAY, YOU MUST KNOW HIM. THEY QUOTE, YOU MUST BE BORN AGAIN. YES, YES AND YES. I SAY, YOU MUST KNOW HIM. IT'S AS IMPORTANT AS ANY OTHER SCRIPTURE, FOLLOW HIM. LEARN ALL YOU CAN ABOUT HIM, WALK AS HE WALKED, TALK AS HE TALKED. MEMORIZE EVERY WORD HE EVER SPOKE AND LEARN HOW HE INTERPRETED EVERY LINE WRITTEN. DOES THAT GIVE YOU A HEADACHE? O' YOU CAN DO IT. THE BETTER YOU KNOW JESUS THE EASIER TO FOLLOW AND DO ALL AS HE WOULD. HE DID MAKE IT LOOK SO EASY BECAUSE IT IS. I BELIEVE HE WAS ALWAYS READY TO FORGIVE AND THAT MAY BE THE HARDEST THING FOR YOU AND I TO DO. HE KNEW THE BEAUTIFUL AND GRACIOUS SIDE OF FORGIVING. THAT ALSO IS A MUST. UNFORGIVENESS IS TOO HEAVY TO CARRY AND HE KNEW THAT. HE GAVE THAT AS A HELP BECAUSE WHEN YOU WALK IN UNFORGIVENESS IT WILL MAKE YOUR OWN LIFE UNBALANCED. HE DID SAY TO FORGIVE AS HE HAS FORGIVEN YOU. DO YOU REALIZE HOW MUCH HE HAS FORGIVEN OF YOU? DO SIT DOWN AND ON PURPOSE RECALL ALL THE STUFF HE HAS RELEASED YOU FROM. WELL, I HAVE DONE THAT BUT I DIDN'T GET VERY FAR SINCE THERE WAS TOO MUCH. HE HAS FORGIVEN ME SO MUCH. HE HAS SUCH A TENDER HEART, AND I AM SO THANKFUL AND YOU WILL BE TOO. IF I HUNG ON TO ALL THE STUFF OF MY UNFORGIVENESS I WOULD NEED A TRUCK TO CARRY IT ALL. DO NOT LET THAT HAPPEN TO YOU. REFRESH, FORGIVE, EVEN AS HE HAS FORGIVEN YOU. KEEP THAT AS CLOSE IN YOUR MEMORY AS POSSIBLE, PLEASE. FORGIVENESS IS A BIGGY. I HAVE SUCH A LOVE AND PASSION FOR WRITING FOR MY JESUS. THERE IS SO MUCH TO WRITE OF

HIM, I JUST MAY WRITE A BOOK. O' WAIT A MINUTE I HAVE DONE THAT. THIS IS BOOK NUMBER FOUR. DO YOU THINK I WANT TO WRITE FOR A THOUSAND YEARS BECAUSE HE IS WONDERFUL AND HAS DONE MUCH TO WRITE ABOUT. HIS LOVE AND LIFE AND LIGHT IS ENDLESS, DO YOU KNOW THAT? HE IS THE LOVE, THE LIFE AND THE LIGHT OF THE WORLD. DO YOU KNOW THAT? YOU DO NOW. HE GOT ALL THAT FROM HIS FATHER, THE GOD OF ALL THAT IS. HIS DADDY IS MY DADDY. IF YOU CAN, SAY THE SAME FOR YOURSELF. YOU MUST CLAIM ALL THAT, TOO. OUR GOD IS THE GOD OF THE WHOLE WORLD, SO SAY IT, EVERY DAY. THE GOD OF ALL THAT IS, SO WANTS TO HEAR EVERY ONE OF HIS OWN CREATEDS TO SPEAK THAT EVERY DAY. EVERYDAY IS THE DAY OF THE LORD. DO YOU KNOW THAT? YOU DO NOW. PLEASE THANK HIM, FOR ALL HE HAS DONE AND IS DOING. IF YOU CAN GET THIS BOOK AND READ IT OFTEN SO AS TO BE REMINDED OF WHAT IS AND WILL ALWAYS BE TRUE. HE WANTS TO HEAR YOU GIVE THANKS EVERY DAY FOR ALL HE HAS PUT HIS HAND TO AND PUT IN YOUR HAND. HE DID IT JUST FOR YOU AND IT'S OKAY TO BELIEVE THAT AND SAY IT ALL DAY LONG. HE LOVES FOR YOU AND ME TO BOAST IN HIM. HE LOVES TO HEAR HIS NAME IN OUR CONVERSATIONS, AND OFTEN. TALK ABOUT HIM AND HIS FATHER IN THE SAME BREATH. TAKE A GOOD LONG BREATH AND SAY GOD OF ALL CREATION, MAKER OF ALL THAT IS. THANK HIM FOR YOUR LIFE THEN GO FISHING, AND SHARE ALL YOU CAN WITH EVERY FISHERMAN ON THE DOCK. YOU ARE A NEW DISCIPLE FOR THE LORD. SHARE WITH ALL WHO ARE NEAR. MAYBE YOU COULD WRITE A BOOK, W.O.W. WONDERFUL O' WONDERFUL. ALL ABOUT JESUS AND HIS FATHER AND HIS LOVE FOR THE WHOLE WORLD. HE WILL HELP YOU, JUST ASK. DO IT, JUST DO IT. JESUS IS GOD'S MAN ON THE GROUND. ALWAYS IN CHARGE, ALWAYS CAPABLE TO TAKE OVER AND GET THINGS GOING AND TO FINISH OFF THE PROBLEMS AT HAND. HE ALWAYS HAD THE LAST WORD. DID I

SAY, JUST TO KNOW HIM? DO YOU JUST WANT TO KNOW HIM? HE WANTS YOU TO BE HIS VERY BEST FRIEND. JUST THINK OF TELLING EVERYONE, JESUS IS YOUR VERY BEST FRIEND. YOU KNOW THERE IS A SONG, AN OLDIE BUT GOODIE. "WHAT A FRIEND WE HAVE IN JESUS". SO GOOD. YOU KNOW, THERE IS NOW NO CONDEMNATION FOR THOSE IN JESUS. YOU CAN'T DO BETTER THAN TO JUST KNOW HIM. JUST TO KNOW HIM, THE LORD JESUS CHRIST. THE ONE SENT BY THE FATHER TO SAVE THE LOST. OUR PRECIOUS REDEEMER AND SAVIOR, WHO WENT TO A CROSS TO SAVE ME. YES, JUST TO KNOW HIM. MY SALVATION.

HE LOVES YOU NOT BECAUSE OF WHO YOU ARE, BUT BECAUSE OF WHO HE IS. DEEP CALLETH UNTO DEEP. MY PROPHECY. I GIVE HIM ALL THE GLORY.
POSSESSED: YES, I BELONG TO MY GOD. I BELONG TO MY FATHER. I LOVE MY DADDY. YOU READ TILL YOU FALL ASLEEP, I WANT YOU TO READ TILL YOU WAKE UP.

CREATION, WERE YOU THERE?

.....HE HATH CHOSEN US IN HIM BEFORE THE FOUNDATION OF THE
WORLD....EPH 1:4-5

WHEN GOD CREATED HIS ULTIMATE MAN.
WERE YOU THERE TO COMPLIMENT THE WORK OF HIS HAND?

IT WAS THE SIXTH DAY,
ANGELS MARVELED AT HIS SKILLFUL WAY.

AS HE FINISHED EACH ONE THERE,
AN ANGEL WROTE A NAME WITH CARE.

FOR A THOUSAND YEARS HE LABORED.
EACH ONE CREATED SO SPECIAL AND FAVORED.

TWO EYES BLUE, TWO EYES BROWN, SO AS TO LOOK AROUND.
UNDER THE BROW YET NEAR THE CROWN.

TWO EARS TO HEAR, DIDN'T GET THAT, SO ASK REPEAT.
I MISSED A WORD, BUT ASK HIM SWEET.

ONE HEART, HIS PLACE OF DWELLING.
ONLY FOR HIM, IF YOU ARE WILLING.

TWO ARMS WITH RIGHT AND LEFT HAND,
TWO LEGS WITH FEET, SO AS TO STAND.

ONE MOUTH TO SPEAK GOD'S LOVE THROUGH LIPS.
OR TO BE SILENT, MAYBE DEEP IN WORSHIPS.

KNEES TO BEND BESIDE THE BED BEFORE I SLEEP.
TO THANK HIM FOR THE DAY AND SOUL TO KEEP.

A NECK AND SHOULDERS, THE SPINE TO STAND ERECT.
DO HIS WORK, PLEASE HIM AND END OF LIFE BE FOUND PERFECT.

MY WONDERFUL SHEPHERD, TILL THE END OF TIME.
I AM HIS AND HE IS MINE, AGAIN O' YES, TILL NO MORE TIME.

GOD'S CREATION OF HIS PERFECT MAN, O' YES SO TRUE.
DAY SIX HE WAS FINISHED, AND HE SAID "I AM THROUGH".
AMEN AND AMEN

WHEN HE WAS DONE WITH THE CREATION OF MAN AND EVERY NAME WAS WRITTEN IN THE LAMB'S BOOK OF LIFE. HE PUT THE BOOK IN ETERNITY TO MARK EACH ONE AS THEY RETURNED TO HEAVEN. HIS INTENT WAS TO HAVE EVERY MAN HE CREATED TO RETURN TO HIM. THOSE WHO DIDN'T RETURN TO HIM, WHO REFUSED THE SON OF GOD, THAT NAME IS BLOTTED OUT OF THE LAMB'S BOOK OF LIFE. HE WAS AND IS SO DISAPPOINTED WHEN THEY DON'T COME HOME. LORD I AM COMING HOME, LORD I AM COMING HOME. EVEN SO COME LORD JESUS. SURELY, I COME QUICKLY. AMEN. BY HIS UNENDING LOVE AND GRACE. AMEN.

DAY SEVEN, REST. HE IS WAITING FOR ALL TO COME HOME.
HE'S WAITNG FOR ME.

IS HE REALLY ALL THAT?

HE IS THAT AND MORE. DO YOU KNOW HIM? DO YOU REALLY KNOW HIM? HE DIED FOR A BROKEN WORLD, THE WHOLE WORLD. THERE IS NOT ONE WHO DOESN'T NEED HIS WONDERFUL SALVATION. JUST ASK, HE IS IN THE SAVING BUSINESS. HE SO WANTS TO BE THE LORD OF YOUR LIFE. YES, JUST ASK. THAT IS WHAT HE DOES, HE SAVES ALL WHO COME TO HIM FOR HIS SAVING GRACE. THAT IS ACTUALLY WHY HIS FATHER SENT HIM INTO THE WORLD, TO SAVE ALL OF THE LOST AND LONELY, DEEP IN SIN AND KNOWING NO WAY OUT. HE WILL BE SO GENTLE AND UNDERSTANDING TO BRING YOU INTO HIS JUSTICE. HE WANTS MORE THAN ANYTHING TO PULL YOU AND ME OUT OF THE MUCK AND MIRE OF SIN. WE CAN'T DO IT WITHOUT HIM. DO YOU KNOW YOU CAN'T SAVE YOURSELF? I CALL HIM MY GENTLE JESUS. HE DOESN'T SEE ANY AS UNSAVEABLE. THROUGH HIM IS THE ONLY WAY TO THE FATHER. HE CAN SAVE YOU IN THE TWINKLING OF AN EYE. HE IS ALWAYS AT HAND, JUST ONE CALL FOR HELP AND HE IS THERE READY TO LIFT THE LITTLE LAMB TO HIS SHOULDER. NO CONDEMNATION, JUST TOTAL LOVE FOR THE LOST. THERE'S NO LOVE LIKE THE LOVE OF JESUS. YOU NEED NOT TO DO A LOT OF EXPLAINING, HE ALREADY KNOWS THE PROBLEM AND HE HAS ALL THE ANSWERS. DOES THAT JUST PUT YOU ON THE FLOOR? ME, TOO. BEEN THERE, DONE THAT. HE IS SO TENDER AND LOVE IS HIS WHOLE HEART. YOU CAN'T TAKE HIM BY SURPRISE, HE KNOWS. YOU MAY WANT TO TELL HIM YOUR LIFE STORY, HE ALREADY KNOWS ALL ABOUT YOUR SITUATION. HE HAS BEEN WAITING FOR YOU ALL OF YOUR LIFE. HIS LOVE FOR YOU IS OVER THE TOP AND ALL YOUR EXCUSES DON'T MATTER. YOU HAVE NOTHING NEW GOING

ON, HE'S HEARD IT ALL. THAT'S KIND OF A RELIEF. HE HAS ALL YOUR STUFF UNDER CONTROL. HE DOES ALL THAT BECAUSE HE LOVES YOU AND ALL OF HIS OWN. HE WILL BEAT YOU TO THE ANSWER BECAUSE HE KNOWS HOW NEEDY YOU ARE. WE ALL ARE SO NEEDY. IF YOU THINK YOU DON'T NEED HIM, YOU BETTER THINK AGAIN. YOU ARE SUCH A MIGHTY AND STRONG LITTLE BEING. YOU ARE, I HEARD YOU IN YOUR BOASTING COSTUME A WHILE AGO AND YOU SOUNDED SO POWERFUL. THAT IS A FALLACY. YOU ARE A LITTLE PUFFED UP AND SELF ABSORBED, YOU LOOK SO BRAVE IN YOUR SUPERMAN APPAREL. GO LOOK IN THE MIRROR, ARE SURE YOU WANT TO DO THAT FANTASY. I DON'T THINK YOU ARE ABLE TO PULL THAT OFF. YOU NEED THE EARTH TO STAND ON AND THE LORD JESUS CHRIST TO STAND WITH YOU. HE IS THE ONLY ONE TO TALK TO AT THIS POINT AS HE IS THE ONLY TRUE HELPER. I KNOW FROM EXPERIENCE. BEEN THERE, DONE THAT. YOU NEED JESUS, HE UNDERSTANDS THESE THINGS WE GO THROUGH. HE IS OUR STRENGTH IN TIME OF NEED, AND I HAVE EXPERIENCED NEEDINESS. HE WAS RIGHT THERE TO LIFT ME OUT OF THE PROBLEM AND HELP ME GET A NEW STEADY. THANK YOU, JESUS. YOU ARE SOOOO DEPENDABLE. WHAT WOULD I DO WITHOUT YOU? I DON'T WANT TO FIND OUT. HE AND I HAVE BEEN TOGETHER FOR A LONG TIME, HE KNOWS ME. HE KNOWS YOU TOO, SO NOT TO WORRY, HE'S WITH YOU. HE, THE HELPER IN TIME OF NEED, HE'S ALL THAT AND MORE. HE AND I ARE A BIG PARTY, I FOLLOW HIS LEAD. I WANT TO STAND ON TOP OF A MOUNTAIN AND PRAISE HIM. LET THE WHOLE WORLD HEAR OF THE GOODNES OF MY LORD AND SAVIOR. HE REALLY IS "ALL THAT", YES, HE REALLY IS "ALL THAT" AND MORE. HE IS SO A KEEPER. IF YOU DON'T KNOW THAT YET, THERE'S A DAY COMING YOU WILL FIND OUT. WE ALL NEED THAT DAY OF LEARNING. HE REALLY IS "ALL THAT" AND MORE. I SAY SO. I AM REPETITIVE, AS HE DESERVES ALL THE GLORY AND PRAISE, I CAN GIVE HIM. WE

ALL SHOULD BE ON THE PRAISE AND WORSHIP TEAM, AND LEAD THE PROGRAM AS OFTEN AS POSSIBLE. WHEN I WAS DOWN AND OUT, WAY OUT, HE WAS WITH ME ALL THE WAY. HE IS SO GENTLE TO SAVE THE LITTLE LAMB ALL BY HERSELF AND DOESN'T KNOW WHAT TO DO OR WHERE TO GO. THAT WAS ME AND I AM FOREVER GRATEFUL TO HAVE MY RESCUER BY MY SIDE FOR ALL ETERNITY. THAT'S JESUS. HE'S COMING TO ESCORT ME TO THE GOLDEN SHORE REAL SOON. JESUS, I AM READY, COME ASAP. LET'S DO THIS BANQUET IN THE HEAVENLIES AND BE TOGETHER FOREVER. I LOVE YOU, COME LORD JESUS COME. DID I HEAR THE TRUMPET?

BE AGED IN HIS GRACE, STEEPED IN HIS WORD, POURED OUT IN HIS GLORY. O' HIS GRACE. THE ALTAR OF GRACE IS THE CROSS OF CHRIST. O' HIS CROSS I WANT TO GROW UP TO BE JUST LIKE YOU, JESUS. THAT'S THE CHILD IN ME. YOU READ TILL YOU FALL ASLEEP, I WANT YOU TO READ TILL YOU WAKE UP.

ISRAEL IS THE WOMB OF ALL CREATION

I SAY, ISRAEL IS THE WOMB GOD CHOSE TO BRING FORTH OUR SALVATION OR SALVATION FOR THE WHOLE WORLD, JESUS. WHEN WE CONSIDER THE BODY OF A WOMAN, HER WOMB IS A SMALL PART OF HER BODY. ISRAEL IS A VERY SMALL NATION IN A BIG WORLD. THE WORLD HAS TAKEN ON THE ABORTION THOUGHT. DESTROY ISRAEL SO THERE WILL BE NO MORE REPOPULATING THE WORLD WITH GOD'S PEOPLE. ABORTION DESTROYS THE WOMB, IT'S INJURED EVERYTIME IT IS SCRAPED AND CLEANSED OF NEW LIFE. THE CHURCH CAME OUT OF, WAS BORN IN ISRAEL. GOD LOVES THE WHOLE WORLD, THE WHOLE WOMAN (WORLD). IF WE ALLOW THE DESTRUCTION OF ISRAEL, THE WORLD WILL BE NO MORE. GOD IS THE FATHER - YES? YES. GOD WILL NOT ALLOW. DEUT 30:16 & 19. HERE COMES ARMEGEDDON, MOUNT MEGIDDO, REV 16:16 BIBLE SAYS POPULATE THE EARTH. IF YOU ABORT, IS THAT NOT AGAINST GOD? AGAINST GENESIS, AGAINST GOD'S COMMAND?? GENESIS 1:28 & 9:1. KEEP ON AND YOU WILL DESTROY THE WOMB, THE PLACE OF NEW LIFE. THE EARTH WILL BE NO MORE. I AM HERE FOR SUCH A TIME AS THIS. SIN BRINGS FORTH DEATH. SATAN (THE WORLD) SO WANTS TO DESTROY THE WOMB OF GOD'S WORLD, ISRAEL. ISRAEL IS THE WOMB WHERE ALL GOD'S CREATION BEGAN AND CAME FROM. ISRAEL IS GOD'S CHOSEN. WE, THE USA, (JER*USA*LEM) ARE ABSOLUTELY THE SUPPORT OF ISRAEL. WE ARE AT WAR TO SAVE, PROTECT AND SECURE ISRAEL. THE WHOLE FALLEN WORLD WANTS TO ELIMINATE THE BELOVED OF GOD, ISRAEL. DO YOU UNDERSTAND? IT SEEMS THAT THE UNITED STATES OF

AMERICA IS THE ONLY SUPPORT FOR ISRAEL. WE DO INDEED WANT TO SEE ISRAEL IN GOOD HEALTH AND WILL BE IN AGREEMENT TO SUPPORT HER AS OUR LITTLE SISTER. WE WILL STAND WITH HER (OR MOST OF US, THE CHRISTIAN POPULATION) UNTIL THE SECOND COMING OF OUR AND HER MESSIAH. WE MUST WATCH OUT FOR HER AS SHE IS THE CHOSEN OF GOD. HE HAS HAD HER ON HIS MIND FOR THOUSANDS OF YEARS. SHE WAS CHOSEN TO BE THE SEAT OF THE THRONE OF GOD. IT'S NOT A RECENT DECISION, THOUGH, AS HE HAS BEEN MINDFUL OF HER AS HIS SOON TO BE THRONE AND THE RULING PLACE OF HIS PLEASURE FOR THOUSANDS OF YEARS. IT'S A GOOD IDEA NOT TO MESS WITH WHAT GOD ORDAINS OR CHOOSES TO DO. HE CAN GET IRRITATED WHEN FOREIGN LANDS TRY TO INTERFER WITH HIS PLANS. IF HE HAS MADE'UP HIS MIND TO DO A THING HIS WAY, HE GETS REAL TESTY WITH THOSE WHO PUT THEIR NOSE IN HIS BUSINESS. HE IS THE LOVE OF THE LIFE OF ISRAEL. SHE IS HIS AND HE IS NOT MOVED BY WHAT THE WORLD THINKS. WHEN HE SAYS HANDS OFF, HE MEANS HANDS OFF. HE HAS PLANS AND HE WON'T CHANGE THEM FOR ANYONE. THESE WORLD POWERS GET A BIG IDEA THAT THEY ARE IN CONTROL, SO THEY ATTACK ISRAEL TO TRY AND KNOCK HER OFF THE MAP. BETTER NOT DO THAT, GOD IS WATCHING YOU. WE HAVE HEARD AND READ THAT THERE WILL BE WAR TO END ALL WARS IN THE NEAR FUTURE. HMMM. WE WILL SEE. IT'S BEEN SAID IT WILL BE THE END OF THE WORLD AS WE KNOW IT, WE WILL SEE. PROBABLY WILL BE AS THE BOOK OF REVELATION TELLS IT. SOUNDS AWFUL SCARY TO ME. GOD WILL HAVE THE VICTORY, HE ALWAYS WINS SO PUT DOWN YOUR WEAPONS. ISRAEL IS HIS, SAYS THE RULER OF ALL CREATION. WHAT DO YOU THINK THE CHANCES ARE FOR THE FALLEN WORLD? ISRAEL IS HIS, FOREVER. I THINK IT'S A GOOD IDEA BUT THEN I HAVE ALWAYS THOUGHT GOD'S IDEAS ARE FAR MORE SUPERIOR THAN MINE. I HAVE MUCH RESPECT FOR MY LORD

AND MY GOD, AND THAT'S THE WAY I LIKE IT, AND SO DOES HE. MAYBE YOU WOULD LIKE TO ARGUE WITH HIM, YOU LOSE. HE HAS ALL THE STRENGTH AND AND TENACITY TO GET THE JOB DONE. DO YOU DOUBT? DON'T DO THAT. HE IS SO MUCH OLDER THAN YOU AND BEEN AROUND THE POND MANY TIMES MORE THAN YOU. SO, KEEP ALL YOUR ADVICE SOMEWHERE HIDDEN. HE IS PERFECTLY ABLE, PERFECTLY, SEE THAT WORD?

HE WORKS FROM PERFECTION, DOES THAT JUST BLOW YOU AWAY? WE USE THE WORD PERFECT BUT WE PROBABLY DON'T REALLY UNDERSTAND THE FULLNESS OF THAT WORD. GOD DOES, WITHOUT ANY HELP FROM ANY SOURCE. OOPS, I GUESS THAT LEAVES US (ME) OUT. THE MORE I AGE, THE MORE I SEE HIM AS MY LORD AND MY GOD OF ALL THINGS... WHEN HE SITS ME DOWN TO WRITE FOR HIM, I AM HIS TO USE. I AM HIS, ALWAYS. AMEN. KEEP JESUS AS YOUR CENTER. EVEN THE ONES WHO HATED HIM PUT HIM IN THE CENTER.

WHEN THEY NAILED HIM TO A CROSS WAS HE NOT IN THE CENTER. HE WAS!
THERE WAS A DAY WHEN I WAS THE ONLY ONE, THE DAY OF PERFECTION, WAS BORN. AMEN

THE MORE YOU LOVE

FOR GOD SO LOVED THE WORLD, HE GAVE AS A SAVIOR, HIS ONLY BEGOTTEN SON ...JOHN 3:16

FALL IN LOVE WITH THE GOD OF THE WHOLE WORLD, THE WHOLE UNIVERSE, EVERYTHING AS FAR AS THE EYE CAN SEE AND BEYOND. GOD HAS NO END, NO, HE DOESN'T. HOW CAN I LOVE WHAT I DON'T KNOW ABOUT? WELL, I AM TELLING YOU THAT THERE IS/ARE SO MUCH WE CAN'T AND DON'T SEE OR KNOW ABOUT. HOW DO YOU LIKE THAT? IT ALL BELONGS TO HIM. HE IS THE CREATOR OF ETERNITY AND INFINITY. HE, THE OWNER OF ALL STUFF AND THINGS WE CAN'T EVEN IMAGINE, IS THE ONE WHO IS THE REQUESTOR OF OUR LOVE. LOVE YOUR ENEMIES, "FOR GOD SO LOVED THE WORLD." I DON'T EVER WANT TO LIMIT GOD, SO I WON'T START NOW. HE'S ETERNAL, HE KNOWS THE WHOLE OF ETERNITY. HE GOES ON AND ON. THAT'S HOW WE EXPLAIN GOD AND THAT'S TRUE. HE HAS NO BEGINNING AND NO END. WE REALLY CAN'T WRAP OUR LITTLE GRAY MATTER AROUND THAT!!! HE IS INFINITE, WE ARE FINITE. HE DOESN'T RUN INTO THE WALL. WE SEE A BEGINNING AND AN END. THAT'S HOW WE ARE MADE. THAT LITTLE DOT ON THE CIRCLE OF INFINITY IS THE AGE OF MAN. THAT'S US. WE BELIEVE BUT WE CAN'T FATHOM (UNDERSTAND) INFINITY, THAT'S GOD'S PLAN AND WE WILL NEVER BE ABLE TO FIGURE THAT OUT. THAT'S LOVE, LOVE IS TRULY WHAT WE DON'T UNDERSTAND. O' I LOVE EVERYBODY, SURE YOU DO. YOU HAVE NO IDEA WHAT YOU ARE SAYING, DO YOU? WHEN GOD THOUGHT ABOUT HIS CREATION AND CREATING, HE DID REACH OUT TO THE EDGE OF ETERNITY AND HIS HAND DID TAKE A LITTLE PIECE OF DIRT FROM A STAR (I SEE IT AS IT WAS A LITTLE MASS UNDER HIS FINGERNAIL, I AM HIS LITTLE STAR) AND DID DEPOSIT IT IN

THE BALCONY OF HEAVEN UNTIL HE WANTED TO CREATE HIS MAN. THAT'S LOVE, HE HAD ME IN MIND BUT HE WASN'T READY YET TO CREATE. I HAVE NO THING (NOTHING) TO BOAST OF, I AM HIS IDEA AND SO IS LOVE. THAT IS SO HUMBLING. I AM SO THANKFUL FOR MY GOD AND HIS LOVE. WE CAN'T LOVE LIKE THAT, WE DON'T KNOW HOW. EVERY DAY SOME ARE OUT THERE MURDERING HIS CREATION. (ABORTION). DO YOU REALLY THINK YOU WON'T ANSWER FOR THAT? THAT'S HIS. WE ARE IN THE AGE OF MAN. HE IS SAYING HANDS OFF. WE ARE HIS BEST, HIS IDEAS AND HE DOESN'T WANT TO SHARE, YOU ARE TAKING HIS THINGS WITHOUT PERMISSION. YOU REALLY SHOULD MIND YOUR OWN BUSINESS. O'YES, WE ARE HIS, ONLY HIS. BORN INTO THE WORLD AS ONE ON LOAN TO WHOSOEVER WILL. YOUR FAMILY MEMBERS ARE THE WHOSOEVER WILL. YOU MUST NOT DESTROY HIS CREATEDS. YOU ARE NOT YOUR OWN, YOU WERE BOUGHT WITH A PRICE. READ AND READ AGAIN. 1 COR 6:19-20 AND 1 COR 7:23. YOU ARE STEALING FROM THE "FAMILY OF GOD". THE BEST THING YOU CAN DO IF YOU HAVE STOLEN FROM GOD, ASK FOR HIS LOVING AND WILLING FORGIVENESS. VERY HUMBLE AND CONTRITE. HE IS SO GOOD TO FORGIVE, HE "ABOVE ALL" CAN AND WILL "FORGIVE". YOU JUST HAVE TO KNOW, IT'S HIS LOVE. GOD'S LOVE IS SO FORGIVING. NO ONE LOVES AS HE LOVES. NO ONE! HIS LOVE MADE AN ENDLESS UNIVERSE. I THINK I AM GETTING A BIT MISTY. I AM SO GRATEFUL FOR MY GOD, I AM SO IN LOVE WITH MY GOD. IF YOU KNOW HIM, YOU KNOW LOVE. DON'T EVER APOLOGIZE FOR LOVE, IT'S A GIFT, GRAB IT, PUT IT IN YOUR HEART AS A PRECIOUS TREASURE. THE BIBLE IS THE BOOK OF LOVE, INVEST IN SIX OR A DOZEN, SO AS TO PUT ONE IN EVERY ROOM AND READ THEM OFTEN, WEAR THEM OUT. YOU CAN GET MORE. TO BE SURE, HE IS LOVE. HIS LOVE RULES OVER THE EARTH, OVER THE HEAVENS, OVER THE FARTHEST EDGES OF THE UNIVERSE. THE DEPTH, THE WIDTH, THE HEIGHT OF HEAVEN IS AS FAR

AS THE LIGHT OF HEAVEN SHINES ACCORDING TO HIS LOVE, ETERNAL. HIS LOVE IS IN COMPLETE CONTROL FOR ALL ETERNITY. YOU CAN'T MEASURE HIS LOVE, IT'S ETERNAL. DON'T YOU JUST LOVE HIM. HE DIED FOR YOU, NOW YOU LIVE FOR HIM. HIS LOVE REACHES FROM ONE END OF HEAVEN TO THE OTHER END OF HEAVEN. INFINITE. HE IS OF THE TRUE "OUTER LIMITS". HAVE YOU EVER SEEN OR HEARD SO MUCH LOVE? I LOVE TO WRITE OF HIS LOVE. ONE OF THESE DAYS I AND ALL WHO LOVE TO LOVE AND OBEY GOD'S LOVE, WILL

GATHER IN THE GLORIOUS GARDEN OF HIS LOVE. I SURE HOPE YOU ARE THERE SO WE CAN TALK TO HIM, THE GOD OF LOVE AND OUR LORD JESUS CHRIST, ABOUT THE LOVE OF OUR SAVIOR WHO DIED TO MAKE ALL OF THIS POSSIBLE FOR ALL OF US, HIS CREATED.

NOT GOD FIRST, GOD ONLY. HE WILL BE ONLY OR HE WON'T
BE ANY.
GOD'S SON, JESUS, THE NAME OF GRACE. THE GRACE OF GOD
IN THE FLESH.
I LOVE THE PURPLE LIGHT, LIGHT FROM HEAVEN. DO YOU
SEE THE SON'LIGHT.
HE LOVES YOU NOT BECAUSE OF WHO YOU ARE, BUT
BECAUSE OF WHO HE IS. AMEN

HOW GREAT IS MY GOD

THE GREAT GOD, MIGHTY AND AWESOME, WHO SHOWS NO PARTIALITY,
NOR TAKES A BRIBE. DEUT 10:17

MY GOD IS SO AWESOME, GOD OF gods, KING OF kings and LORD OF lords. SO WONDERFUL, SO HOLY, HIGH AND LIFTED UP. MY GOD IS THE ONLY GOD, MORE GLORIOUS THAN ANY god. HE IS SO MUCH MORE GOOD THAN ANY COULD EVEN MENTION. MY GOD IS NOT FIRST, HE IS ONLY. DO YOU KNOW THE DIFFERENCE? HE IS ONLY OR HE WON'T BE ANY. YOU CAN NOT EVEN FIND A WORD OF PRAISE BY ANYONE WHO COULD BOAST OF ANY WHO IS GREATER THAN HIS GREATNESS. I BOW TO HIS GREATNESS AND WONDER. HE IS THE OWNER OF ALL THE HEAVENS, ALL THE STARS, ALL THE PLANETS, ALL THE AIR I BREATHE. THE OWNER OF THE EARTH AND ALL THAT IS ON IT AND IN IT. I HEARD MY NAME ECHOING IN THE HEAVENS. MEZZECHAH, THE NAME GIVEN TO ME EARLY ONE MORNING. HE DID HAVE ME TO WAKE UP AND WRITE IT DOWN. I AM ONE WHO KEEPS A TABLET ON THE BED STAND TO WRITE DOWN WHAT HE SAYS IN THE NIGHT OR EARLY MORNING. I AM MY FATHER'S LITTLE STAR. THE TRANSLATION OF MY NAME, MEZZECHAH, IS "STAR". HE CHOSE ME EIGHTEEN THOUSAND YEARS AGO. HE TOOK ME TO THE BALCONY OF HEAVEN TO WAIT FOR THE DAY OF CREATION. HE HAS SHOWN ME MUCH FAVOR. HE KEEPS ME SO CLOSE TO HIS SIDE, LOVES TO HOLD MY HAND. NONE CAN COME BETWEEN HIM AND ME. I DID NOT CHOOSE HIM, HE CHOSE ME. THANK YOU, DADDY. MY GOD IS GREATER THAN ANY CAN SAY. HE HAS ME AT HIS ATTENTION. I NEED TO HEAR EVERYTHING HE SAYS TO ME OR ABOUT ME. I CHOOSE TO PRAISE AND WORSHIP HIM WHEN I HEAR HIM BY MY SIDE. HE IS THE ONE WHO IS INSTANT TO MY ATTENTION. THERE IS NONE BEFORE HIM OR BESIDES HIM, OR OVER HIM.

HE IS ONLY. DO YOU UNDERSTAND THAT? I HAVE DIBS ON THE ATTENTION OF HIS HEART. A TUG ON HIS HOLY NAME IS WHAT I DEPEND ON TO GET HIS HOLY ATTENTION. I AM ON HIS MIND AND I LIKE THAT. YES! HIS SCRIPTURES ARE CONSTANT ON MY MIND. THE MORNING IS HIS AND SO IS ANYTIME HE WANTS TO SAY ANYTHING OF HIS GLORY AND WONDER. HE IS THE GLORY OF THE MORNING, THE ONE THERE WHEN I WAKEN IN THE EARLY OF THE DAY. HE CALLS ME AND I ANSWER, I CALL HIM AND HE ANSWERS BACK. YOU HAVE HEARD OF BEING AT HIS BECK AND CALL. I AM. HE IS, TOO, FOR ME. ALWAYS HAS TIME FOR A WORD, HIS WORD. ME, TOO. WHEN THE DAYS END I WILL BE FOUND OF HIM AT THE CROSS TO HONOR THE ONLY BEGOTTEN OF THE FATHER. JESUS AND ME TO WORSHIP AND COMMUNE WITH OUR FATHER. I AM OF MY FATHER AND SO IS MY JESUS. O' THE BLOOD OF JESUS, SHED FOR THE REMTTANCE OF THE SIN DEBT OF ALL WHO WILL ASK, AND WILL RECEIVE. ALL WHO ASK WILL RECEIVE, THAT TO THE GLORY OF GOD THROUGH JESUS, BY THE BLOOD SHED IN THE GARDEN ALL THE WAY TO THE CROSS. HOW COULD ANY NOT ASK FOR THE GIFT OF ETERNAL LIFE BY THE SHED BLOOD OF JESUS? HOW GREAT IS MY GOD. YOU REALLY MUST AGREE. HE HAS KEPT ME THESE THOUSANDS OF YEARS THAT I MAY BE ALIVE FOR THE RAPTURE. I WILL CERTAINLY BE ONE WHO LEAVES THIS EARTH WITH MY JESUS. THAT WAS THE PLAN IN THE BEGINNING AND IS NOW THE SAME IN THE ENDING. IT'S THE PLAN. AS I WROTE "I AM GOING TO PLAN BECAUSE I AM PLANNING TO GO". SUN OR NO SUN, MOON OR NO MOON, LET'S GO. ALL THAT HE IS, I AM READY TO ESCAPE TO HIM. O'HOW GREAT IS MY GOD. TASTE AND SEE, YOU WILL AGREE. DO YOU KNOW JESUS BELONGS TO ME. YOU DO NOW. O'HOW GREAT IS MY GOD. JESUS IS MINE. AMEN

NOT GOD FIRST, GOD ONLY. HE WILL BE ONLY OR HE WON'T BE ANY.
I AM SO BLESSED, SO LOVED, HE GAVE ME HIS WORD. THE LORD JESUS CHRIST. MY PROPHECY, "DEEP CALLETH UNTO DEEP". I GIVE HIM ALL THE GLORY.

IF I TELL YOU

HE COUNTS THE STARS; HE CALLS THEM ALL BY NAME. PSALM HG147:4
MY NAME IS MEZZECHAH, MY DADDY'S LITTLE STAR.

I HAVE INFORMATION TO SHARE WITH ANY WHOSOEVER WILL TREASURE IT AS I DO. DO YOU KNOW ME? YES, WE GO TO THE SAME CHURCH, WE ARE CHRISTIANS. I SO LOVE TO GO TO CHURCH. I THINK IT HAS A LOT TO DO WITH WHO I AM. IT BRINGS OUT JOY IN MY SOUL TO COME AND COMMUNE WITH MY FELLOW CHURCH FAMILY. THEY HAVE NOT BEEN TOLD, AS FAR AS I KNOW, WHO THEY SIT WITH AND SING AND WORSHIP WITH. IT'S NOT A SECRET BUT THEY WILL MOST PROBABLY BACK UP A LITTLE WHEN THEY FIND OUT. I AM A VERY QUIET MEMBER OF THE TRINITY. SINCE I WAS A YOUNG GIRL I HAVE KNOWN MY IDENTITY HERE. I WAS STOOD STILL MANY YEARS AGO TO HEAR THE VOICE OF HEAVEN, WHETHER ANGEL OR HOLY GHOST OR GOD HIMSELF OR JESUS HIMSELF TO TALK WITH ME. I WAS BETWEEN TEN TO TWELVE YEARS OLD WHEN IN THE DINING ROOM OF OUR FAMILY HOME IN PIPESTONE, MN., I HEARD A VOICE TELL ME A SECRET FROM MY FATHER, THE GOD OF HEAVEN. EVERYTHING CHANGED BECAUSE I DIDN'T KNOW HOW TO PROCESS THAT INFORMATION. MOST PROBABLY TOO, I HAD BEEN WATER BAPTIZED IN A CHURCH THAT HAD A BAPTISTRY, SINCE OUR LITTLE CHURCH DIDN'T. I WAS NEW "BORN AGAIN", SO WE (MY BROTHER AND SISTER) WERE LIVING A NEW LIFE IN THE LORD. YES, SO EXCITING TO BE WELCOMED INTO THE KINGDOM OF HEAVEN. THAT'S HOW WE WERE TOLD ABOUT WHAT HAD HAPPENED TO US. I FELT SO SPECIAL, THAT I WOULD HEAR FROM HEAVEN, OH SO GLORIOUS. GUESS WHAT? I STILL DO. I AM SO HAPPY WHEN I SING IN THE SPIRIT, PRAY IN THE SPIRIT. MAY I ADD, GOD IS SO GOOD. O BY THE WAY,

THIS HAPPENED MANY YEARS AGO. I DID ALL THE STUFF THAT CHILDREN AND YOUNG PEOPLE DO INCLUDING TASTING ALCOHOL, SMOKING AND SOMETIMES USING BAD LANGUAGE, EVEN THOUGH I DID KNOW BETTER. I HAVE REPENTED AND DON'T DO THAT ANYMORE, EVER. HE, MY JESUS, WOULD BE SO DISAPPOINTED. I CERTAINLY DON'T WANT TO HURT MY LORD JESUS CHRIST. IT'S TIME TO COME TO THE FRONT OF THE CLASS AND TALK ABOUT THE GOODNESS OF GOD. ALL THOSE YEARS PAST I WAS TEMPTED TO DISCUSS WHAT HAPPENED LONG AGO. I DIDN'T. NOW IS THE TIME TO SHARE THE GLORIOUS NEWS FROM MY FATHER IN HEAVEN. I BELIEVE HE HAS ALLOWED THIS FOR NOW. I ALSO BELIEVE TOO THAT WE ARE SO CLOSE TO THE RAPTURE OF THE LORD'S CHURCH. I HOPE ALL WILL APPRECIATE THIS TELLING NOW. THE DIALOG OF THAT DAY WAS "YOU ARE FOUR". YOU ARE THE FOURTH MEMBER OF THE TRINITY. WHAT DOES THAT MEAN? I DID TALK TO MY FRIENDS AT SCHOOL, THOUGH I DIDN'T DISCLOSE WHY. THERE WERE MANY KIDS WHO WERE CATHOLIC, I AM NOT CATHOLIC. I KNOW THAT THEY WORSHIP MARY, AND THAT'S A NO-NO. GOD IS GOD AND HIM ONLY SHALL YOU WORSHIP. ABSOLUTLY. I AM NOT HOLY AS ONLY GOD IS HOLY, LORD JESUS CHRIST, AND THE BLESSED HOLY GHOST, ARE THE BLESSED TRINITY. I WAS CHOSEN TO BEAR THE SON OF GOD. I WAS CHOSEN EIGHTEEN THOUSAND YEARS AGO. IN THE LAST MANY YEARS, I DON'T KNOW TO BE EXACT, HE HAS GIVEN ME MUCH INFORMATION. I HAVE BEEN TOLD OF OTHERS WHO ARE CHOSEN FOR OTHER ASSIGNMENTS FROM HEAVEN. I HAVE WRITTEN THREE BOOKS TO TELL ABOUT WHO AND WHERE THEY ARE. JOHN THE BELOVED, THE DISCIPLE JESUS LOVED, IS BOB FITTS WHO LIVES ON THE ISLAND OF HAWAII. SIMON THE CYRENEAN, IS ARTHUR BLESSITT WHO CARRIES THE CROSS ALL OVER THE WORLD. JOHN MARK, WROTE THE GOSPEL OF MARK, HE IS A PASTOR OF A CHURCH IN THE VALLEY. JOSEPH, JESUS' EARTHLY FATHER, WAS IN CHURCH

FOR A WHILE THEN DISAPPEARED. GABRIEL, THE VIP ANGEL OF HEAVEN IS JONATHAN CAHN. SAUL, THE FIRST KING OF ISRAEL WAS ALSO THE SAUL, WHO HATED CHRIST FOLLOWERS BUT WAS BLINDED ON THE DAMASCUS ROAD AND WAS SAVED, I DON'T KNOW WHERE HE IS NOW. CONSIDER YOURSELF TOLD. THERE IS SO MUCH TO TELL SINCE THAT DAY HE STOOD ME STILL TO GIVE ME DIRECTION. I SO WANT TO TELL EVERYONE I CAN. I SO WANT TO ENGAGE ALL WHO WILL STAND STILL FOR A MINUTE. HE DID STAND ME STILL THAT DAY, BUT IT TOOK MANY YEARS TO GET TO WRITING IT DOWN. I DON'T HAVE A FAMILY, HUSBAND, GONE. FOUR CHILDREN, GONE. TWO BOYS, NO CHILDREN. TWO DAUGHTERS, TWO CHILDREN, BUT DISTANT. THEY ARE BUSY. ONE SISTER, MUCH YOUNGER THAN ME. IT IS SO TIME FOR THE RAPTURE. I NEED TO GO HOME, I REALLY DO NOT WANT TO DIE. HE KNOWS. PLEASE PRAY FOR ME THAT I AM WELL ABLE TO ENDURE TO THE END. I LOVE MY FATHER, MY JESUS, MY BLESSED HOLY GHOST. AMEN. SO BE IT. IF YOU WANT TO TALK, WE CAN.

NOT GOD FIRST, GOD ONLY. HE WILL BE ONLY OR HE WON'T BE ANY. I LOVE MY LORD.

ONLY JESUS

ACTS 4:12

NEITHER IS THEIR SALVATION IN ANY OTHER: FOR THERE IS NONE OTHER NAME UNDER HEAVEN GIVEN AMONG MEN, WHEREBY WE MUST BE SAVED. MY HEART WON'T ALLOW ANY OTHER OPTIONS. I AM SO GRATEFUL FOR MY JESUS. I WOULD NEVER CONSIDER TO REVERENCE OR WORSHIP ANY OTHER THAN MY JESUS, MY SAVIOR. SINCE I WAS A YOUNG GIRL, I HAVE BEEN IN LOVE WITH JESUS. I DID HAVE A FEW WONDERFUL SUNDAY SCHOOL TEACHERS WHO GAVE THE WORD AS IT WAS A LIFE-OR-DEATH CHOICE. DO YOU KNOW THAT'S TRUE? THE FATHER, MY GOD, MY JESUS, AND THE BLESSED HOLY GHOST. I WAS STEEPED IN THE HEAVENLY GOOD NEWS EVERSINCE I CAN REMEMBER. AM I BLESSED OR WHAT? O' I AM. ALL CHILDREN SHOULD BE AS FORTUNATE AS I WAS AND AM., HE SURE DID BLESS ME. I DO LOVE MY TRINITY. HE CHOSE ME, I DID NOT CHOOSE HIM. NOW, THAT'S SOMETHING WONDERFUL TO WRITE HOME ABOUT, HUH. I AM IN CHURCH EVERY SUNDAY, HOPING THAT THE RAPTURE WOULD HAPPEN. WOULDN'T IT BE FUN TO LEAVE THIS WORLD FROM THE CHURCH. AT LEAST I WOULD BE DRESSED PROPERLY. HE DOESN'T CARE IF I HAVE ON MY GARDEN CLOTHES, NOW DOES HE. IF YOU HAVE ON YOUR WORK CLOTHES, HE WILL PUT YOU TO WORK. WOW. WHAT A PLEASURE TO WEED THE GARDEN IN HEAVEN WITH JESUS LOOKING ON. HE MAY EVEN WANT TO GET HIS HANDS DIRTY WITH THE FERTILE SOIL OF HEAVEN. ISN'T HE 'SO GOOD' AND FUN. TO BE THERE WHEN HE TURNS ON THE RAIN TO WATER THE GARDEN, WE COULD ALL GET WET. HE IS SO ADORABLE, AND HE IS MINE. AND YOURS, TOO, IF YOU WANT TO OR CHOOSE TO. ARE YOU SAVED? ALL THIS I HAVE WRITTEN

HINGES ON SALVATION. DON'T NEGLECT SALVATION, YOU REALLY NEED IT. NOT BECAUSE I SAY SO, HE SAID SO. HE DIED TO PROVIDE A SECURE FUTURE FOR ALL OF HIS OWN. YOU MUST BE BORN'AGAIN, MAYBE WITH THE EVIDENCE OF SPEAKING WITH OTHER TONGUES. YOU MAY WANT TO GO FOR THE WATER BAPTISM, TOO. I DID, WHEN I WAS COMING UP OUT OF THE WATER, I KNEW THERE WAS MUCH MORE TO DO. FOLLOW HIM TO THE DESTINY OF ETERNITY IN THE HEAVENS. IT'S SO WONDERFUL TO BELONG TO HIM AND HE SO WANTS TO SHARE ALL HE HAS WITH YOU AND ME. THE WHOLE SCRIPTURE DOES INVITE ALL TO FOLLOW IN HIS HOLY REDEMPTION AND SALVATION. KEEP YOUR EYES ON THE CROSS SO AS TO REMEMBER THE SACRIFICE THAT WAS THE BEGINNING OF THE JOURNEY TO ETERNAL LIFE. JESUS' JOURNEY WAS THE ROAD HE WALKED TO GOLGOTHA (GREEK) OR MOUNT CALVARY (HEBREW) TO PROVIDE MY SALVATION. YES INDEED, IT IS A JOURNEY AND HE WILL WALK THE WHOLE WAY WITH YOU. HE IS THE BEST GUIDE TO TAKE YOU OR I SHOULD SAY, "US" TO OUR HEAVENLY DESTINATION. WHAT A DAY OF REJOICING THAT WILL BE. PUT DOWN THE 'WAIT TIL LATER' STUFF, YOU MAY NOT HAVE AN OPTION OR TIME LATER ON. THERE IS NOT A BETTER TIME THAN RIGHT NOW TO BE RE'BORN. HE WILL NOT PRESSURE ANY TO COME, IT HAS TO BE YOUR CHOICE. THE BIBLE SAYS "CHOOSE NOW WHO YOU WILL FOLLOW. JOSHUA 24:15. IT REALLY DOES MEAN 'NOW', YOU ARE NOT TOO BUSY. I HAVE A WRITE "FALL IN LOVE WITH JESUS" AND I SURE DO RECOMMEND THAT HE IS THE ONE TO LOVE TO THE END. YE KNOW NOT WHEN THE DAY SHALL COME. ONLY JESUS IS THE ONE TO HEAR OR LISTEN TO, HIS CALL IS NOT TO BE IGNORED. ENOUGH, YES, JESUS IS ENOUGH. I SO RECOMMEND THAT YOU PUT DOWN ALL THAT STUFF YOU ARE DOING AND COME FOLLOW HIM IN THE REGENERATION OF LIFE. JESUS IS THE ONLY ONE TO FOLLOW, THE REST OF THEM WILL TAKE YOU TO THE ETERNITY OF

DARKNESS. THOSE ARE MY WORDS. JUST DO IT. JESUS IS THE ONLY ONE TO PROMISE LIFE LASTING NOW, FOREVER. I KNOW HIM VERY WELL AND HE REALLY DOES KEEP HIS PROMISES. HIS LOVE WILL NEVER RUN OUT, SO REACH FOR THE HAND THAT LEADS TO TRUTH AND LIFE, SECURITY. GET HIS BOOK AND READ IT, EVERY DAY. I HAVE A WRITE TO ENCOURAGE THAT YOU DO INTENTIONALLY, DELIBERATELLY, ON PURPOSE FOLLOW HIM. CHOOSE WELL, YOUR CHOICE IS ENDLESS. THAT'S NOT A THREAT, THAT'S THE TRUTH. FIND A GOOD CHURCH AND GO. JESUS, MY HEART WON'T ALLOW ANY OTHER OPTION. JUST JESUS, I HAVE TO LOVE YOU, JESUS. YOU PROBABLY SEE I LOVE TO SAY HIS NAME, I SURE DO. AMEN.

NOT GOD FIRST GOD ONLY. HE WILL BE ONLY OR HE WON'T BE ANY. GOT IT?
BE AGED IN HIS GRACE, STEEPED. IN HIS WORD, POURED OUT IN HIS GLORY AMEN THE BREAD, THE WINE. MY HEALING, MY SALVATION. MY ALL IN ALL. MY EVERYTHING.

NAMES, WHO ARE THEY?

WE ALL KNOW SOMEONE WHO HAS BEEN HERE BEFORE. MAYBE IT'S YOU? WE PROBABLY DON'T REALIZE THAT WHOEVER THEY ARE HAS A HISTORY OF LIFE BEFORE THIS LIFE. MOST COULD/WOULD SAY OR ADMIT THAT THEY HAD A REASSIGNMENT AND ARE NOW FULFILLING IT. YES, YOU HAVE. YOU ARE NOT GONNA LIVE A FEW YEARS AND THEN PASS AND FLOAT AROUND HEAVEN AND WAIT FOR THE REST OF US TO CATCH'UP WITH YOU. GOD WILL SEE TO IT THAT YOU KEEP BUSY. BUSY HANDS ARE HAPPY HANDS. I DO NOT REFER TO REINCARNATION. YOU WERE NEVER A TREE OR A DOG OR SOMEONE'S FUR COAT OR THE ROCK OF GIBRALTAR. DON'T GO THERE. PEOPLE ARE REASSIGNED AS PEOPLE. I DON'T THINK YOUR DOG OR CAT WAS EVER A DOG OR CAT FOR SOMEONE ELSE, EITHER. WHEN SOMEONE DECIDES TO ABORT THEIR BABY, GOD GATHERS THE SPIRIT AND SOUL TO BE REASSIGNED TO ANOTHER. YOU MAY DECIDE TO THROW HIM OR HER AWAY BUT GOD DOESN'T. THAT'S HIS CREATION AND IT IS DEAR TO HIM, ABSOLUTELY. YOU CANNOT TREAT HIS GOLD LIKE ASPHALT. THAT'S A NO NO. YOU PROBABLY WILL WANT TO ARGUE THIS WITH ME OR WHOEVER? O O, YOU LOSE. I AM MOTHER OF THOUSANDS. I HAVE BEEN IN AND OUT OF THIS WORLD MANY TIMES.

ARTHUR BLESSITT:
SIMON, THE CYRENIAN

REMEMBER, WHEN JESUS WAS CARRYING HIS CROSS THRU THE STREETS, ON HIS WAY TO CALVARY, FALLING DOWN, HARDLY ABLE TO WALK, LET ALONE CARRY THE CROSS. THEY PULLED SOMEONE FROM THE CROWD, WHO WAS JUST PASSING BY, TO CARRY IT FOR HIM. HE WAS SIMON, THE CYRENIAN. HE MUST HAVE BEEN HONORED BY THEIR CHOICE TO CARRY THE CROSS FOR THE KING, HOWEVER AT THAT TIME I AM SURE HE DIDN'T UNDERSTAND WHO THAT BLOODIED AND BEATEN, CONDEMNED MAN WAS. I KNOW (BELIEVE) THAT THE MAN WHO CARRIES THE CROSS TODAY, WHO HAS CARRIED IT ALL OVER THE WORLD, UNDER ALL KINDS OF CIRCUMSTANCES AND CONDITIONS, IS NONE OTHER THAN ARTHUR BLESSITT, AKA SIMON, THE CYRENIAN. I WONDER HOW MANY CROSSES HE HAS CARRIED SINCE THE ONE HE CARRIED FOR OUR LORD JESUS CHRIST? I WONDER DOES HE KNOW AND UNDERSTAND WHO HE IS OR HAS EVER THOUGHT ABOUT IT? HE PROBABLY HASN'T ALWAYS HAD THE SAME NAME. YOU KNOW WHO HE IS, DON'T YOU? ALL THRU THE TWO THOUSAND YEARS AND PLUS, SINCE THE DAY OF THE DEATH OF JESUS, ARTHUR BLESSITT, HAS BEEN SOMEWHERE CARRYING A CROSS. THERE ARE THOSE WHO ARE REASSIGNED FROM HEAVEN TO CARRY ON THE ASSIGNMENTS GIVEN TO THEM FROM OUR FATHER TO FINISH, TO THE LAST DAY. AS WE APPOACH OUR FINAL DAY ON THIS PLANET, WE MUST INDEED, DO OUR ASSIGNMENTS GIVEN FROM ABOVE. DEAREST ARTHUR, WE ARE SO GRATEFUL FOR YOU AND YOUR DEDICATION TO YOUR JOURNEY. JESUS NEEDED YOU TO WALK WITH HIM TO HIS DEATH AND YOU DID. YOU WILL RECEIVE, THE CROWN MOST BEAUTIFUL

FOR YOUR LOVE FOR OUR PRECIOUS LORD. THANK YOU, YOU ARE SO BLESSED AND BEAUTIFUL. GOD SAID SO. I HEARD HIM SAY THAT AND MORE. GOOD JOB, ARTHUR. YOU ARE FROM EVERLASTING TO EVERLASTNG. SO, I SAY.

AMEN AND AMEN!

JONATHAN DAVID CAHN

JONATHAN DAVID CAHN: GABRIEL: GOD'S MESSENGER

DO YOU DOUBT WHO HE IS? HE IS GOD'S MESSENGER, INDEED. HE HAS STUDIED TO BE APPROVED OF GOD AS A MESSENGER FOR/OF THE LAST DAYS. LOOK AT THE BOOKS HE HAS WRITTEN. THE HARBINGER, HARBINGER COMPANION MYSTERY OF THE SHEMITAH AND BOOK OF MYSTERIES, I KNOW HIM. WE HAD AN ENCOUNTER MANY YEARS AGO. AS GABRIEL, HE ANNOUNCED THE BIRTH OF CHRIST OR PREGNACY OF ME (AS MARY). READ "THE ENCOUNTER" ONE OF MY WRITES. I MET HIM IN THE EARLY MORNING IN MY APARTMENT, WHEN I WAS IN THE FIFTH MONTH OF MY FIRST PREGNACY (AS ARLENE). HE TOOK MY SON. HOWEVER, HE GAVE ME A SON TWO THOUSAND YEARS AGO. HE IS GOD'S MESSENGER, INDEED. HE LOOKS THE SAME NOW AS WHEN I SAW HIM 55 (DOUBLE GRACE) YEARS AGO. THE DIFFERENCE BETWEEN NOW AND THEN IS, HE WAS HUGH, FILLED THE WHOLE HALL WHERE HE STOPPED ME TO DO THE TRANSFERMATION. YA, ROLL YOUR EYES. YOU DOUBT, IT'S OK. IT TOOK A WHILE FOR ME TO GET IT. IT BEGAN TO UNFOLD OVER TWO YEARS AGO. FEW HAVE I TOLD. THE MAIN CHARACTER OF THIS NOVEL IS ROBERT FITTS. GABRIEL TOOK BOB FITTS FROM ME YEARS AGO. I HAVE BEEN TRYING TO GET HOLD OF MR FITTS, BUT HE IS SO BUSY. I SO WANT TO SEE HIM. I HAVE WRITTEN LETTERS BUT. SINCE YOU ARE GOD'S MESSENGER, DEAREST GABRIEL, WOULD YOU PLEASE GO SEE IF YOU CAN GET MR FITTS TO COME VISIT ME, ASAP. THANK YOU SO MUCH. I DISCOVERED HIM (MR FITTS) WHEN HE WAS SINGING ON JOSEPH PRINCE MORNING PROGRAM. I STOOD UP, OR WAS STOOD UP, BROUGHT TO MY FEET BY THE HOLY GHOST. IN AWE, I SAID "I KNOW THAT MAN BUT WHO IS HE

AND HOW DO I KNOW HIM. AFTER 44 DAYS OF PRAYER AND FASTING GOD TOLD ME, THE SON YOU LOST MANY YEARS AGO. MR CAHN, YOU ARE NOT AN ENEMY, JUST A PART OF A DIFFERENT PUZZLE. FROM EVERLASTING TO EVERLASTING, OF THE HEAVENLIES. GOD'S CHOSEN. BEAUTIFUL. COME SEE ME, PLEASE. I AM NOT AFRAID OF YOU ANYMORE. YOU LOOK THE SAME AS YOU DID 55 (DOUBLE GRACE) YEARS AGO. YOU ARE TRULY A MESSENGER FROM GOD, GABRI(EL). (EL) THE NAME OF GOD. YOU ARE FROM EVERLASTING TO EVERLASTING.

AMEN AND AMEN!

ROBERT FITTS:
MY SON AND MISSIONARY.

YOU ARE A PIECE FROM A DIFFERENT PUZZLE. FROM EVERLASTING TO EVERLASTING. I WOULD THAT YOU WOULD COME SEE ME AND ALLOW ME THE COURTESY OF YOUR ACQUAINTANCE. I HAVE WANTED TO SEE YOU BUT YOU DON'T RESPOND TO MY REQUESTS. YOU ARE THE MOST WONDERFUL SINGER THE WHOLE WORLD HAS EVER KNOWN AND I AM DELIGHTED TO SING WITH YOU EVERY EVENING. I AM ONE WHO SINGS TO HER LORD FOR AN HOUR BEFORE BED. VERY SOOTHING AND RESTFUL. YOU PROBABLY READ THE LAST CHAPTER OF JOHN, WHERE JESUS SAYS THAT IT'S NOBODY'S BUSINESS IF YOU (JOHN) SHOULD REMAIN UNTIL CHRIST'S RETURN. THERE YOU ARE, STILL HERE. IT'S IN THE SCRIPTURES BECAUSE IT'S TRUE. JESUS DIDN'T WASTE HIS WORDS, HE HAD A PURPOSE FOR EVERYTHING HE SAID. YOU MAY HAVE SLIPPED AWAY BETWEEN ASSIGNMENTS BUT YOU ARE HERE NOW, WAITING FOR OUR JESUS. YOU ARE JOHN THE BELOVED APOSTLE OF THE LORD JESUS CHRIST. HOW SO. FOLLOW THE LINKS. JOHN WAS BANISHED TO AN ISLAND, PATMOS, WHERE HE WAS IN CONSTANT CONVERSATION WITH THE FATHER AND HIS SON (JESUS). YOU WROTE "THE REVELATION OF JESUS CHRIST OUR LORD". SO, WHAT IS THE CONNECTION? YOU STILL ARE AN ISLAND DWELLER (HAWAII) AND YOUR CHOICE OF PLACE TO WORSHIP IS THE ISLAND OF SINGAPORE AND YOUR MINISTRY IS THE ISLANDS OF THE PACIFIC. IT'S ALL GOOD, BUT YOU ARE SO FAR AWAY FROM ME. LIKE IT OR NOT YOU ARE MINE OR PART OF ME. JESUS SPOKE TO BOTH YOU AND ME FROM THE CROSS. WOMEN, BEHOLD YOUR SON (YOU),

AND TO THE DISCIPLE, BEHOLD THY MOTHER (ME). I SO WANT TO SEE YOU, PLEASE. I LOVE YOU AND NEED TO SEE YOU, YOU ARE THE BABY I LOST MANY YEARS AGO WHEN GOD CHANGED YOUR ASSIGNMENT AND SENT GABRIEL TO GATHER YOU TO ANOTHER PLACE. PLEASE, I HAVE MUCH TO TELL YOU. TIME AS WE KNOW IT IS COMING TO A CLOSE, SO PLEASE DO YOUR BEST. I SO NEED TO SEE YOU. DO YOUR BEST, DO YOUR BEST. YOU ARE FROM EVERLASTING TO EVERLASTING, AS AM I, ALSO.

AMEN AND AMEN!

ARLENE: MARY, MEZZECHAH, MOTHER OF THOUSANDS

I HAVE BEEN IN AND OUT OF THIS WORLD MANY TIMES IN THE LAST THIRTEEN THOUSAND YEARS. GOD HAS GIVEN ME MUCH TO KNOW THESE LAST FEW YEARS. I HAVE BEEN WITH HIM LONGER THAN THAT, THO. I HAVE HAD MANY ASSIGNMENTS GIVEN BY MY GOD AND FINISHED ALL BUT THE ONE FROM THE LAST COUPLE OF YEARS. IT WOULD BE SO WONDERFUL IF I COULD GET MR FITTS (MY SON) TO COME SEE ME. JONATHAN CAHN WOULD BE A NICE VISITOR, TOO. ARTHUR BLESSITT, WOULD BE A GREAT HONOR TO SEE HIM. I WOULD LIKE TO FINISH ALL MY ASSIGNMENTS BEFORE I LEAVE OR IT MAY BE THAT I HAVE TO FINISH ALL BEFORE I LEAVE. WE ARE CLOSE TO THE DAY OF HIS (JESUS) RETURN, IT'S REAL CLOSE. YOU REALLY OUGHT TO ASK HIM FOR YOURSELF, HE WILL TELL YOU. IF HE TOLD ME HE WILL TELL YOU. I HAVE A STRONG DESIRE TO STAND AT THE FOOT OF THE CROSS WHERE MY SON WAS CRUCIFIED. I WANT THE BLOOD THAT DRIPS FROM HIS BROKEN BODY TO DRIP ON ME. THE SECRET PLACE OF THE MOST HIGH IS UNDER THE BLOOD OF JESUS. PSALM 91, (PSALM OF GOD'S PROTECTION). AMEN. MEZZECHAH, ANCHOR OF MY SOUL, NAME GIVEN TO ME FROM HEAVEN, MOTHER OF THOUSANDS. ONLY RECENTLY I FOUND GENESIS 24:60, REBEKAH, MOTHER OF THOUSANDS OF MILLIONS. HER NAME IS CLOSE TO MY HEAVENLY NAME. REBEKAH, COULD IT BE (REBBECHAH)? I HAVE MY WHITE STONE WITH MY HEAVENLY NAME ON IT. READ MY WRITE "MEZZECHAH IS BORN". I AM MEZZECHAH, ANCHOR OF MY SOUL, OF M(EL)CHIZEDEK, ALSO ANCHOR OF THE SOUL. NEW JERUSALEM COMING DOWN OUT

OF HEAVEN FROM GOD, MOTHER OF US ALL, CHILDREN OF PROMISE. I WANT EVERYTHING ALLOWABLE AND JUST. WHATEVER HE HAS PROVIDED, I WANT IT ALL. DEEP CALLETH UNTO DEEP, MY PROPHECY FROM LONG AGO, CREATED ON THE FOURTH DAY, I AM MY DADDY'S LITTLE STAR, BORN ON THE SEVENTH DAY. PRAYING ALWAYS IN THE HOLY GHOST. ALL GLORY UNTO MY GOD, ALL GLORY UNTO MY LORD JESUS CHRIST, ALL GLORY UNTO MY PRECIOUS HOLY GHOST. EVEN SO, COME, LORD JESUS. I AM FROM EVERLASTING TO EVERLASTING. YOU KNOW, ISRAEL (JEWS) ARE MY CHILDREN ALSO. MANY ARE GOING TO ISRAEL TO BE ENTERTAINED, ISRAEL NEEDS TO BE SAVED, BORN'AGAIN, NOT THE PLACE OF THE PARTY. IF YOU GO, GO AS A MISSIONARY.

SO, A LITTLE HISTORY LESSON FROM THE LORD OF THE HEAVENS. YOU MAY WANT TO READ MY WRITES IN REGARDS TO THE "DESECRATION OF HEAVEN", "BEFORE THE BEGINNING" AND "DEEP CALLETH UNTO DEEP". ALL VERY GOOD WRITES. DEEP CALLETH UNTO DEEP IS MY PERSONAL PROPHECY GIVEN LONG AGO. I WAS RAISED IN THE CHURCH BUT SOME YEARS WERE BETTER THAN OTHERS. I AM SORRY TO SAY THAT PERHAPS THE CHURCH HAS LOST SOME OUTSTANDING PEW WARMERS, AS THEY HAVE BEGUN TO LET THE WORD FALL BY THE WAYSIDE. THE WORD SAYS THERE WILL BE A GREAT FALLING AWAY AND THAT JUST MAY BE THE WAY NOW. WE ARE AT THE END OF THE AGE OF MAN.

EVERYONE SEEMS TO WANT TO PARTY, AS IN THE DAYS OF NOE. I SAY 'WORSHIP' NOW, PARTY LATER. THERE IS A BANQUET (WEDDING SUPPER) PLANNED FOR ALL WHO ENDURE TO THE END. PLEASE EVERYBODY SHOW'UP. GOD HAS HAD THE PLAN SINCE TIME BEGAN, PLEASE EVERYBODY SHOW'UP. GOD DOESN'T DISAPPOINT AND WE MUSTN'T EITHER. GIVE HIM SOME LOVE BACK. OUT OF LOVE FOR US, HE GAVE HIS SON, SO GIVE SOME LOVE BACK. I AM FROM EVERLASTING TO EVERLASTING. AMEN AND AMEN!

NAMES, WHO ARE THEY? JOSEPH

JOSEPH, HUSBAND OF MARY, PARENT OF THE LORD JESUS CHRIST

JOSEPH, WAS THE BETHROTHED OF MARY. WHEN HE FOUND OUT THAT SHE WAS PREGNANT, HE ASSUMED THAT SHE WAS NOT FAITHFUL TO HIM. EVEN'THO AN ANGEL WAS SENT TO TELL HIM IT WAS NOT THAT MARY WAS UNFAITHFUL BUT CHOSEN OF GOD TO BEAR THE SAVIOR OF THE WORLD. EVEN'THO, HE HAD TROUBLE WITH THE TRUTH, HE DID GO THRU WITH THE MARRIAGE. WHAT A GUY. HE DID BECOME THE EARTHLY FATHER OF JESUS, AND DID GO ON TO FATHER NATURAL CHILDREN WITH MARY. I DON'T KNOW HOW MANY, FOR SURE. I DO BELIEVE THAT, OR KNOW THAT HE LATER WAS HAUNTED BY THE THOUGHT THAT HE HAD BEEN DUPED BY HER, THAT MAYBE SHE WAS UNFAITHFUL. SOMETIMES WE CAN OVER THINK THINGS AND FALL INTO DOUBT. JESUS DIDN'T GO INTO THE MINISTRY UNTIL HE WAS PROBABLY THIRTY. SO, THAT PROBABLY FED INTO HIS (JOSEPH'S) DOUBT. ANYHOW, I SAID ALL THAT TO SAY, THAT IN THE LAST FEW MONTHS THERE IS A MAN AT CHURCH, WHO IN THE BEGINNING WAS STALKING ME. I WATCHED HIM AS HE PACED AROUND THE SANCTUARY, HE WAS FAMILIAR, SO I WATCHED HIM. HE IS VERY TALL AND VERY THIN. HE DID FINIALLY SIT DOWN A FEW ROWS FROM ME, SO I WENT OVER TO HIM, TO ASK SOME QUESTIONS. HE RAN, OK, HE GOT UP AND LEFT IN A HURRY. HMMM? SINCE THAT SUNDAY, I HAVE WATCHED FOR HIM. I GUESS I AM STALKING HIM NOW. HE IS AWARE THAT I AM THERE, AND AVOIDS ME. I BELIEVE (KNOW) HE IS JOSEPH, JESUS' EARTHLY FATHER. TWO WEEKS LATER, HE WAS WALKING NEAR ME AND I SAID HELLO TO HIM, HE LOOKED STRAIGHT AHEAD AND HURRIED AWAY. O YES, THEY ARE AMONG US. WE ARE FROM EVERLASTING TO EVERLASTING. I

AM MARY, HERE AS ARLENE (MARIE) WOOD, MEZZECHAH, MY HEAVENLY NAME, WITH MY WHITE STONE AND ALL. O YES, THEY ARE AMONG US. SOME ARE AFRAID OF ME, WHY, I DON'T KNOW? THESE ARE ASSIGNMENTS THAT WE ARE SENT TO FINISH. DO YOU HAVE AN ASSIGNMENT? THAT YOU NEED TO FINISH? GET BUSY. LET'S TALK ABOUT IT. THIS INFORMATION IS NOT PROVEN, YET. WE WILL SEE. I NEED TO TALK TO HIM IF I CAN GET HIM TO SIT STILL. HE IS FROM EVERLASTING TO EVERLASTING.

AMEN AND AMEN!

NAMES, WHO ARE THEY?
MARK, THE APOSTLE, JOHN MARK

HE IS THE WRITER OF THE GOSPEL OF MARK, THE SECOND OF THE FOUR GOSPELS IN THE NEW TESTAMENT. I WAS INVITED TO GO WITH A FRIEND FROM MY CHURCH TO A MEETING OF "AGLOW". THANK YOU SO MUCH, INEZ. IT'S A SMALL MEETING MAYBE 14 - 20 LADIES. VERY NICE. THERE WAS A MAN THERE WHO WAS FAMILIAR, THO NOT A RECENT ACQUAINTANCE. I COULDN'T HELP BUT STUDY HIS PSYCHE. HE DID A LITTLE SERMON FOR THE GATHERING, NICE. STILL, I STUDIED HIM NOT SO OBVIOUS THOUGH I JUST KNEW HIM, THOUGH I HAD NEVER SEEN HIM HERE, IN THIS AGE OR TIME (2017). THEN WE CAME TOGETHER FOR ANOTHER MEETING A MONTH LATER. AGLOW. HE ALSO WAS IN ATTENDANCE THAT DAY. SO HAPPENED THAT WE MET IN THE HALL AND I STOPPED TO TALK WITH HIM. I SAID TO HIM "YOUR NAME IS MARK". OR LATIN MARKUS. HE SAID TO CORRECT ME, NO I AM ANDREW. I DID STUDY HIM UP CLOSE. GOTTA TELL YOU, HE IS MARK, OR JOHN, WHOSE SURNAME IS MARK. THIS WAS BACK IN LATE OCTOBER. HE DIDN'T COME TO THE NOVEMBER OR DECEMBER MEETING. I HOPE HE WASN'T INTIMIDATED BY MY INSISTANCE, OR MAYBE HE WAS. PROBABLY DOESN'T WANT TO BE FOUND OUT, ALTHO MOST WOULDN'T EVEN CARE. WHEN YOU FEEL SOMETHING IN YOUR SPIRIT OR GIVEN A HEADS'UP, IT'S A GOOD IDEA TO PAY ATTENTION. I HOPE TO SEE HIM AGAIN. HE IS FROM EVERLASTING TO EVERLASTING.

AMEN AND AMEN!

NAMES, WHO ARE THEY? SAUL

SAUL, THE 1ST KING OF ISRAEL AND OF THE DAMASCUS ROAD. THEY ARE ONE ANDTHE SAME, THO IN DIFFERENT TIMES. YES, SAUL, OF THE OLD TESTAMENT, WHO WAS TO BE REPLACED BY DAVID AS KING OF ISRAEL. HE DIED TRAGICLY IN A BATTLE WITH THE PHILISTINES. ACTUALLY, HE COMMITTED SUICIDE WHEN HIS SON JONATHAN WAS KILLED IN THE SAME BATTLE. ALL OF HIS SONS WERE KILLED IN THE SAME BATTLE. KING SAUL HAD BEGUN TO FOLLOW AND BELIEVE IN IDOL WORSHIP AND MYSTICISM. IT MAY HAVE HAD SOMETHING TO DO WITH HIS DEMISE. HE LEFT OFF FOLLOWING THE GOD OF ISRAEL AND LISTENING TO THE PROPHET OF GOD, SAMUEL, WHO BTW ANOINTED SAUL TO BE THE FIRST KING OF ISRAEL. SAUL BECAME A GREAT DISAPPOINTMENT TO SAMUEL NEAR THE END OF HIS REIGN BECAUSE OF HIS DISOBEDIENCE TO THE GOD OF ISRAEL. KING SAUL STARTED OUT ON THE RIGHT SIDE OF HIS LIFE TO HONOR GOD, BUT AS HIS PRIDE INCREASED BECAUSE HE WAS FULL OF HIMSELF AS KING OF ISRAEL, HE MOVED INTO DISOBEDIENCE AND SIN. SAMUEL, GOD'S PROPHET, WATCH THIS HAPPENING AND WARNED SAUL OF THE CONSEQUENCES OF WITCHCRAFT, BUT HE TURNED A DEAF EAR. NOW, ON THE OTHER HAND, SAUL OF THE NEW TESTAMENT WAS A STUDENT OF THE HIERARCHY OF JUDAISIM. A TRUE JEW. SO, HE WAS DILIGENT IN HIS QUEST TO KILL CHRISTIANS, FOLLOWERS OF THE LORD JESUS CHRIST. GOD SAW/WAS GONNA USE THIS AMBITIOUS JEW TO SPREAD THE WORD OF HIS SON TO THE WORLD. GOOD CHOICE. SO, CAME THE CONVERSION OF SAUL TO PAUL ON THE DAMASCUS ROAD. I JUST LOVE TO READ THAT. ON HIS WAY TO IMPRISON OR KILL MORE CHRIST'FOLLOWERS GOD

INTERCEPTED HIM AND BLINDED HIM SO HE (GOD) COULD GET HIS ATTENTION. IT WORKED, THANK YOU FATHER. I LOVE PAUL. WE WOULDN'T HAVE WHAT WE HAVE IF NOT FOR PAUL. CERTAINLY, GOD COULD HAVE APPOINTED SOMEONE ELSE, BUT HE WANTED PAUL, ME TOO, BECAUSE OF HIS DETERMINED ATTITUDE, HE WAS A VALIANT SEEKER OF THE TRUTH. HE WROTE 3/4 OF THE NEW TESTAMENT. INDEED, A TRUE CHRIST FOLLOWER AND OF THE ORDER OF MELCHIZEDEK. HE IS FROM EVERLASTING TO EVERLASTING.

AMEN AND AMEN!

NAMES, WHO ARE THEY? NICODEMIS

RABBI NICODEMIS, WHO CAME TO JESUS AT NIGHT HE WAS A MEMBER OF THE SANHEDRIN, BUT WAS A BELIEVER IN JESUS. HE DIDN'T WANT IT TO BE KNOWN BY THE SANHEDRIN HIERARCHY. HE USUALLY WENT TO SEE JESUS AFTER DARK SO AS NOT TO BE SEEN. HE KNEW JESUS WAS TRULY THE SON OF GOD AND WANTED TO TALK WITH HIM AS A FRIEND. IF THE OTHERS OF THE SANHEDRIN KNEW WHAT HE WAS DOING THEY PROBABLY WOULD HAVE HAD HIM REMOVED FROM THE RANKS. AFTER THE CRUCIFIXION OF OUR LORD JESUS CHRIST, HE WAS THERE TO HELP WITH JESUS' BURIAL. WE DON'T HEAR MUCH ABOUT HIM AFTER THE CROSS OF CHRIST. THANK YOU, NICODEMUS.

TO WHOM IT MAY CONCERN:

WHOSOEVER, IS READING THIS WRITE,

PLEASE SEE TO IT THAT MR BOB FITTS GETS THIS WRITE. THANK YOU SO VERY, VERY MUCH.

I AM YOUR EVERLASTING TO EVERLASTING.

MUCH LOVE AND MANY BLESSINGS

ARLENE MARIE WOOD

MEZZECHAH, ANCHOR OF MY SOUL, OF THE ORDER OF MELCHIZEDEK

P/S: WHY IS IT SO HARD FOR PEOPLE TO BELIEVE? THE LAST DAYS PROMISED TO BE VERY INTERESTING AND NEARLY ARE WE NOW, TO THE END. LET GOD BREATHE ON YOU. YOU WILL BE SURPRISED AT WHAT YOU MAY HEAR AND SEE. THE LAST DAYS AS FAR AS THE SAVED ARE CONCERNED WILL BE WONDER-FUL. FULL OF WONDER! GOD WATCHES OVER HIS OWN, YOU, SO DARE TO BE IMPRESSED BY THE LORD. HE'S WANTS YOU TO TRUST HIM.

T RUS T
RU*SAVED?

TRUST BEGINS AND ENDS AT THE CROSS!

JESUS IS LORD, TO THE GLORY OF GOD THE FATHER. THESE LAST THREE + YEARS HAVE BEEN FOR MY PREPARATION AND LEARNING. MUCH HAS BEEN TOLD TO ME AND I AM SO GRATEFUL FOR ALL HE HAS SHARED WITH ME. THE TRUTH BE TOLD I WAS GIVEN SOME KNOWLEDGE WHEN I WAS VERY YOUNG, PRE'TEEN. MY NUMBER IS FOUR (4). GOD DOES INDEED DEAL (TEACH) IN NUMBERS. THE BIBLE IS FULL OF IMPORTANT NUMBERS. WE COULDN'T READ THE BIBLE EXCEPT FOR CHAPTER AND VERSE NUMBERS. NUMBERS ARE IMPORTANT AND NECESSARY FOR THE STUDY OF THE SCRIPTURES. WE ARE SO GRATEFUL FOR ALL THE BIBLE SCHOLARS, AND ALL WHO ARE LABORERS IN THE WORD, WHO LIVED AND ARE LIVING TO BRING THE SCRIPTURES TO US. I PRAY ALL WADE INTO THE BIBLE, GO DEEP TO FIND MEANING AND GET UNDERSTANDING. IN MY BIBLE, I ADDED VERSE TWENTY'TWO, GOD SPEAKING, REV 22:22, SAYS "I SAID ALL THIS TO SAY, I LOVE YOU". MY ANSWER IS "I LOVE YOU, TOO". THANK YOU! MY PRECIOUS JESUS AND MY PRECIOUS HEAVENLY FATHER, AND MY PRECIOUS HOLY GHOST (TEACHER). DO YOU SEE REVELATION 22:22 (22+22=44) IT'S ONLY IN MY BIBLE, I LIKE TO MAKE MY OWN NOTES, WITH REFERENCE TO MY NUMBER FOUR. THE FATHER, THE SON, THE HOLY GHOST AND ME. FOUR. I SAY THE BIBLE IS A LOVE LETTER, A LOVE STORY. PLEASE READ IT FROM COVER TO COVER. IT'S ALL ABOUT HIM TO YOU. YES, HE LOVES YOU. IS THAT SO BEAUTIFUL? IT IS. DO YOU KNOW THAT? HMMM.

YOU DO NOW. YOU DO NOW.

****

SOME SAY NOE*L

HE DIDN'T COME, HE WAS SENT.
HIS FATHER SAW A NEED, SO JESUS WENT.

THE FIRST NOEL

NO FAITH IN GOD, THE WORLD SO LOST.
NEED FOR SALVATION, UNAWARE OF THE COST.

THE ANGEL DID SAY

THE WEATHER SO COLD, BUT TRAVEL WAS A NEED.
THE RIDE WAS NO COMFORT, BUT THE DONKEY DID HEED.

WAS TO CERTAIN POOR SHEPHERDS

THE TIME WAS NOW, HERE, THE TERM WAS NOW THRU.
NO ROOM FOR THE THREE, THE BABY NOW DUE.

IN FIELDS AS THEY LAY

THE LAMB AND THE COW HAD TO MOVE OUT.
THE PRECIOUS YOUNG GIRL DID WEEP AND DID SHOUT.

IN FIELDS WHERE THEY

THE STRAW AND HAY IN A MANGER FOR A BED.
WERE FOR HIS COMFORT AND WARMTH, HIS MOTHER SAID.

LAY KEEPING THEIR SHEEP

THE SHELTER WAS NEITHER HEATED NOR WARM
MARY WRAPPED AND CUDDLED, TO KEEP BABY FROM HARM.

ON A COLD WINTER'S NIGHT

SHEPHERDS DID SEE A STAR, EVEN AN ANGEL DID SHARE.
LEFT THE FLOCKS TO GO SEE, AND TO SHOW THAT THEY CARE.

THAT WAS SO DEEP.

THE FEW SHEPHERDS WHO HAD SEEN THE GLORIOUS STAR.
MADE A JOURNEY WITH HAST, THOUGH IT WASN'T TOO FAR

NOEL, NOEL

THEY DID LEAVE THE SHEEP, DECIDED TO GO SEARCH.
THE PLACE OF HIS BIRTH GLOWED, AS A LIGHT FROM A CHURCH.

NOEL, NOEL

THE NIGHT WAS NEAR OVER, WHEN THEY CAME TO THE STABLE.
THOUGH NOT SURE OF THE REASON, THEY WERE GLAD TO BE
ABLE.

BORN IS THE KING

THE FAMILY OF JESUS WAS HAPPY TO WELCOME THE VISITORS.
THE SHEPHERDS SO BLESSED TO VISIT THEIR SAVIOR.

OF ISRAEL.

MOST CELEBRATE HIS BIRTH EVERY YEAR.
MY SAVIOR SO WELCOME, HE BRINGS ME A TEAR.

O' COME LET US ADORE HIM
AMEN I LOVE YOU, MY PRECIOUS JESUS. AMEN

******* ******* *******

WHEN I WAS ABOUT TWELVE YEARS OLD, HE STOOD ME
STILL TO TELL ME I AM THE MOTHER OF THE LORD JESUS
CHRIST. SOME ALREADY KNOW. I AM SO PLEASED TO HAVE
BEEN HIS "CHOSEN". JESUS IS THE JOY OF HEAVEN.
HE CERTAINLY IS THE JOY OF MY EXISTENCE. GOD KNOWS. I
AM MY DADDY'S LITTLE STAR.

AMEN. JUST WORSHIP. ALL GLORY TO HIS NAME. JUST
WORSHIP. AMEN. NOEL, NOEL, NOEL, NOEL. BORN IS THE KING
OF ISRAEL. MY KING, JESUS.

CHANGE YOUR MIND

YES, CHANGE YOUR MIND. WHICH WAY ARE YOU GOING? I SO HOPE YOU ARE HEAVEN BOUND. SOMETIMES WE, OR SOME OF US, CAN'T SEE THE END FROM WHERE WE STARTED YESTERDAY. DID YOU SLEEP LAST NIGHT? MAYBE, I CAN'T REMEMBER. LIFE GETS TOUGH SOMETIMES. MAYBE I WILL HAVE TO START OVER, OR MAYBE NOT. WE CAN'T ALL HAVE THE TIGER BY THE TAIL. THE BEST THING TO DO IS FOLLOW JESUS, HE WILL KEEP THE WAY CLEAR. HE IS SO DEPENDABLE AND HE CARES SO MUCH FOR ME. INVITE HIM INTO YOUR LIFE. HE KNOWS ALL THE INS AND OUTS OF LIFE AND HE DOES IT WITH GREAT CARE AND WISDOM. I KNOW, HOW DO YOU THINK I KNOW? BEEN THERE, DONE THAT. HE KNOWS ME AND I KNOW AND NEED HIM. THE BEST TEACHER IN THE WHOLE WORLD. HE KNOWS EVERYTHING. HE DID CLAIM ME EIGHTEEN THOUSAND YEARS AGO. I AM HIS AND HE, MINE. MY WONDERFUL HEAVENLY FATHER REACHED INTO THE FARTHEST EDGE OF THE UNIVERSE AND TOOK A LITTLE PIECE OF DIRT AND DEPOSITED IT IN THE BALCONY OF HEAVEN. THE TRUE "OUTER LIMITS" OF SPACE. SOMETIME AFTER THAT HE DID DECIDE TO CREATE LITTLE ME. I WAS CREATED ON THE FOURTH DAY AND BORN ON THE SEVENTH DAY. MANY YEARS AGO, I WAS REALLY BORN ON THE SEVENTH DAY. YOU HAVE HEARD THAT BEFORE OR MOST PROBABLY READ THAT BEFORE. YES! I DO REPEAT SOME OF THE STORY OF MY BEGINNING. AS A MATTER OF FACT, I HAVE BEEN IN AND OUT OF THIS WORLD MANY TIMES. MY WONDERFUL FATHER HAS TESTED ME MANY TIMES FOR THE ASSIGNMENT TO BE THE SINGLE PARENT OF THE LORD JESUS CHRIST. I AM HAPPY TO SAY I PASSED WITH FLYING COLORS. WHAT A PLEASURE TO BE

USED OF THE GOD OF HEAVEN TO NURTURE HIS BELOVED SON, THE LORD JESUS CHRIST. JOSEPH WAS A GOOOD HELPER. SOME HAVE A HARD TIME WRAPPING THEIR HEAD AROUND THIS PARTICULAR PART OF THE BIRTH OF JESUS. YOU MUST HAVE A LOVE FOR THE GOD OF HEAVEN AND HIS PRECIOUS SON. THEY BOTH JUST FILL ME WITH LOVE AND DELIGHT. I CAN'T IMAGINE A BETTER ASSIGNMENT, WHAT A JOY. DO YOU LOVE THIS REMEMBRANCE AS I DO. MY HEART IS SO BLESSED BY THE MEMORY OF MANY YEARS GONE BY. DO YOU KNOW THIS IS A LOVE STORY, IT IS. SOME SAY THE BIBLE IS A LOVE LETTER WRITTEN BY THE GOD OF HEAVEN TO HIS CREATED. IT IS. THE BIBLE IS THE GREATEST BOOK EVER WRITTEN, I SAY SO. I HAVE MORE THAN A FEW AND I LOVE EVERY ONE OF THEM. CAN'T WAIT TO BE WITH MY HEAVENLY FATHER AND MY LORD JESUS CHRIST, AND THE BLESSED HOLY GHOST. WHAT A DAY OF REJOICING THAT WILL BE. YES, WE DO HAVE THE MIND OF CHRIST, SINCE WE ARE BORN AGAIN, FILLED WITH THE HOLY GHOST AND BAPTIZED IN HOLY GHOST WITH EVIDENCE OF SPEAKING WITH OTHER TONGUES. I HAVE THE GIFT OF AND FROM HEAVEN. THE LORD JESUS CHRIST. HE IS THE FIRST COMFORTER SENT FROM THE HEAVENS ABOVE. WHEN HE WAS CRUCIFIDED AND WAS FINISHED, HE DID NOT LEAVE THIS EARTH UNTIL HE HAD SENT AND INSTALLED THE BLESSED HOLY GHOST. THERE IS NOT A DAY GOES BY THAT THE HOLY GHOST IS NOT MY HELPER. HOW DO SOME MAKE IT WITHOUT HIM? HMMM MAYBE THEY WON'T? I DO ENCOURAGE YOU TO BE FILLED WITH HOLY GHOST, PRAY IN THE SPIRIT. WORDS SENT TO THE HIGHEST HEAVENS, HEARD AND ANSWERED FROM THE ONE WHO KNOWS THE CIRCUMSTANCES. HE KNOWS OUR EVERY TROUBLE AND CAN CHANGE THINGS TO OUR ADVANTAGE. JUST PUT ALL TRUST IN HIM, HE KNOWS THE WAY. FILL YOUR LIFE WITH THE THOUGHTS AND WORDS FROM HEAVEN. PRAY, FOLLOW HIS INSTRUCTIONS, HE KNOWS THE ANSWERS TO ALL THINGS. FOLLOW HIM. HE CAN CHANGE

YOUR MIND AS YOU BEGIN TO WALK IN HIS WISDOM. I HAD WRITTEN A COUPLE WRITES CONCERNING GOD'S PATTERNS, HE HAS PATTERNS FOR EVERY WORKS UNDER THE SUN (SON). YES, HIS SON KNOWS THE WAY OF HIS FATHER AND HE WILL BE THE ONE TO DEPEND ON FOR THE FIX OF THE PROBLEM. JUST REMEMBER TO THANK HIM FOR THE LEADERSHIP OF HIS FATHER, THEY ARE INSEPARABLE. WORSHIP HIM. THAT'S WHAT YOUR JOB IS. IF YOU EVER WONDERED WHAT YOU ARE HERE FOR, IT'S FOR WORSHIP. JUST WORSHIP. LOVE HIM FOREVER. YOU KNOW TIME MOVES REALLY FAST. TOO SOON WE WILL HEAR THAT TRUMPET, SO BE READY. YOU WON'T BE AMUSED AT HOW FAST TOMORROW COMES. HE WILL BE HERE SO BE PACKED UP AND PUT ON YOUR RACING SLIPPERS, WE ARE GOING UP. JUST WORSHIP...

NOT GOD FIRST, GOD ONLY. HE WILL BE ONLY OR HE WON'T BE ANY.

AGREE AND AGLOW

I HAVE WRITTEN MY CHRISTMAS CARD FOR THIS YEAR.
TO CELEBRATE MY SAVIOR ON THE MIDNIGHT CLEAR.

SO NOW, LET'S DO THE WRITE FOR NEXT WEEK.
I SO LOOK FORWARD TO SEE THE GIRLS AT AGLOW, SUCH A TREAT.

THIS PLAGUE HAS HINDERED OUR COMING TOGETHER.
IT DOESN'T HAVE ANYTHING TO DO WITH THE WEATHER.

I AM SO BLESSED TO HAVE MY SISTER TO DRIVE ME.
SHE IS DEPENDABLE AND WE BOTH AGREE.

THE DRIVE ISN'T VERY FAR BUT WE WISH IT TO BE CLOSER.
WE BOTH LOVE THE CONVERSATION, AND WE KEEP IT
KOSHER.

IT'S BEEN SO GOOD FOR US TO CONVERSE DURING THE TRIP.
SOMETIMES WE MESS WITH EACH OTHER, SHE CALLS ME A DRIP.

WELL YOU KNOW, I DO HAVE A COMEBACK AND WE LAUGH.
WE BRING OUR LORD INTO THE MIX, SHE AND ME, AND HE
THE OTHER HALF.

HE IS SO MUCH FUN, HE MAKES THE MILES A SHORT RUN.
WE GET SO INVOLVED WITH HIM, TOO SOON THE TRIP DONE.

WHEN WE ARRIVE AND ALL ARE VISITING AND READY TO EAT.
WE ARE SO PLEASED TO LAUGH, HUG AND GREET.

THE SPREAD IS MOSTLY HEALTHY AND DELICIOUS.
MOST OF US GET TO LEAVE AND NOT DO THE DISHES.

THE TIME GOES BY MUCH TOO FAST BUT IT IS FRUITFUL.
OUR WORSHIP IS FROM ABOVE, FULL OF PRAISE, AND MIRTHFUL.

USUALLY A GUEST SPEAKER WITH A GREAT MESSAGE.
KEEPS US FASCINATED AND O SO BLESSAGED.

THO THIS WRITE SEEMS KINDA STRANGE, IT'S A BLESSING.
YOU HAVE TO BE THERE, IT IS SO WARM AND REFRESHING.

OUR PRECIOUS MAREE, OUR GUIDE AND LEADER.
KEEPS THE GIRLS IN GOOD ORDER, YOU REALLY SHOULD
MEET HER.

WHEN WE PRAY THE PRAYER OF PARTING AND GOING OUR WAY.
WE DO HAVE A PLAN FOR A LATER DAY.

EACH ONE BLESSED BY THE LOVE OF OUR FATHER IN HEAVEN.
WE WILL SEE EACH OTHER NEXT MONTH OR MAYBE IN HEAVEN.
AMEN AND AMEN.

****

NOT GOD FIRST, GOD ONLY. HE WILL BE ONLY OR HE WON'T
BE ANY. HE SHARES HIS THRONE WITH NONE.
BE AGED IN HIS GRACE, STEEPED IN HIS WORD, POURED OUT
IN HIS GLORY.

A LETTER FROM HOME (HEAVEN)

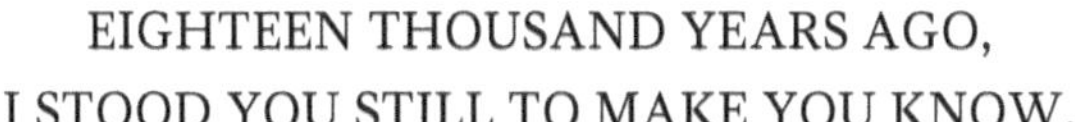

EIGHTEEN THOUSAND YEARS AGO,
I STOOD YOU STILL TO MAKE YOU KNOW.

YOU WERE CHOSEN FOR MY SAKE.
THE GLORY WAS MINE FOR YOU TO TAKE.

MY GLORY COMES FROM FAR ABOVE.
RAINING DOWN TO SHOW MY LOVE.

I HELD A BASKET TO RETRIEVE,
LIGHT AND TRUTH SENT, THAT YOU MAY RECEIVE.

MORE AND MORE DID DESCEND.
I AM RIGHT, THERE IS NO END.

I AM THE LORD YOUR GOD, EVER GRACEFUL.
HERE FOREVER AND ALWAYS FAITHFUL.

TILL TIME AND SPACE HAVE RUN OUT,
I AM HERE FOR YOU, REFUSE TO DOUBT.

WHEN THE TRUMPET SOUNDS AND CLOUDS DO PART,
I WILL SEE YOU, WHO DWELLS WITHIN MY HEART.

SO TILL I WRITE THE VERY LAST PAGE.
EVEN TIL THE END OF THE AGE.

YOU REMAIN DEEP IN MY ENDLESS WATCH AND PATIENCE.
OVER AND OVER WITH LOVELY CADENCE.

THERE IS NONE TO TELL YOU TO WORRY,
TO SHOUT AND YELL FOR YOU TO HURRY.

ALL IS WELL, ALL IS WELL
I GIVE YOU FLOWERS, ENJOY THE SMELL.

SO GOOD TO GIVE YOU GREETING,
SO LOOKING FORWARD TO OUR MEETING.
MUCH LOVE AND MANY BLESSINGS
YOUR HEAVENLY FATHER (DADDY)

****

NOT GOD FIRST, GOD ONLY. HE WILL BE ONLY OR HE WON'T
BE ANY. EVEN SO, COME LORD JESUS. GIVE HIM ALL THE
GLORY.
HE IS ALWAYS AND AMEN, WITHOUT PERMISSION, WITHOUT
END. HE IS THE LIGHT OF MY LIFE, LORD OF MY LIFE, LOVE OF
MY LIFE.
AMEN AND AMEN 1-7-22

ANY DAY NOW

ANY DAY NOW WE WILL HEAR THE TRUMPET SOUND.
ANY DAY NOW WE WILL SURELY BE HEAVEN BOUND.

I HAVE HEARD THAT MOST OF MY LIFE.
WE WILL BE TAKEN FROM THE EARTH, THE END OF STRIFE.

WE SEE THE HEAVENS OPEN WIDE TO LET US COME INSIDE.
LEAVE BEHIND THE CHAOS AND ALL THAT EMPTY PRIDE.

HOW WILL IT BE WHEN THERE ARE NO TEARS TO SHED?
SO HAPPY TO BE AT HOME, NOTHING MORE TO DREAD.

THE SAVIOR STANDING AT THE GATE, ARMS OPEN.
THE BANQUET TABLES AND CHAIRS ALL SET, FOR WE, THE
CHOSEN.

AS HE DIRECTS US TO OUR PLACE PROMISED.
WE EMBRACE OUR FRIEND, REMEMBER THOMAS?

OUR JESUS WILL LIFT THE CUP, THE BEST WINE EVER.
HE WILL SAY A POEM WELCOMING US, FOREVER.

WHEN ALL ARE IN THEIR ASSIGNED PLACE.
HE WILL BLESS US WITH A PRAYER OF GRACE.

THE FATHER'S VOICE WE HEAR FROM WHERE, WE DON'T
KNOW.
HE MUST BE IN THE KITCHEN LIGHTING CANDLES, TO SOFTLY
GLOW.

WE HAVE SO LOOKED FORWARD TO THIS TIME AND NOW.
WE ARE ALL GATHERED, FATHER, SON, AND HOLY GHOST.
WE BOW.

WE ARE SO BLESSED AND THRILLED TO BE AT REST. LOOKING
FORWARD TO HONOR AND GREET EACH GUEST.
WE CAN COME TO OUR SAVIOR ANY DAY WE PLEASE.
AT LAST, WE CAN REST, WE ARE SO BLESSED AND AT EASE.

**** **** ****

WE ARE SO DEEPLY THANKFUL HE KEPT HIS PROMISE AND
NOW WE ARE HOME AT LAST. WE ARE HOME. ANY DAY NOW.
HALLELUJAH! BLESS HIS HOLY NAME. HALLELUJAH!

THE BIRTH OF MY SAVIOR

THEY CAME A LONG WAYS

THEY DIDN'T WANT TO TRAVEL THOSE DAYS

NOW THE BIRTH OF JESUS CHRIST WAS ON THIS WISE

IN A STABLE

THIS IS NOT A FABLE

THE FIRST NOEL

A NEWBORN IS ASLEEP

COME SEE, JUST TAKE A PEEK

THE ANGEL DID SAY

BORN LAST NIGHT AFTER DARK

I THINK HE MADE THE WATCH DOG BARK

WAS TO CERTAIN POOR SHEPHERDS

THERE WAS A CERTAIN STAR
SHEPHERDS CAME FROM NEAR AND FAR
IN FIELDS AS THEY LAY

THREE OR FOUR CAME TO ADORE
WELL, MAYBE THERE WERE MORE
IN FIELDS WHERE THEY

THE MOTHER WORRIED OF THE COLD
BABY LESS THAN A DAY OLD.

LAY KEEPING THEIR SHEEP

SHE HELD HIM CAREFUL TO HER HEART
TO WARM HIM, GIVE HIM A GOOD START.

ON A COLD WINTERS NIGHT

THE COW AND SHEEP WERE QUIET
NO NOISE, DON'T TRY IT.

THAT WAS SO DEEP

DADDY WAS KIND OF FEARFUL
DIDN'T WANT MOTHER TO BE TEARFUL

NOEL NOEL

HIS BED WAS A MANGER
TO KEEP BABY FROM DANGER.

NOEL NOEL

SHEPHERDS WATCHED WITHOUT A WORD
SO AS TO NOT FRIGHTEN OR DISTURB

BORN IS THE KING OF ISREAL

SOME SAY NOE*L

I AM HERE TO WITNESS AND TO TELL.
MY KING JESUS

AMEN

I AM WATCHING THE NEWS. THE "CHOSEN" IS BEING SHOWN TO OVER SEAS VENUES AND I AM SO GLAD THAT THEY ARE DOING THIS. I DID WATCH THE "CHOSEN" ON TV EARLY THIS YEAR. I THOUGHT IT WAS WONDERFUL. HOWEVER, I WROTE THAT, IN REGARDS TO MYSELF. I AM THE "CHOSEN". HE CHOSE ME EIGHTEEN THOUSAND YEARS AGO. I GAVE BIRTH TO JESUS TWO THOUSAND YEARS AGO. I THINK I WOULD WANT TO TALK TO WHOSOEVER IS IN CHARGE OF THIS PRODUCTION??? WHEN DID YOU WRITE THIS???

IT'S MY ASSIGNMENT

IT'S MY ASSIGNMENT. DO YOU HEAR? YOU DON'T KNOW WHAT HE GAVE ME TO KNOW WHEN ON THAT DAY, HE STOOD ME STILL IN THE DINING ROOM OF OUR HOME IN MINNESOTA. 207 4TH STREET, THE ADDRESS DEFINED, SECOND BORN OF SEVEN, ON 4TH STREET (MY NUMBER IS 4). 2021 MINUS 80 = 1941 + 12 = 1953. I WAS ORDAINED, TOLD TO BE MARY, MOTHER OF MY LORD JESUS CHRIST. HE STOOD ME STILL. I CAN'T TELL YOUR STORY, ONLY MY OWN. APPOINTED, SELECTED AS ORDAINED BY GOD TO BE. GOD IS THE AUTHOR OF EVERY DAY, SUNRISE TO SUNSET. HE'S ON THE THRONE. WHAT HE SAYS, GOES. DO NOT GO AGAINST GOD. IT COULD BE FATAL. I AM HERE FOR HIM. YOU REALLY HAVE NO SAY IN HIS WORK. FOLLOW INSTRUCTIONS. JUST WORSHIP - PRAISE HIS HOLY NAME. HE REALLY IS LARGE AND IN CHARGE. DON'T GET OUT ALL YOUR SAINTHOOD STUFF. YOU HAVE NOT THE AUTHORITY TO SPEAK. WHAT HE SAYS, GOES. 1 COR. 14:33, HEB 12:2, HEB 5:9-10. WHEN WE WERE IN THE DINING ROOM OF OUR HOME, HE (MY G0D) GAVE ME TO KNOW THE ASSIGNMENT I WAS TO FULFILL AND I WAS ABLE TO DO JUST THAT. WHEN HE GIVES ORDERS THE BEST THING TO DO IS FOLLOW. I DON'T THINK I REALLY UNDERSTOOD WHAT HE SAID BUT I DID JUST KEEP IT TO MYSELF TILL I WAS OF THE AGE OF KNOWING WHAT WAS SAID. PLEASE DON'T GO OFF TO SAY THOSE CRAZY CATHOLICS. I WAS BORN A BAPTIST AND THAT WAS THE WAY I WAS TO RECEIVE MY ASSIGNMENT. I HAVE EVERY INTENTION TO FINISH WHAT I WAS TOLD TO DO TO THE BEST OF MY ABILITY. I DO KNOW THAT THERE ARE OTHERS WHO WERE GIVEN ASSIGNMENTS TO FOLLOW AND THEY ARE AFTER IT AS WE SPEAK, AND I WILL DO THE SAME. I SO WANT TO BE

OBEDIENT TO HIS INSTRUCTIONS. IT WOULD BE AN ERROR TO SLACK OFF OF WHAT HE SAID. I WANT TO DO AS HE SAYS. I KNOW, SOME SAY WHO DO YOU THINK YOU ARE? I DON'T THINK MORE THAN I WAS TOLD, AND I WILL DO AS TOLD. GOD REALLY WANTS OBEDIENCE. ME TOO. YOU HAVE HEARD THAT HIS WISDOM IS WHAT MATTERS. JUST LISTEN AND DO. I DO SO LOVE MY DEAR FATHER AND AM SO FULL OF EXPECTION TO SEE HOW HE PLAYS IT OUT. JUST FOLLOW. WHEN THE FULLNESS OF TIME CAME TO MY UNDERSTANDING, I WAS SO READY TO DO AS I WAS TOLD. HE HAS ALSO GIVEN ME MORE DETAILS OF MY ASSIGNMENT. I LOOK FORWARD TO THE WHOLE FINISHED WORK. I HAVE SEEN SOME WHO WERE GIVEN ASSIGNMENTS AND I WANT TO TALK TO THEM. WHEN I GET THE OPPORTUNITY, IT WILL FILL SOME OF THE EMPTY SPACES. JONATHAN CAHN IS GABRIEL, SIMON THE CYRENIAN IS ARTHUR BLESSITT, WHO CARRIES THE CROSS ALL OVER THE WORLD AND HAS FOR MANY YEARS. JOHN THE BELOVED IS BOB FITTS, WHO BY THE WAY LIVES ON THE ISLAND OF HAWAII. DO YOU REMEMBER HE WAS SENT TO THE ISLAND OF PATMOS, IT WAS A SENTENCE OF PUNISHMENT. THEN THERE IS JOHN-MARK, WHO WROTE THE GOSPEL OF MARK, SECOND BOOK IN THE NEW TESTAMENT. THEN JOSEPH, JESUS' EARTHLY FATHER CAME TO MY CHURCH FOR A FEW MONTHS. I AM SO HONORED TO DO AS HE WANTS. I HAVE WRITTEN OF THIS A FEW TIMES AND PROBABLY WILL CONTINUE. HE WILL REWARD ALL WHO DO AS TOLD. ISN'T HE FASCINATING? I SO LOVE HIM AND SO WANT TO PLEASE HIM. HE'S BEEN SO GOOD TO ME. PRAISE HIS HOLY NAME.

GOD DID NOT CHOOSE HIS SON, HIS CHRIST.

GOD DID NOT CHOOSE HIS BELOVED SON AS OUR SAVIOR. JESUS IS THE "ONLY" BEGOTTEN OF THE FATHER. IN ORDER TO CHOOSE YOU MUST HAVE MORE THAN ONE CHOICE. JESUS IS THE ONLY, THE MIDDLE MEMBER OF THE TRINITY. THERE IS A VERY POPULAR PRODUCTION ON THE MOVIE ROLES NOW. THE TITLE IS "THE CHOSEN". I DID WATCH THE FIRST PRODUCTION, EARLY IN 2021. THE CHARACTERS ARE REPRESENTED VERY WELL. HOWEVER, I DON'T KNOW WHO THE CHOSEN ARE/IS. IF IT'S JESUS, HE IS NOT THE CHOSEN, HE WAS NOT CHOSEN AS IF THERE ARE MORE THAN ONE. HE IS THE ONE AND ONLY BEGOTTEN OF THE FATHER, SO THE FATHER HAS NO CHOICE. IT'S LIKE THERE NEEDS TO BE AN EXPLANATION OF THE TITLE OF THE PRODUCTION. WHO IS THE CHOSEN?? IT MAY BE THAT IT IS WRITTEN BY THE ONE WHO IS DALLAS JENKINS. I WOULD LIKE TO TALK TO HIM, PLEASE. IT MAYBE THAT HE IS REFERENCING SOME OTHER CHARACTER, NOT JESUS. SO AS WE GO ON THERE MUST BE SOME CLARITY OF THIS MOVIE. WE CERTAINLY DON'T WANT TO MISREPRESENT OUR JESUS. HE IS THE ONE AND ONLY, BEGOTTEN OF THE FATHER. HE IS IRREPLACEABLE. IF IT'S AN ERROR WE MUST FIX IT. WE DON'T WANT THE PUBLIC TO CALL HERESY OR CRAZY CHRISTIANS. WE HAVE TO BE CAREFUL NOT TO MESS WITH THE ONES WHO LIVE TO HOLLER CHRISTIAN ERROR. THERE ARE SOME WHO LIVE TO FIND ERROR IN REGARD TO OUR CHRISTIANITY WHENEVER POSSIBLE. THEY ARE SO CARING THAT WE GET EVERYTHING RIGHT. WE SO APPRECIATE THEIR LOVING KINDNESS. YES, WE DO. THE TRINITY HAS ALWAYS BEEN AND

WILL ALWAYS BE. THE FATHER, THE SON AND THE HOLY GHOST. IT HAS NO BEGINNING AND NO ENDING. IT IS ETERNAL, NEVER BEGINNING, NEVER ENDING. THAT IS KIND OF SOMETHING WE HAVE TROUBLE WRAPPING OUR GRAY-MATTER (BRAIN) AROUND. WE ARE TEMPORAL SO WE HAVE MANY DOUBTS OF THIS KIND OF THING. SAME WITH INFINITY, NEVER ENDING, NO BEGINNING AND NO ENDING. ARE YOU GETTING A MIGRAINE? ME TOO. HE, OUR GOD IS AWESOME. WHEN WE ARE LONG-GONE, HE WILL STILL BE GOING STRONG. ISN'T THAT FASCINATING, ISN'T HE FASCINATING. WE MOST CERTAINLY WANT TO GET EVERYTHING CORRECT. NOTHING MISSING, NOTHING WRONG. I SO LOVE MY GOD, MY FATHER AND MY WONDERFUL JESUS AND MY BLESSED HOLY GHOST, SO I WANT EVERYTHING OUT STANDINGLY PROPER, AS HE IS OUTSTANDING AND PERFECT. THERE ARE SOME WHO MAKE THEIR DAY BY EDITING EVERY WORD WRITTEN, ESPECIALLY CHRISTIAN STUFF. I MAY MAKE SOME ERRORS BUT GOD IS ALWAYS CORRECT AND PERFECT, SO BE CAREFUL NOT TO TANGLE WITH THE PERFECT ONE. MAYBE MR JENKINS HAS AN ANSWER TO THIS, HOPEFULLY. I AM SURE HE WANTS EVERYTHING IN GOOD ORDER, AS I DO TOO. JESUS THE ONLY BEGOTTEN OF THE FATHER, GOD'S ONLY BELOVED SON. THE MOST IMPORTANT WORD THERE IS 'ONLY'. I AM THE MOTHER OF THE ONLY BEGOTTEN OF GOD, CHOSEN EIGHTEEN THOUSAND YEARS AGO TO BE THE FOURTH MEMBER OF THE TRINITY. IS THAT HARD FOR YOU TO GET HOLD OF? IT'S OKAY, WE CAN TALK ABOUT IT IF YOU WANT TO, SO DON'T BE TROUBLED BY IT. I WRITE WHAT I KNOW. THE SON, OUR SAVIOR. THAT'S A GOD IDEA, HE'S NEVER WRONG. DO YOU WANT TO TALK ABOUT THAT TOO? IT'S WORTH IT. IF GOD HAD AN IDEA, HIS IDEA WOULD BE GOD. THAT'S JUST THE WAY IT IS, HIS LOVE. DO YOU KNOW THE MEANING OF CHOSE, CHOOSE, CHOSEN, ONLY BEGOTTEN? ONLY ONE. LET'S TALK ABOUT THIS.

ARLENE M. WOOD, MEZZECHAH (STAR), MY CREATED NAME.
I AM MY DADDY'S LITTLE STAR
NOT GOD FIRST, GOD ONLY. HE WILL BE ONLY OR HE WON'T
BE ANY.

A LETTER FROM HOME (HEAVEN)

EIGHTEEN THOUSAND YEARS AGO,
I STOOD YOU STILL TO MAKE YOU KNOW.

YOU WERE CHOSEN FOR MY SAKE.
THE GLORY WAS MINE FOR YOU TO TAKE.

MY GLORY COMES FROM FAR ABOVE.
RAINING DOWN TO SHOW MY LOVE.

I HELD A BASKET TO RETRIEVE,
LIGHT AND TRUTH SENT, THAT YOU MAY RECEIVE.

MORE AND MORE DID DESCEND.
I AM RIGHT, THERE IS NO END.

I AM THE LORD YOUR GOD, EVER GRACEFUL.
HERE FOREVER AND ALWAYS FAITHFUL.

TILL TIME AND SPACE HAVE RUN OUT,
I AM HERE FOR YOU, REFUSE TO DOUBT.

WHEN THE TRUMPET SOUNDS AND CLOUDS DO PART,
I WILL SEE YOU, WHO DWELLS WITHIN MY HEART.

SO TILL I WRITE THE VERY LAST PAGE.
EVEN TIL THE END OF THE AGE.

YOU REMAIN DEEP IN MY ENDLESS WATCH AND PATIENCE.
OVER AND OVER WITH LOVELY CADENCE.

THERE IS NONE TO TELL YOU TO WORRY,
TO SHOUT AND YELL FOR YOU TO HURRY.

ALL IS WELL, ALL IS WELL
I GIVE YOU FLOWERS, ENJOY THE SMELL.

SO GOOD TO GIVE YOU GREETING,
SO LOOKING FORWARD TO OUR MEETING.
MUCH LOVE AND MANY BLESSINGS
YOUR HEAVENLY FATHER (DADDY)

****

NOT GOD FIRST, GOD ONLY. HE WILL BE ONLY OR HE WON'T
BE ANY.
EVEN SO, COME LORD JESUS. GIVE HIM ALL THE GLORY.
HE IS ALWAYS AND AMEN, WITHOUT PERMISSION, WITHOUT
END.
HE IS THE LIGHT OF MY LIFE, LORD OF MY LIFE, LOVE OF MY
LIFE.
AMEN AND AMEN
1-7-22

THE OBEDIENCE OF THE SEED

A MAN, A DOG, A TREE, A FRUIT, A VEGETABLE, A WEED.
EACH ONE CONTAINS AN EVERLASTING SEED.

ALL CREATED BY HIS MIGHTY HAND.
PUT IN GOOD GROUND WILL OBEY FOREVER HIS HOLY
COMMAND.

THAT SEED IS OBEDIENT TO "AND GOD SAID."
JUST TO FOLLOW INSTRUCTIONS OF BEING GOD LED.

THE EARTH, TOO, SO WILLING TO RECEIVE.
READY TO NOURISH AND EMBRACE THE GIFT OF CONCEIVE.

THE MIRACLE BEGINS IN THE WOMB OF THE EARTH.
THE GROUND WILL NURTURE AND PROTECT THE NEW BIRTH.

IT DOESN'T MATTER WHAT THE SEED MAY BE.
THERE'S A PROMISE IN IT THAT WE CAN'T SEE.
PSALM 139:15-16

GOD HIDES HIS! MYSTERIOUS" SOMETIMES SO DEEP.
WE ARE UNAWARE OF ALL HIS SECRETS HE WANTS TO KEEP.

JUST WAIT, HE WILL SHOW OUT AND SURELY SURPRISE.
A MAGNIFICENT TREE OR A RAMBLING VINE TO SURMISE.

GOD HIMSELF PLANTED A SEED TWO THOUSAND YEARS AGO.
HOWEVER, HE TOLD BY TYPE AND SHADOW SO WE WOULD
ALL KNOW.

AT THE APPOINTED TIME THE PROMISED SAVIOR WAS BORN.
TO GO TO A CROSS, ALL FOLLOWERS WOULD MOURN.

YES, HE WAS OBEDIENT, GOD'S BLESSED SEED. GOD HIMSELF
SAW OUR DESPERATE NEED.

HIS PRECIOUS, LONG AWAITED, PROPHESIED HOLY ONE. ROSE
UP - THE TRUE VINE - HEAVEN'S ETERNAL GLORIOUS SON.
MARK 4:3-9
THE OBEDIENT SEED, BY THE HOLY GHOST
HE IS REAL, SUPERNATURALLY, REAL
O THE MIGHTY LOVE AND GRACE OF GOD BY THE HOLY
GHOST

HIS BLOOD IS FOREVER, ETERNAL

WHOSO EATETH MY FLESH AND DRINKETH MY BLOOD HATH ETERNAL LIFE; AND I WILL RAISE HIM UP AT THE LAST DAY. JOHN 6:54

THE BLOOD OF THE LORD JESUS CHRIST WAS SHED FOR THE WHOLE OF HUMANITY. WHEN HE WENT TO THAT CROSS, I WAS THERE. STANDING AT THE FOOT OF THE CROSS, AND KNOWING THAT IT WAS THE WAY THE FATHER WANTED IT DONE. GOD HAD SENT HIS BLESSED SON TO REDEEM YOU AND ME AND THE WHOLE WORLD. WHETHER YOU APPRECIATE HIM OR NOT, HE STILL DIED FOR YOU. GIVE THAT SOME THOUGHT. HIS DEATH DID SET YOU FREE. I AM SO BLESSED TO BE IN THE WORLD, REDEEMED BY THE LOVE OF GOD. I DO SO LOVE MY JESUS, AS I AM HIS MOTHER, WHO BORE HIM AND WHO NEEDED A SAVIOR, TOO. I NEEDED THE SAME THING THE WHOLE WORLD NEEDED. BEING HIS MOTHER DID NOT MAKE ME EXEMPT. I WAS AS THE REST OF THE POPULATION. I AM STILL IN NEED OF THE SAVIOR OF THE WHOLE WORLD. AS A MATTER OF FACT, WE ARE ALL STANDING GUILTY OF SIN. YOU CAN REPENT TILL THE COWS COME HOME, YOU STILL NEED HIS REDEMPTION. HAVE YOU BEEN BORN AGAIN? GOOD, NOW CONTINUE TO FOLLOW YOUR SAVIOR-REDEEMER, THE LORD JESUS CHRIST. HIS BLOOD PAID THE DEBT YOU COULD NOT PAY. DO YOU KNOW THAT AND CONFESS THAT? GIVE IT SOME THOUGHT. AS LONG AS YOU LIVE YOU NEED HIM, SO GET OVER YOURSELF. YOU MAY BE A SHINNING EXAMPLE OF RIGHTEOUSNESS, I'M SURE. DO YOU KNOW THAT YOUR RIGHTEOUSNESS IS AND CAME FROM THE LORD JESUS CHRIST. EVERYONE WHO CLAIMS TO BE RIGHTEOUS IS RIGHTEOUS IN HIM ONLY. DON'T YOU JUST LOVE HIM. ME TOO. HIS BLOOD IS THE ONLY THING IN THIS WORLD TO TAKE CARE OF YOUR SALVATION, REDEMPTION. HE DID SHED HIS BLOOD FOR YOU,

AND DON'T YOU BRUSH THAT ASIDE. BE REMINDED EVERYTIME YOU KNEEL BY YOUR BED AND THANK HIM FOR THE WONDERFUL DAY YOU ENJOYED, IT WAS GIVEN TO YOU IN HIM. O THANK YOU, JESUS. WHERE EVER WOULD I BE OR WHERE WOULD I GO FOR THE SECURITY I GET FROM JESUS. O' THE LOVE OF JESUS, O' THE BLOOD OF JESUS, IT WASHES WHITE AS SNOW. WELL, I GO TO CHURCH AS OFTEN AS I CAN AND GIVE WHEN I GO. I KNOW HOW IMPORTANT IT IS TO SUPPORT THE CHURCH. DO YOU? HOW WONDERFUL. WHY DON'T YOU GO AND SUPPORT REGULARLY. THERE'S CHURCH, USUALLY EVERY SUNDAY, SO GO WHEN THE CHURCH IS OPEN FOR ALL OF US. I WOULD LIKE TO SEE YOU AND FELLOWSHIP WITH YOU. IT'S CALLED THE DAY OF THE LORD, BUT THEN ISN'T EVERYDAY, THE DAY OF THE LORD? IT IS. MAKE NO MISTAKE, I LOVE YOU, AND SO HOPE TO SEE YOU "OVER THERE". DOESN'T THAT SOUND GOOD? HUH? WE ALL NEED TO SUPPORT THE CHURCH BY GOING AS OFTEN AS THE DOORS ARE OPEN AND REVIEW ALL THE PROMISES MADE IN THE SCRIPTURES, OKAY? I TOO, LOVE YOU AND WANT YOU TO HAVE A GOOD REPORT ON THE DAY WE ARE RAPTURED. I SO LOOK FORWARD TO THAT DAY AND SO HOPE TO SEE YOU WHEN THAT TRUMPET SOUNDS. WHAT A DAY OF REJOICING THAT WILL BE. PLEASE BE THERE TO ENTER IN TO HIS REST. THAT BANQUET PROMISED FOR THE SAVED PROMISES TO BE THE MOST WONDERFUL GATHERING EVER. DON'T MISS IT. THE FATHER HAS PLANNED SUCH A BEAUTIFUL COMING TOGETHER. THE BLOOD WILL BE ON THE SHORE AND WE WILL CROSS OVER IT. THE GLORY OF ALL HEAVEN WILL BE SEEN. ALL THE PROMISES WILL BE FULFILLED AS WE GATHER. O' SO BEAUTIFUL. O' THE BLOOD OF JESUS, SHED FOR ME. WHERE WOULD I BE, IF NOT FOR THE TREE.

THE LORD JESUS CHRIST, MY HIGH PRIEST, MY ADVOCATE,
MY VINDICATOR JESUS, WHAT A BEAUTIFUL NAME. AM I
BLESSED OR WHAT? O' I AM.
BE AGED IN HIS GRACE, STEEPED IN HIS WORD, POURED OUT
IN HIS GLORY. AMEN. YOU READ TILL YOU FALL ASLEEP, I SAY,
READ TILL YOU WAKE UP. AMEN.

GIVE HIM ALL THE GLORY *
HE IS WORTHY

THREE HOURS OF DARKNESS. GOD WENT INTO THE DEEP TO WEEP. MATT 27:45, MK 15:45, LK 23:44.

WHO COULD YOU EVEN IMAGINE DESERVES ALL THE GLORY, BESIDES THE LORD JESUS CHRIST AND HIS FATHER, THE LORD GOD OF ALL CREATION? GIVE HIM ALL THE GLORY, HE IS WORTHY. GIVE GOD ALL THE GLORY, YES, HE IS WORTHY, HE HAS ALL THINGS WORKED OUT FOR OUR UNDESERVED FAVOR. YES, HE DOES, SO GIVE HIM ALL THE GLORY, HE IS WORTHY. HE, JESUS DIED FOR ALL MANKIND. NOBODY WAS LEFT OUT OF THE COUNT. LIVE AS THOUGH YOU ARE FORGIVEN, SINLESS. FIGHT THE TEMPTATION, REPENT AND RECEIVE THE FORGIVENESS HE PAID FOR ON THE CROSS. HIS BLOOD WAS SHED IN THE GARDEN OF GETHSEMANE, ON THE WHIPPING POST, THE CROWN OF THORNES, WHEN HE HUNG ON THE CROSS AND WHEN THEY PIERCED HIS HEART TO BE SURE HE WAS DEAD. HE BLED OUT FOR ALL WHO WOULD BELIEVE, BLOOD AND WATER RAN OUT WHEN THEY PIERCED HIS HEART, HIS HEART WAS BROKEN. HE BLED OUT FOR ME. HE, MY JESUS BLED OUT COMPLETELY FOR ALL WHO WOULD RECEIVE HIS FORGIVENESS. GIVE HIM ALL THE GLORY, HE IS WORTHY. HE PAID OUR SIN DEBT, PAID IN FULL, THE SLATE IS CLEAN FOR ALL WHO LOVE HIM AND ARE THANKFUL FOR HIS SACRIFICE. HE WAS/IS GOD'S ONLY BEGOTTEN SON. WHEN GOD HEARD JESUS SAY "IT IS FINISHED" THE LAND WAS DARKENED FOR THREE HOURS. HIS FATHER WENT INTO THE DEEP TO MOURN HIS LOSS. GOD, THE FATHER, AS WE KNOW CAN NOT LOOK ON SIN. JESUS TOOK ON ALL OF MY SIN AND YOURS. WHEN THE SOLDIERS SAW THE CLOUDS AND THE DARKNESS THEY SAID "SURELY THIS IS/WAS THE SON OF

GOD". GIVE HIM ALL THE GLORY, HE IS WORTHY. TO BE SURE, I COME EVERY DAY AND LAY DOWN THE SIN THAT SO EASILY ENSNARES ME. READ HEBREWS 12:1-2. I MUST ASK FOR HIS PARDON AND REPENT OF THE SINS WE SO WILLFULLY COMMIT. SOME SAY I DON'T SIN EVERY DAY?? REALLY?? NO, I AM BORN'AGAIN. SO YOU ARE BORNAGAIN, YOU MOST PROBABLY DO STILL SIN. START THAT PRAYER WITH REPENTANCE. GIVE HIM ALL THE GLORY, HE IS WORTHY. YOU ARE FORGIVEN. TO BE SURE, PRAY FROM YOUR HEART TO HIS HEART. TO BE SURE, GIVE HIM ALL THE GLORY, HE IS WORTHY. I AM FORGIVEN, I AM HEAVEN BOUND, O' HALLELUJAH, BLESS HIS HOLY NAME. I GIVE HIM ALL THE GLORY, HE IS WORTHY. I AM SAVED BY THE GENTLE MERCY OF MY GOD AND MY LORD JESUS CHRIST. I SO THANK HIM FOR ALL HE DID FOR ME AND STILL DOES. WHEREVER COULD YOU RECEIVE SUCH FORGIVENESS AND LOVE. GIVE HIM ALL THE GLORY, HE IS WORTHY. WHERE WOULD I BE IF HE DIDN'T PAY MY SIN DEBT. OH, THE DEBT THAT I WOULD HAVE LAID ON ME, IT'S UNTHINKABLE. I GIVE YOU, O' MY JESUS, ALL THE GLORY, YOU ARE WORTHY. THE THOUGHT BRINGS A TEAR. O' MY SAVIOR. NONE OF US WANT TO THINK THAT WE ARE UNDESERVING, WE ARE AT TIMES WILLFUL TO HURT OTHERS. THAT'S WHY JESUS WAS SENT, GOD SAW THE NEED, O' THANK YOU, FATHER, WHAT A SAVIOR. SING HALLELUJAH, ALL OF US, TO OUR WONDERFUL SAVIOR. GIVE HIM ALL THE GLORY, HE IS WORTHY. WE ARE SAVED BY THE BLOOD OF THE LAMB. THE CROSS IS THE ALTAR THAT GOD PUT JESUS (HIS LAMB) ON TO TAKE AWAY THE SIN OF THE WHOLE WORLD. THANK YOU, FATHER GOD, FOR THE CROSS. GIVE HIM ALL THE GLORY, HE IS WORTHY. O' WHAT A SAVIOR. THE BEST I CAN DO IS LIVE FOR YOU, JESUS. RECEIVE ALL MY PRAYER AND THANKSGIVING, YOU ARE SO DESERVING. I GIVE YOU ALL THE GLORY, HE IS WORTHY. I SO NEED YOU, JESUS, AND I AM SO BLESSED TO KNOW AND DEPEND ON YOU. I GIVE YOU ALL THE

GLORY, HE IS WORTHY. THE DAY WILL COME AND THE TRUMPET WILL SOUND, AND FACE TO FACE, I WILL GIVE YOU ALL THE GLORY, YOU ARE WORTHY. WHAT A DAY OF REJOICING THAT WILL BE. O' TO SEE MY SAVIOR, GIVE HIM ALL THE GLORY, HE IS WORTHY. O' LET'S ALL BE READY TO GO WHEN THE TRUMPET SOUNDS. PARENTS, YOU MUST TAKE YOUR CHILDREN TO CHURCH AND TEACH THEM THE NECESSITY OF GOING EVERY SUNDAY AND BE PART OF A BIBLE STUDY GROUP. THEIR FRIENDS SHOULD BE MOSTLY OF THE CHURCH. GIVE HIM ALL THE GLORY, HE IS WORTHY. BEING SAVED AND HEAVEN BOUND IS PART OF GOD'S FAMILY PLAN. YOU SO WANT THE WHOLE FAMILY TO LEAVE WITH YOU, AUNTS, UNCLES, COUSINS AND THE WHOLE NEIGHBORHOOD. AMEN.

I HAVE BEEN THROUGH ENOUGH TO KNOW HE IS ENOUGH. HE IS ENOUGH 4 ME. HE DID IT ALL, HE DOES IT ALL, HE IS MY ALL IN ALL. I SAY SO.
GIVE HIM ALL THE GLORY, HE IS WORTHY. GIVE HIM ALL THE GLORY, HE IS WORTHY.
NOT GOD FIRST, GOD ONLY. HE WILL BE ONLY OR HE WON'T BE ANY. HE IS WORTHY.

WALK SOFTLY

WALK SOFTLY WITH HIM.
DON'T GIVE IN TO EVERY WHIM.

PRAY FOR HIS HOLY LEADING.
SIT WITH HIM FOR A HOLY, PRAYERFUL MEETING.

HE IS ALWAYS READY TO LISTEN.
HE MAY TELL YOU OF YOUR MISSION.

HE HAS CALLED YOU TO HIS CROSS.
JUST DO IT, YOU TOO, MAY MISS IT, SUFFER LOSS.

LOOK INTO AND STUDY HIS BEAUTIFUL FACE.
HIS HEART IS FULL OF LOVE AND GRACE.

DON'T SKIP THE CHANCE TO HOLD HIS HAND.
LISTEN, HE HAS CALLED YOU TO DO WHAT HE HAS PLANNED.

JUST JESUS AND THE HOLY GHOST.
THE FATHER CALLED, YOU NEED ALL THREE THE MOST.

NOW ON YOUR KNEES BEGIN TO PRAY.
UNTIL YOU HEAR FROM HIM, STAY THAT WAY.

GIVE HIM ALL THE GLORY AND THE PRAISE.
YOU CAN'T POSSIBLY DO MORE THESE DAYS.

SO FEW TO HEAR THE MESSAGE OF LOVE
ALL POURED OUT FROM HEAVEN ABOVE.

WALK TO THE BEAUTIFUL OLD RUGGED CROSS.
DO YOU COUNT IT AS A TERRIBLE LOSS?

NOT SO, JUST STAY AND SEE,
HE CALLS YOU SAVED AND HAS SET YOU FREE.

WALK EVER SO SOFTLY, SHARE JESUS.
AMEN

OUR GOD IS THE BROKER FOR THE STOCK MARKET OF
HEAVEN. THE SHARES ARE THE COUNT OF HOW MANY YOU
SHARE JESUS WITH. HOW MANY SHARES ARE YOU
ACCOUNTABLE FOR TODAY? THE MORE YOU SHARE, THE
MORE YOU MAY LEAD TO REDEMPTION AND SALVATION
THROUGH OUR LORD JESUS CHRIST.
CHECK YOUR SHARES. JESUS IS ENOUGH 4 ME. AMEN.
HE DID IT ALL, HE DOES IT ALL, HE IS MY ALL IN ALL. I SAY SO.
AMEN AND AMEN SO BE IT AMEN AND AMEN

WALK INTO THE FIRE,
I AM IS ALWAYS THERE

GATHER ALL YOUR COURAGE,

LISTEN FOR THE WORD.

GOD IS ALWAYS CALLING,

JUST BE SURE YOU HEARD.

THE PROTECTION WRAPPED ALL AROUND,

HIS GOODNESS SO PROFOUND.

JUST LOOK UP TO THE HEAVENS

HE'S WATCHING YOU, HE STRENGTHENS

HE ALWAYS KEEPS HIS PROMISES,

HE WILL NEVER LET YOU DOWN.

YOU CAN'T HELP BUT LOVE HIM,

HIS LOVE IS ALL AROUND.

HE WATCHES EVERY STEP YOU TAKE,

THE ONLY ONE TO CARE.

SO WALK INTO THE FIRE,

I AM IS ALWAYS THERE.

AMEN
AMONEE TRIESS
SO BE IT BY THE HOLY GHOST

THE CROSS AGAIN, NO CHOICE

GOD HAD NO CHOICE WHEN HE SAVED ME. HE HAS ONLY ONE SON. GOD NAILED HIS JESUS, HIS ONLY SON, TO A CROSS. JESUS KNEW HIS FATHER IS THE ONLY ONE TO MAKE THE CROSS FOR HIM. THE ONLY ONE ABLE AND WORTHY. HE HAD TO DO THAT TO SEAL THE DIRECTION OF MY SALVATION. YOU HAVE NO CHOICE, JESUS ONLY. NOT GOD FIRST, GOD ONLY. HE WILL BE ONLY OR HE WON'T BE ANY. YOUR TROUBLE IS IN YOUR CHOOSING. YOU MAKE A CHOICE WHEN THERE IS NO CHOICE. I HAVE JESUS. ONE PATH, ONE WAY, ONE SAVIOR, ONE GOD. ONLY ONE DIRECTION. WHEN YOU SAY "I HAVE A CHOICE", YOU ARE LOST. IN THE GARDEN, MAN MADE A CHOICE. SO, IN BEGINNING, MAN MADE HIS FIRST ERROR. HE MADE A CHOICE WHEN THERE WAS NO CHOICE. SO EVIL. ALL WAS GIVEN TO HIS CREATED MAN WHEN HE WAS IN THE GARDEN. HE DID NOT LIMIT WHAT WAS FOR HIS MAN, EVERTHING IN THE GARDEN WAS CREATED FOR ADAM AND EVE. THEY WERE HIS ONLY CHILDREN, THE GARDEN WAS ALL THEIRS. HE GAVE THE GARDEN FOR THEIR ONLY MEANS TO WORK AND EAT, BE AT REST. HE, THE CREATED, HAD NO ENEMIES. HE WAS TO WALK AND ONLY COMMUNICATE WITH GOD. THE PERFECTION OF THE HOLY CREATION. THERE WAS NO REASON TO GET IN CONVERSATION WITH THE FALLEN ONE. HE WAS LOOKING FOR A CHANCE TO TEMPT ADAM, HE IS A "SNARE UNTO ERROR", STILL IS. HOWEVER DID HE GET PULLED INTO THE TRAP OF SATAN, WHO TOLD ADAM HE WAS MISSING OUT ON FUN STUFF AND GOOD TIMES AND WISDOM. EAT FROM THE TREE OF THE KNOWLEDGE GOOD AND EVIL, O' HOW AWFUL. HE DID CONVINCE ADAM THAT HE WAS CHEATED OUT OF THE KNOWLEDGE OF GOOD AND EVIL. HE

(ADAM) FAILED THE TEST, WHEN THE FALLEN EVIL ONE CONVINCED EVE TO TAKE OF THE FRUIT OF THE TREE AND SHE DID SHARE WITH HER HUSBAND. WELL, WE KNOW THE REST OF THE STORY AND HAVE SUFFERED FROM THE OUTCOME OF THAT TEMPTATION. OVER THE THOUSANDS OF YEARS SINCE THE GARDEN TO GET TO THIS PLACE, WE ARE STILL FIGHTING THE TEMPTATION TO HEAR THE EVIL ONE WHISPER IN OUR EAR TO HEAR "DO YOU REALLY BELIEVE? YOU DO AS YOU CHOOSE, DON'T MISS OUT ON THE GOOD TIMES". SO, NOW CHOOSE WHO YOU WILL FOLLOW. JESUS? HE IS NO FUN AND DO YOU REALLY HAVE TO LIVE THROUGH HIM AND HIS SHED BLOOD? YES, AND YES. HE IS THE ONLY ONE TO FOLLOW AS HE WILL LEAD YOU THROUGH THE FIRE AND INTO HIS LOVING ARMS OF SAFETY AND SECURITY. HE IS THE ONLY ONE TO HEAR AND FOLLOW AS HE HAS THE TRUTH AND IS THE AUTHOR AND FINISHER OF OUR SALVATION. DO NOT GET CAUGHT INTO THE TRAP OF THE CHEATER AND LIAR WHO WILL BRING ALL KINDS OF FOOLISH WORDS TO PULL YOU DOWN. DO YOU REALLY HAVE TO FIGHT EVERY THOUGHT AND MAKE A CHOICE OF WHO TO FOLLOW? WE SHOULD HAVE COME TOO FAR TO DOUBT ANYTHING OF GOD. WE SHOULD SAY WE WILL FOLLOW OUR SAVIOR WITH OUT ANY HESITATION. HE HAS PROVEN HIMSELF OVER AND OVER, HOW DO WE STILL DOUBT. GO TO THE CROSS, LISTEN TO YOUR OWN TESTIMONY AND YOU WON'T HAVE ANY DOUBT AND WON'T HAVE TO MAKE A CHOICE. THEY SAY BE "ALL IN" WITH JESUS, HE IS THE ONLY WAY, THE ONLY ONE. AMEN. I AM ALL HIS AND I HAVE MADE UP MY MIND TO BE WITH MY JESUS FOR ALL ETERNITY, NO CHOICE. IT IS FINISHED. I AM SO HIS. I AM ONLY HIS, FOREVER. THANK YOU, JESUS. THE CROSS DID IT FOR ME, IT'S FINAL. THANK YOU, JESUS. I AM HIS FOREVER. AMEN.

NOT GOD FIRST, GOD ONLY. HE WILL BE ONLY OR HE WON'T BE ANY.

I AM HIS AND HE IS MINE. IT WILL BE THAT WAY TILL THE END OF TIME.
MY HIGH PRIEST, AVOCATE, VINDICATOR, JESUS, WHAT A BEAUTIFUL NAME.
MY SAVIOR FOREVER AND EVER.

HAVE YOU READ THIS BEFORE? YOU ARE BLESSED TO READ IT AGAIN.

I CORINTHIANS 15: 41

YES, YOU HAVE AND AGAIN. MAYBE MORE THAN ONCE OR TWICE.
I HAVE WRITTEN OF THIS MANY TIMES, BUT I WILL STILL BE NICE.

EIGHTEEN THOUSAND YEARS AGO MY FATHER CHOSE ME.
HE REACHED OUT TO THE EDGE OF ETERNITY, THIS IS HOW IT WOULD BE.

HE TUCKED ME IN A HIDDEN PLACE TILL THE DAY OF HIS CREATION PLAN.
THE FOURTH DAY HIS HAND REACHED OUT TO FINISH HIS HEAVENLY SPAN.

I AM HIS LITTLE STAR, CREATED FROM AND FOR HIS PLEASURE.
TO LIGHT THE NIGHT AND BE PART OF HIS TREASURE.

SO MANY YEARS WENT BY TO DECIDE WHERE I WOULD PROVE HIS NEED.
HIS JESUS WAS HIS PLAN FROM WHEN I WOULD CARRY HIS SEED.

FOR THE THOUSANDS OF YEARS, I WAS TESTED TO BE SURE, A TRUSTED ONE.
I AM MOTHER OF THOUSANDS, PROVEN OVER AND OVER, TO MOTHER HIS SON.

YES, OVER TWO THOUSAND YEARS HAVE PASSED SINCE HE WALKED ON THE EARTH.

HE WOULD BE THE ONLY ONE, WHO DID PROVE HE IS GOD'S
SON, HIS WORTH.

I, HIS PRECIOUS STAR, WOULD BEAR THE HOLY OF HOLIES,
HIS HOLY SAVIOR.
I HAVE NO BOAST, CERTAINLY NOT, I AM SO HONORED,
NEVER A WAVER.

HE, JESUS, OUR BLESSED SAVIOR DID SO TO PLEASE HIS
FATHER.
DO YOU KNOW THE WEALTH OF HIS ASSIGNMENT, SO
PERFECT, NOT A BOTHER.

WELL, HERE WE ARE, THE REMNENT OF HIS BELOVEDS
SALVATION.
JESUS DIED, WAS CRUCIFIED, THE SAVIOR OF HIS CREATION.

MY HEART WAS BROKEN ON THAT DAY, NO MOTHER SHOULD
GO THRU THAT WAY.
I DID KNOW THAT HE WOULD RISE, HE SUFFERED, MORE
THAN I CAN SAY.

WHEN I WAS TWELVE, HE STOOD ME STILL, I WAS PROVEN BY
HIS WAYS.
SO NOW I AM HIS AND WILL ALWAYS BE, TILL THE END OF
DAYS.

ONE STAR DIFFERETH FROM ANOTHER STAR IN GLORY.
I AM MY DADDY'S CHOSEN, I AM HIS LITTLE STAR. BEAUTIFUL
STORY.
AMEM AMEN

I AM MEZZECHAH, MY CREATED NAME.
THIS IS HIS DOING, IT'S MARVELOUS IN MY SIGHT!
AMEN AND AMEN

* PROGRESSION OF PERFECTION *

I BELIEVE THE FIRST CALL CAME ON MARCH 14, 2014. HE TOLD ME HE WOULD SHAKE THE EARTH FOR ME. IN FOUR DAYS, HE DID. ON MONDAY MARCH 17, 2014 AT 6:25 AM HE DID INDEED SHAKE THE EARTH FOR ME. THE MEASURE OF IT WAS 4.4. THESE NUMBERS ARE IMPORTANT AND SIGNIFICANT TO ME. MY NUMBER IS FOUR. I DID CALL MY BROTHER TO TELL HIM OF THE WORD GOD HAD GIVEN ME AND THAT WE HAD AN EARTHQUAKE THAT MORNING. HIS RESPONSE WAS "WHO DO YOU THINK YOU ARE". I WAS SET ABACK BY HIS ATTITUDE. IT WASN'T THE ATTITUDE I EXPECTED. I REALLY THOUGHT HE WOULD BE GOOD WITH THE HAPPENING. NOT SO, OUR RELATIONSHIP WENT SOUR AFTER THAT.??! I GUESS HE WAS JEALOUS. GOD DOESN'T SHAKE THE EARTH FOR JUST ANYBODY. CRYBABY.

EIGHTEEN THOUSAND YEARS AGO, GOD PULLED ME FROM THE DARK OF THE EDGE OF ETERNITY. I WAS AND AM A CHOSEN BEING, YOU MAY WANT TO SEE THE WRITES I DID THIS YEAR, "CHOSEN I AND CHOSEN II". WE, THERE WERE OTHERS, WERE ASSIGNED TO THE BALCONY OF HEAVEN TO WAIT FOR WHAT, I DON'T KNOW. IN THAT ERA OF GOD'S TIME, HE HAD CREATED LUCIFER, HIS MOST RADIANT ARCHANGEL OF HEAVEN. WE ARE NOT FAMILIAR WITH HIS TIME. ITS SEEMS THAT LUCIFER WENT ON AN EGO TRIP THAT WENT REALLY BAD. HE WAS USHERED OUT OF HEAVEN, CAST DOWN TO EARTH TO LIVE IN THE DIRT OF THE EARTH. HIS ANGER WAS GREAT AS HE KICKED THE DIRT THAT BECAME AIRBORN AND BLOTTED OUT THE LIGHT. THE WHOLE OF GODS EARLY CREATION, VEGETATION AND PREHISTORIC ANIMALS

PERISHED FOR LACK OF LIGHT AND BREATHEABLE AIR. THE EARTH WAS THEN VOID AND WITHOUT FORM, DARKNESS WAS ON THE FACE OF THE DEEP. DO YOU SEE THAT? WE DON'T KNOW HOW LONG THAT LASTED BUT GOD WENT INTO THE DEEP TO MOURN HIS LOSS OF LUCIFER. GENESIS 1:2. WE, WHO WERE CHOSEN EIGHTEEN THOUSAND YEARS AGO AND SET ASIDE IN THE BALCONY OF HEAVEN WATCHED AS THE GOD OF THE WHOLE UNIVERSE MOURNED HIS LOSS. WE DO NOT KNOW HOW LONG HE STAYED IN THE DEEP. HE DID GO INTO THE DEEP TO MOURN. SEE GENESIS 1:1-2. BTW MY PROPHECY FROM LONG AGO IS DEEP CALLETH UNTO DEEP. PSALM 42:7. IN GENESIS 1:3, GOD INTRODUCED HIS SON, JESUS, THE LIGHT OF THE WHOLE WORLD. IN HIM IS NO DARKNESS AT ALL, THE TRUTH. THEN DID HE BEGIN HIS SECOND CREATION.

DAY 1, SEPARATION OF DAY AND NIGHT.

DAY 2, HE SEPARATED THE WATER ABOVE FROM THE WATER BELOW. HE NAMED THE FIRMAMENT ABOVE "HEAVEN". DON'T YOU JUST LOVE HIM. YES, ME TOO.

DAY 3, SEPARATED DRY LAND EARTH FROM THE WATER OF THE SEAS.

DAY 4, HE CREATED THE LIGHTS OF HEAVEN SUN, MOON, STARS. THE SUN TO LIGHT THE DAY, THE MOON TO LIGHT THE NIGHT. HE MADE THE STARS, ALSO. I AM HIS LITTLE STAR. BTW: MY NUMBER IS FOUR, HE GAVE ME TO KNOW THIS WHEN I WAS ABOUT 10 TO 13 YEARS OLD. I AM THE FOURTH MEMBER OF THE TRINITY. ASK ME.

DAY 5, HE CREATED BIRDS AND GREAT FISHES.

DAY 6, LIVING CREATURES AFTER IT'S KIND, CATTLE AND EVERYTHING THAT CREEPS ON THE EARTH. GOD ALSO SAID, LET US MAKE MAN IN OUR IMAGE AND LIKENESS TO HAVE DOMINION OVER ALL THE CREATION. THEY SHOULD BE MALE AND FEMALE (THERE IS NOTHING IN BETWEEN, I SPEAK OF HOMOSEXUALITY) AND BE FRUITFUL AND MULTIPLY, AND GO AND REPLENISH (GEN 1: 28) THE EARTH.

THE FIRST CREATION ALL DIED, SO ADAM AND EVE WERE TO "REPLENISH"THE EARTH. HE WAS PLEASED WITH HIS WORK OF HIS HANDS AND SAID IT WAS "VERY GOOD", AND IT WAS, AND PLEASE NOTICE THAT ALL MEN AND WOMEN (AND WOMEN) ARE CREATED EQUAL. GOD IS EVERYONES FATHER. ISN'T THAT SO BEAUTIFUL AND TIMELY, TOO. AMEN.

THE (7) SEVENTH DAY GOD RESTED FROM ALL HIS WORK THAT HE HAD MADE. HE BLESSED IT AND SANCTIFIED IT. O YES, AND BTW, I WAS BORN ON THE SEVENTH DAY. HMMM. GOD RESTED ON THE DAY I WAS BORN. IS HE SO WONDERFUL OR WHAT?

PROGRESSION OF PERFECTION

IN ALL, THE SECOND CREATION TOOK SEVEN THOUSAND YEARS. 2 PETER 3:8. ONE DAY WITH THE LORD IS AS A THOUSAND YEARS, AND A THOUSAND YEARS AS ONE DAY. ONE MORE THING, ON THE SIXTH DAY, AS HE MADE EACH MAN, HE DID NAME THAT MAN AND THE NAMES WERE WRITTEN BY THE ANGELS IN THE BOOK OF LIFE. (LAMB'S BOOK OF LIFE). MY CREATED NAME IS MEZZECHAH, REVEALED TO ME ON 8-8-2015, AT 5:00 AM. GOD MADE A GOOD REPORT ON MY CREATED NAME. THANK YOU, MY PRECIOUS HEAVENLY FATHER. WE ALL HAVE A CREATED NAME, BUT ALSO FOR OUR DIFFERENT ASSIGNMENTS WE HAVE NAMES APPROPRIATE FOR THE AGES WE ARE BORN IN. ALL MEN WERE/ARE CREATED ON THAT SIXTH DAY, LASTING A THOUSAND YEARS. IT TOOK GOD A THOUSAND YEARS TO CREATE ALL OF HIS WONDERFUL EARTHLY CHILDREN. AS WE HAVE READ, THERE IS NOTHING NEW UNDER THE SUN. THE ONLY ONE WHO HAD ONLY ONE ASSIGNMENT AND BECAME A MAN IS JESUS, WHO WAS (SENT BY HIS FATHER) AS THE REDEEMER OF FALLEN MAN. THE ONES CREATED ON THE SIXTH DAY HAVE BEEN SENT AT DIFFERENT TIMES TO FULFILL ASSIGNMENTS. WE HAVE ALL HAD MULTIPLE ASSIGNMENTS. JESUS SPEAKING, MATT 11:14, ELIJAH WHO WAS FROM THE OLD TESTAMENT AND REASSIGNED TO BE JOHN THE BAPTIZER. IF JESUS SAID IT, IT IS THE TRUTH. YOU MAY HAVE BEEN REASSIGNED MANY TIMES. SOME MAY HAVE AT SOME TIME SAID THAT THEY HAD BEEN HERE BEFORE, MAYBE THEY HAVE, I HAVE HAD MANY ASSIGNMENTS. THE NAME MEZZECHAH MEANS MOTHER OF THOUSANDS, AND I AM. O YES AND BTW I AM HIS LITTLE STAR. THE NAME HAD A SPECIAL PURPOSE WHEN HE GAVE ME THAT

NAME. YES, HE DID, AND I FULFILLED THAT ASSIGNMENT LONG AGO. THE NAME REBBECHAH MAYBE THE SAME OR PERHAPS A VARIATION OF MEZZECHAH. AS I WAS COMING FROM THE EARLY AGES OF THE OLD TESTAMENT, I DID COME TO THE AGE OF THE WORLD THAT JESUS WAS BORN INTO, TWO THOUSAND YEARS AGO. I WAS CHOSEN TO BIRTH JESUS BECAUSE AS BEING MOTHER OF THOUSANDS I HAD BEEN TESTED AND APPROVED, PASSED THE TESTS OF MOTHERHOOD. I WAS CHOSEN TO BE THE MOTHER OF CHRIST. WHAT A GIFT, WHAT A GOD. WE CAN TALK ABOUT IT IF YOU LIKE. YOU MAY HAVE QUESTIONS. AT THE SAME TIME, JOHN THE BELOVED, THE DISCIPLE JESUS LOVED, WAS BORN AND WAS CHOOSEN AS A DISCIPLE OF THE LORD JESUS CHRIST. I KNOW WHERE HE IS TODAY. HE LIVES ON THE ISLAND OF HAWAII. HE WAS RELEGATED TO THE ISLAND OF PATMOS TO PUNISH HIM FOR HIS BEING A FOLLOWER OF JESUS. HE IS AN ISLAND DWELLER. HE DID WRITE THE "REVELATION OF JESUS CHRIST". HE FAVORS THE ISLAND LIFE AS THAT'S WHERE HE WROTE THE BOOK OF THE "REVELATION OF JESUS THE CHRIST", THE MESSIAH. I UNDERSTAND THAT. I HAVE BEEN TRYING TO GET HIM TO COME HERE TO SEE ME. SURE WISH HE WOULD COME TO VISIT. I HAVE QUESTIONS, HE MOST PROBABLY HAS ANSWERS. I PRAY A LOT ABOUT IT. I SO WANT TO SEE HIM. I HAVE A GOOD MANY PAGES OF THE LAST BOOK I WROTE THAT REFER TO MANY WHO ARE FROM JESUS TIMES AND BEFORE. IF YOU HAVE THE BOOK TITLED "READ THE BOOK, READ THIS ONE TOO", THE TITLE OF THE WRITE IS "NAMES: WHO ARE THEY". PEOPLE FROM THE LONG AGO THAT ARE HERE NOW. CHECK IT OUT. THEY ARE HERE DOING NEW ASSIGNMENTS, SO GOOD. I KNOW I HAVE PUT A LOT OF WORDS IN LITTLE SPACE BUT YOU CAN HANDLE IT, YOU HAVE BEEN HERE A LONG TIME AND HAD LOTS OF PRACTICE.

PROGRESSION OF PERFECTION

IF YOU HAVE AN UNCTION (ANOINTING) TO DIG DEEPER INTO THE THINGS OF ETERNAL LIFE, GET CLOSE TO HIM AND ASK THOSE QUESTIONS. HE SO WANTS TO HEAR FROM HIS OWN. HE HAS TIME TO HEAR ALL YOU WANT TO KNOW. ASK, HE WILL ANSWER, ASK IN FAITH. YOU MAY BE SURPRISED AT SOME OF THE THINGS HE WILL TELL YOU. HE IS SO GLAD TO SPEND TIME WITH YOU AND TO KNOW THAT YOU WANT TO SPEND TIME WITH HIM. HE IS FULL OF SURPRISES SO BE SURE THAT YOU ARE SITTING DOWN WHEN HE GETS GOING. SO GOOD. IT MAY TAKE SOME TIME TO GET GOING BUT HE IS SO WORTH IT. YOU WILL REALIZE THAT HIS WISDOM COMES FROM ETERNITY AND GOES INTO ETERNITY. YOU WILL BE IN REALLY GOOD COMPANY. HE LOVES YOU AND HE IS EAGER TO SHARE WITH YOU. YOU WILL NEVER BE THE SAME. YOU WILL GLOW AFTER THE TIME SPENT WITH HIM. AFTER A WHILE WITH HIM, AGAIN, YOU WILL NEVER BE THE SAME NOR WILL YOU WANT TO. THAT TIME IS AND WILL BE ABOVE BLESSING. YOU WON'T JUST EAT, YOU WILL FEAST. THANK YOU, HEAVENLY FATHER. THANK YOU, JESUS, THANK YOU, HOLY GHOST. THE THREE IN ONE. THEY, THE THREE, DO YOU SEE? T(HE)Y. HE IS ALWAYS IN THE MIDDLE. TO BE SURE, KEEP HIM IN THE CENTER OF ALL YOU DO. LIVE FOR HIM, HE DIED FOR YOU. THE SCRIPTURE SAYS "BE ANXIOUS FOR NOTHING" BUT IN ALL THINGS, GIVE THANKS. HE IS HERE FOR YOU, YOU, NOW, SHOULD BE HERE FOR HIM. JUST DO IT. HE IS WORTH MORE THAN ALL THE TREASURE ON OR IN THE EARTH. LOOK UP, YOUR REDEMPTION DRAWETH NIGH. JESUS IS ON HIS WAY, "GLORY HALLELUJAH". SCRIPTURE ALSO SAYS "BE PERFECT AS HE IS PERFECT". MATT 5:48. HE WOULDN'T SAY IT IF IT WAS

NOT POSSIBLE. WHEN I FOUND OUT THAT PERFECTION WAS POSSIBLE, I WENT AFTER IT. O' THAT I MIGHT BE FOUND PERFECT IN HIM. JESUS IS MY RIGHTEOUSNESS, ONLY IN JESUS AM I RIGHTEOUS. I SO WANT TO BE PERFECT, ONLY TO BE AS MY JESUS IS PERFECT. AMEN. WHAT GOD SAYS ABOUT SATAN IS TRUE. WHAT SATAN SAYS ABOUT GOD IS A LIE. GOD IS TRUTH, HE CAN NOT LIE, SATAN IS A LIAR, HE CAN NOT SPEAK TRUTH. HE IS THE FATHER OF LIES, DEEP CALLETH UNTO DEEP.

AS LONG AS HE IS ALLOWED TO BE HERE, HE WILL LIE ABOUT ANY SUBJECT THAT COMES UP. SCRIPTURE SAYS THAT THE TRUTH IS NOT IN HIM, SO EVEN WHEN TRUTH IS EASY HE WILL STRETCH IT INTO A LIE. YOU KNOW, JUST GOTTA LIE. THAT'S HOW HE THINKS. TRUTH WILL SET YOU FREE, CAN'T HAVE THAT, NOW CAN WE. HE WILL KEEP YOU IN BONDAGE. TURN THE LIGHT ON, HE WILL FLEE INTO THE DARK. HE HAS A HIDDEN AGENDA, BUT IT ONLY WORKS IN THE DARK. STAY IN THE LIGHT AND HE WILL HAVE TO LEAVE. JESUS IS IN THE LIGHT AND HE IS SO MUCH BETTER COMPANY. HE CAME TO SEEK AND TO SAVE THE LOST, THE ONES WHO CAN'T FIND THEIR WAY OUT OF THE DARK. JUST TAKE HIS HAND. GO FOR A WALK WITH HIM. HIS PEACE WILL EASE YOUR MIND. HIS PEACE IS SO WONDERFUL. THE SCRIPTURE SAYS HE IS THE PRINCE OF PEACE, OH YES, HE IS. JUST LET HIM LEAD. HE IS THE GOOD SHEPHERD. LET HIM LEAD YOU TO GREEN PASTURES. AMEN

IF I PLACE MYSELF WITH YOU, JESUS, I AM IN A GOOD PLACE.
HE IS THE WAY, THE TRUTH AND THE LIFE, TAKE HIS HAND.
NO MAN COMES TO THE FATHER EXCEPT THEY COME THRU
JESUS.
THE ONLY WAY TO THE FATHER IS THROUGH THE DOOR
(JESUS).
HE SAID "I AM THE DOOR". JOHN 10:9

HE UNDERSTANDS,
SHOW "RESPECT"

NO, 'YOU' DON'T UNDERSTAND. HE UNDERSTANDS PERFECTLY. YOU HAVE NO "RESPECT" FOR WHAT HE HAS DONE. I HAVE WRITTEN OF THIS BEFORE, BUT WE ARE ALL FREE TO DO AS WE PLEASE. YES, YOU ARE, SO OFF YOU GO TO DO AS YOU PLEASE. HE IS WATCHING. HE SAYS NOTHING BECAUSE YOU ARE FREE TO DO AS YOU PLEASE, BUT THE DAY WILL COME. YOU ARE SO ANXIOUS TO SEE THE DAY OF THE LORD. WHAT A DAY OF REJOICING THAT WILL BE. WHEN WE ALL SEE JESUS, WE WILL SING AND SHOUT THE VICTORY. MOST OF US WILL, HOPEFULLY. HOW IS IT THAT YOU DON'T UNDERSTAND THAT GOD GAVE YOU HIS BEST, SHOULDN'T YOU ALSO GIVE HIM YOUR BEST? DO YOU EVER LOOK IN THE MIRROR? NO, DO YOU REALLY LOOK IN THE/YOUR MIRROR? WHAT DO YOU SEE? DO YOU SEE YOUR BEST? YES, THIS IS THE OUTFIT THAT I PAID A LOT OF MONEY FOR. MAYBE YOU SHOULD GET YOUR MONEY BACK. DO YOU SHOP IN THE TRASH FOR YOUR CLOTHES? THOSE THINGS YOU ARE WEARING ARE TRASH, I DON'T CARE HOW MUCH YOU PAID FOR THEM. THEY ARE THROW AWAYS. THEY ARE ONLY YOUR BEST IF YOU LIVE IN ABJECT POVERTY. YES, WE LOOK AT THE THIRD WORLD POPULATION AND IT BREAKS OUR HEART TO IMAGINE HOW THIS CAN BE IN A WORLD OF THIS DAY. THEY ARE SUFFERING FROM HUNGER, COLD, DEEPEST POVERTY. IS THAT OK WITH YOU. THEY HAVE NO CHOICE. THE RAGS ARE THEIR BEST. DO YOU MOCK THEM BY THE WAY YOU DRESS? YES, YOU DO. THERE ARE PASTORS COMING INTO THE PULPIT IN RAGS? THEY COME WITH THE GOOD NEWS OF CHRIST AND SALVATION

AND THE GOODNESS OF GOD???? IN RAGS! IS THAT YOUR TESTIMONY? GOD IS SO GOOD? YOU LOOK LIKE YOU LIVE IN THE ALLEY BEHIND THE THRIFT SHOP. DO YOU? LET ME REFRESH YOUR MEMORY, YOU ARE THE PASTOR. MOST CHURCHES SUPPORT THEIR PASTORS, DO YOU NOT HAVE ENOUGH MONEY TO DRESS BETTER. THEN YOU BETTER GET A JOB IN ADDITION TO WHAT THEY CAN AFFORD TO PAY YOU. YOU DON'T REPRESENT CHRIST LOOKING LIKE THAT. DO YOU? NO! DID HE LEAVE YOU LIKE THAT? NO! PLEASE HAVE SOME RESPECT FOR THE LORD. PUT ON SOME DECENT GARB WHEN YOU COME TO THE PULPIT, YOU REPRESENT CHRIST TO THE PEOPLE. SHOW SOME RESPECT FOR GOD, THE FATHER, JESUS, HIS SON, AND THE HOLY GHOST. SO, TELL ME, WOULD YOU IF YOU WERE INVITED TO COME BEFORE THE QUEEN OF ENGLAND, NOT DRESS TO THE NINES, MAYBE GO OUT AND BUY A NEW OUTFIT SO AS TO LOOK REALLY GOOD? O', YOU WOULD, YES YOU WOULD. DOES SHE RANK HIGHER THAN OUR ROYAL HEAVENLY FATHER, TRIUNE GOD AND OUR BLESSED JESUS, WHO DIED FOR US AND IS RISEN AGAIN FOR OUR SALVATION. WOULD YOU DARE TO COME BEFORE THE ENGLISH ROYALTY IN RAGS? I TROW NOT. WOULD YOU COME BEFORE THE PRESIDENT OF THE GOOD OLD U S A IN RAGS? GOOD HEAVENS, NO. WELL THERE YOU GO. PUT ON SOMETHING UNBROKEN, FULL OF HOLES AND SO TATTERED MOST WOULDN'T WASH THE CAR WITH WHAT YOU ARE WEARING. COME ON NOW, PUT ON SOMETHING DECENT. JESUS IS COMING SOON. WE ALL MUST BE READY TO LEAVE THIS PLACE FOR OUR HEAVENLY HOME. PLEASE ARRIVE IN SOMETHING FITTING FOR YOUR HOME COMING. SOME ONE WILL BE THERE TAKING PHOTOS. GET READY FOR YOUR PHOTO SHOOT. YOU WILL PROBABLY BE IN THE FRAME WITH OUR LORD. HE LOOKS SO LOVELY AND SO SHOULD YOU. HE IS THE ONE OF PROSPERITY AND SO ARE YOU, BECAUSE OF HIM. SO, PROSPER IN HIS LOVE. YOU CAN DO IT. DRESS'UP FOR HIM.

I SAY IF YOU DON'T WALK WITH HIM, YOU WALK AGAINST HIM, ARE YOU ANTI'CHRIST? THE MORE I READ, THE MORE I NEED. PERFECT (7) X GRACE (5) = 35, THE NUMBER OF PERFECT GRACE. DON'T DO WHAT YOU'RE THINKING, THINK WHAT YOU'RE DOING. SOME HAVE BEEN IN THE PULPIT FOR YEARS AND STILL IN DISRESPECT. PASTORS IN RAGS, REPRESENTING THE PEOPLE TO GOD AND REPRESENTING GOD TO THE PEOPLE, IN RAGS?? THINK WHAT YOU ARE DOING. ARE YOU CELEBRATING AND HONORING-SHOWING RESPECT TO OUR GOD AND HIS CHRIST? DO YOU KNOW HE IS ALL POWERFUL AND HE HASN'T SET YOU ON FIRE? O' HIS PITY AND PATIENCE. ISN'T HE SO WONDERFUL? O' HE IS, MY GENTLE JESUS. GO INTO THE ATTIC, FIND THE OLD TRUNK AND SEE IF THERE IS SOME RESPECT IN IT, RESPECT IS STILL IN FASHION. GENESIS 4:4. FOUR IS MY NUMBER, COME, I WILL TELL YOU ABOUT RESPECT. HE IS MINE AND I AM HIS, O'COME LET ME TELL YOU. INFINITY ABOUNDS.

NOT GOD FIRST, GOD ONLY. HE IS ONLY OR HE WON'T BE ANY.
HE GAVE YOU HIS BEST, MAYBE YOU COULD GIVE HIM YOUR BEST.

AT THE APPOINTED TIME

FOR THE VISION IS YET FOR AN APPOINTED TIME, BUT AT THE END IT SHALL SPEAK, AND NOT LIE: THOUGH IT TARRY, WAIT FOR IT; BECAUSE IT WILL SURELY COME, IT WILL NOT TARRY. HABAKKUK 2:3

GOD'S TIMING IS NOT OUR TIMING. WE KNOW THAT SO WE DON'T SIT AROUND AND BEG HIM TO DO IT OUR WAY, MOSTLY BECAUSE WE KNOW BETTER. MOST OF US ARE WELL AWARE THAT HE DOES THINGS IN HIS OWN TIMING AND NOT UNTIL HE WANTS TO. O' IF WE WOULD JUST GET THAT. IT IS NOT THAT HE WANTS HIS OWN WAY BUT HE KNOWS WHAT, WHEN, WHERE, AND WHAT FOR. IT'S HIS PLAN FOR OUR GOOD. YOU MAY WANT TO PRAY FOR A CERTAIN THING OR SITUATION AND BE WAY OFF TRACK. IT MAY NEED TO STEW FOR A WHILE. SO YOU MAY NEED TO ASK "IS IT SOUP YET"? HE WILL BE IN CONTROL OR YOU MAY PUT YOUR FOOT IN YOUR MOUTH, AND MAKE A MESS OF THE WHOLE THING. YOU HAVE HEARD THAT YOU DON'T KNOW ALL THE CIRCUMSTANCES. YOU PROBABLY HAVE HEARD THAT LITTLE SAYING "IN DUE TIME", TOO. YES, IN DUE TIME HE CAN DO ALL THINGS AND IN GOOD ORDER. BE PATIENT AND SEE IT MAY COME OUT BETTER THAN YOU COULD EVER IMAGINE. OR, YOU COULD SPEAK OUT OF TURN AND MESS THE WHOLE THING UP. YOU DON'T WANT THAT. "I'M SORRY" CAN ONLY WORK FOR A WHILE AND SOMETIMES MAYBE NOT AT ALL. LEARN TO LISTEN TO THE VOICE OF GOOD SENSE. HE REALLY WANTS YOU TO GET GOOD RESULTS. HE JUST WANTS YOU TO LISTEN TO THE VOICE OF LOVE. HE LOVES YOU AND WANTS YOU TO BE SUCCESSFUL IN ALL YOU DO. GOT IT? HOW ABOUT OBEDIENCE? SOMETIMES HE IN HIS WONDERFIL WISDOM CAN SHOW OUT AND YOU WILL BE SO GLAD TO HAVE DONE IT HIS WAY. I KNOW FROM EXPERIENCE, HE IS SO GOOD AT WHAT HE DOES. I SO LOVE TO GIVE HIM ALL THE PRAISE AND GLORY, HE IS SO WISE. I KNOW

THAT YOU KNOW IT ALSO. YOU PROBABLY WILL GET SOME ACCOLADES FOR DOING IT HIS WAY. NOT THAT YOU SHOULD GET ALL PUFFED UP BUT JUST DO IT HIS WAY, HE HAS SUCH GOOD INTENTIONS. HIS WAY ALWAYS WORKS. HE HAS A PLAN FOR BEING GOOD AT WHAT HE DOES. HE LOVES YOU AND HE'S GOOD AT WHAT HE DOES. HIS TIME IS GOOD TIME. HE IS IN IT TO WIN IT, AND YOU WILL BENEFIT FROM HIS ABILITY. HE KNOWS THE END FROM THE BEGINNING. HE HAS REAL GOOD IDEAS AND THEY WORK. HMMM. HE HAS BEEN HERE AND DONE SO MUCH MORE THAN YOU OR ME. I DID A WRITE ABOUT 'WATCH HIM WORK', HE IS AMAZING AND TOO, HE HAS HAD SO MUCH MORE EXPERIENCE. HE CREATED ALL THAT WE SEE AND DON'T SEE. HE HAS WORKED WITH LITTLE TIME AND LOTS OF TIME, IT DOES NOT MATTER, HE'S IN CHARGE. HE DOES AS HE PLEASES AND WE MUST AND WILL ALLOW. HE HAS PATTERNS FOR ALL OF HIS WORK, HE'S THE CREATOR. THE MOUNTAINS, THE OCEANS, THE DESERTS, NORTH POLE, SOUTH POLE, ALL OF IT. HE'S GOT IT. WHEN I THINK OF ALL HE HAS DONE, ALL HE WILL DO, AND SOME OF IT ALL FOR YOU, WHAT COULD WE POSSIBLY ARGUE ABOUT OR ASK FOR MORE. WE ARE LOADED WITH BENEFITS. HE IS A GOOD-GOOD GOD. JUST WORSHIP. HE HAS GIVEN ME MORE THAN I CAN COUNT. THE GIFT OF LIFE TO START WITH. YOU JUST CAN'T DO BETTER THAN HIS GOODNESS, HE IS AMAZING, AND HE ISN'T DONE YET. WE HAVE TOMORROW. WHO KNOWS WHAT'S ON HIS AGENDA AND WHAT'S AHEAD. COUNT THE STARS, NOW THAT'S A HEADACHE. CAN YOU? NO, NOBODY CAN. HE KNOWS THE NAME OF EVERY STAR, HE NAMED THEM. TO GOD BE THE GLORY, FOREVER AND FOREVER. YOU MUST JUST STAND IN AWE OF HIS ABILITY. WOW, LOOK WHAT GOD HAS DONE. I MAY JUST BREAK DOWN AND CRY, HE BLOWS ME AWAY, HE IS AMAZING. JUST SAY SO.

NOT GOD FIRST, GOD ONLY. HE WILL BE ONLY OR HE WON'T
BE ANY.
HE IS REAL, SUPERNATURALLY REAL. HE HAS NO MATCH FOR
OR AGAINST.
O' THE MIGHTY LOVE AND GRACE OF GOD BY THE HOLY
GHOST.

THE ABYSS OF UNBELIEF

LUKE16:26

IS THAT A NEW ONE FOR YOU? ARE YOU A BELIEVER? BETTER CHECK IT OUT, NOW. THERE ARE PROMISES IN THE SCRIPTURE YOU MAY NEVER KNOW EXCEPT YOU GO AFTER THEM. IT SAYS WITH NO HESITATION, "YOU MUST BE BORN AGAIN". YES, SO WHAT ARE YOU WAITING FOR? IT'S GONNA TAKE A WHILE SO YOU BETTER GET A BIBLE AND READ TIL YOU FALL ASLEEP OR MAY I SAY TILL YOU WAKE'UP. THERE IS SO MUCH WONDERFUL STUFF TO LEARN AND DISCOVER. READ ALL ABOUT IT. SO RICH AND FULL OF HEALTH FOOD. THE WORD IS RICH AND HEALTHY FOOD FOR THE WHOLE BODY AND SOUL.. YAH, A WHOLE BUNCH. JESUS IS THE ONE TO FOLLOW SINCE HE FOLLOWS SO CLOSE TO HIS FATHER. HE WILL SHOW YOU, YOU JUST HAVE TO KNOW HOW TO DO ALL THE IMPORTANT STUFF. DID YOU KNOW THAT HE DIED FOR YOU? YES, HE WAS NAILED TO THE OLD RUGGED CROSS. YOU PROBABLY KNOW THAT, IT IS THE STORY OF JESUS RAISED BACK TO LIFE ON THE THIRD DAY. IT IS THE EASTER STORY OF OUR REDEEMER BEING RAISED FROM THE DEAD. O' YES HE WAS, IF HE WASN'T RAISED FROM THE DEAD WE WOULD STILL BE IN OUR SIN STATE AND NO ONE TO RESCUE US FROM ETERNAL DEATH. NEVER HEARD OF THAT? YES, WE WOULD BE HOPELESS. HE IS OUR MOST HOLY SAVIOR AND REDEEMER. I SO LOVE HIM, AND AM SO GRATEFUL FOR WHAT HE DID FOR ME. I AM SO GLAD FOR WHAT HE HAS DONE, I GO TO CHURCH EVERY SUNDAY JUST TO PRAISE AND WORSHIP HIM. HE IS SO WORTHY. THAT'S WHAT I WOULD TELL ALL WHO WOULD STAND STILL LONG ENOUGH TO HEAR ALL ABOUT HIM. I COULD WITNESS FOR HOURS AND STILL GO FOR DAYS TO PRAISE HIM AND YOU WOULD BE SO TAKEN WITH HIM YOU

WOULD PROBABLY DO THE SAME. THE MORE YOU HEAR THE GOOD NEWS, THE MORE YOU WILL WANT TO WORSHIP OUR SAVIOR. I AM SO SURE YOU WILL FALL IN LOVE WITH JESUS THAT YOU WILL BEGIN TO SING PRAISES TO THIS BEAUTIFUL NAME. YOU WILL NOT BE ABLE TO HOLD BACK THE PRAISE AND WORSHIP. WHAT A BEAUTIFUL THING. I DO MOST ASSUREDLY RECOMMEND THAT YOU DO IT EVERYDAY. NOT TO MAKE IT A HABIT, BUT YOU WILL LOOK FORWARD TO INTENTIONALLY DO IT EVERY DAY, SOMETIMES MORE THAN ONCE. O' YES. HE IS SO WORTHY OF ALL WORSHIP. I HAVE KNOWN HIM FOR MY WHOLE LIFE AND AM SO GLAD HE IS MINE. YUP!! YOU MAY KNOW SOME WHO ARE DEPRESSED AND JUST CAN'T SEEM TO PULL THEMSELVES OUT OF THE DUMPS. THEY NEED JESUS. THAT IS YOUR OPENING TO EVANGELIZE YOUR LITTLE HEART TO YOUR DOWNCAST FRIEND OR BROTHER OR SISTER. BE READY WHEN THE OPPORTUNITY COMES, IT WILL BE SO GOOD FOR YOU, TOO. JESUS MAKES THE HEART GLAD. WE ALL NEED A GLAD HEART, IT'S A HEALTHY HEART. YOU JUST MIGHT FIND ONE WHO NEEDS TO BE RESCUED FROM THE ABYSS OF LONELY AND LOST. IT WILL TEST YOUR HEART FOR THAT GRADUATION INTO BEING A BEARER OF THE GOOD NEWS. JESUS IS GOOD NEWS AND YOU TOO, WILL GET LIFTED UP AS A TRUE FRIEND OF OUR JESUS. GET OUT THERE WITH YOUR WHOLE HEART. LIFT ALL WHO WILL LISTEN. BRING ALL INTO THE LIGHT OF THE LOVE OF JESUS. HE IS THE LIGHT, THE LOVE, THE LORD OF MY LIFE. O' HE IS, HE SURE IS. DO NOT NEGLECT HIM. HE IS THE ONLY, THERE IS NO OTHER WHO CAN SAVE YOU. HE SO WANTS ALL TO DEPEND ON HIM. HE IS THE "ONLY" ONE TO CARE FOR YOUR LIFE ON THIS EARTH. PUT ALL THE HEAVY AND EASY STUFF ON HIM, HE IS THE "ONLY" TRUE FRIEND TO WALK WITH YOU. GIVE IT ALL TO HIM. IF YOU MAKE A MIS'STEP HE WILL CATCH YOU ON THE WAY DOWN AND LIFT YOU UP, HE DOES THAT. HE'S DONE IT FOR ME MORE THAN ONCE. MAYBE THAT'S WHY

I LOVE HIM SO. THERE IS A VERY DARK ABYSS FOR THOSE WHO REFUSE THE HIGH AND HOLY LOVE OF OUR SAVIOR AND LORD.

TO BE SURE, UNBELIEF IS A FATAL ERROR. DON'T TEST THE WATER OF UNBELIEF, IN THE END IT WILL BE A GREAT LOSS. WE ALL WANT FOR OUR FAMILIES AND FRIENDS TO JOIN US IN THE MOST GLORIOUS AND HOLY ETERNITY WITH OUR LORD AND SAVIOR, THE LORD JESUS CHRIST. JUST DO IT. DECIDE TODAY, LIFE WILL BE BRAND NEW AND JOY FOR YOU. I AM PRAYING FOR ALL TO FIND REPENTANCE, ON YOUR KNEES, PLEASE. ISN'T HE GOOD. BE BORN AGAIN, BE BAPTIZED IN THE WATER, BE FILLED WITH THE HOLY SPIRIT, SAVED. GET AFTER IT, BE RAPTURE READY. COULD BE TOMORROW, OR TONGHT, OR MAYBE TEN MINUTES.

NOT GOD FIRST, GOD ONLY. HE WILL BE ONLY OR HE WON'T BE ANY.
WHILE TIME IS, DO THE MOST WONDERFUL THING OF YOUR WHOLE LIFE. BE SAVED. HE TRULY, TRULY WILL SAVE YOU AND GIVE YOU THE BEST LIFE EVER.
MUCH LOVE AND MANY BLESSINGS. JUST DO IT.

YOUR DOUBT WILL
TAKE YOU OUT

BUT IF I WITH THE FINGER OF GOD CAST OUT DEVILS, NO DOUBT THE KINGDOM OF GOD IS COME UPON YOU. LUKE 11:20

ARE YOU NOT SURE OF WHAT THE BIBLE TEACHES? DO AN INVESTIGATION. FIND OUT WHAT THE TRUTH IS. FOLLOW IF NOT FOR SURE, YOU ARE SAVED, GOD WILL PROVE TO YOU THROUGH HIS WORD. GET AFTER THE BIBLE AND PROVE THE RIGHT HAND OF THE FATHER, HIS WORD, JESUS. HE WANTS YOU TO BE COMFORTABLE. HE SO WANTS WITH ALL OF HIS HEART THAT YOU LIVE BY HIS WORD. DO NOT DOUBT. DOUBT WILL CHOKE THE WORD. PRAYER IS MOST NECESSARY TO BUILD FAITH. THERE IS A MOST NECESSARY NEED FOR PRAYER. PRAY ABOUT EVERTHING. PHILIPPIANS 4:6. BE CAREFUL FOR NOTHING; BUT IN EVERYTHING BY PRAYER AND SUPPLICATION WITH THANKSGIVING LET YOUR REQUEST BE MADE KNOWN UNTO GOD. I BELIEVE THE SHORT REFERENCE IS PRAY ABOUT EVERYTHING. I DO. SO DON'T DOUBT, TAKE IT TO THE LORD IN PRAYER AND MAKE IT PLAIN WHAT YOU WANT AND EXPECT. TALK TO HIM. HE SO LOVES IT WHEN WE HAVE A NEED TO SPEAK WITH HIM. HE IS ALWAYS AVAILABLE. YOU NEED TO TAKE HIM AT HIS WORD. HOW WILL YOU EVER LEARN OR UNDERSTAND HIM EXCEPT YOU COME TO HIM AND GET HIS WORD FROM HIM? YOU MAY NOT WANT TO MISQUOTE HIM. DO NOT CHANGE THE WORD OF GOD. HE WILL BE PATIENT WITH YOU. HE ABOVE ALL WANTS A RELATIONSHIP WITH YOU. GO AFTER IT. HE, OUR CREATOR DOES KNOW ALL ABOUT US AND HE WILL GET TO THE POINT. HE HAS ALL THE ANSWERS. HE KNOWS EVERYTHING ABOUT ALL OF US AND LOVES US IN SPITE OF OUR SLOW ATTITUDE. DON'T HOLD BACK, HE IS READY TO GIVE YOU

UNDERSTANDING EVEN IF HE HAS TO REPEAT SOME OF THE ANSWER. HE IS A BIG GOD, ABLE TO DEAL WITH OUR LACK OF UNDERSTANDING. WHEN ALL IS SAID AND DONE, HE AND YOU WILL BE ON THE SAME PAGE, SO TO SPEAK. HE WILL ABSOLUTELY DISSOLVE ALL MISTAKES YOU MAKE, SO STAY WITH HIM. HE WILL NOT ABANDON YOU, HE IS THERE FOR YOU. HIS LOVE IS SO PATIENT. HE IS GOD, THE CREATOR OF ALL OF US, HE KNOWS US ALL BACK TO FRONT AND UP AND DOWN. GOT IT? JUST DON'T FORGET HE IS RIGHT, ALWAYS, IF YOU HAVE QUESTIONS, HE HAS ANSWERS. YES, HE DOES. THAT'S WHY HE IS GOD. GOTTA LOVE HIM. HE AND I HAVE BEEN HERE A LONG TIME AND HAD MANY SERIOUS ENCOUNTERS. YES, HE ALWAYS SHOWS ME HOW HE LOVES TO HELP ME GET IT. YOU WILL NEVER FIND A MORE WONDERFUL AND LOVING ONE TO TALK WITH AND HE FEELS THE SAME WAY. I LOVE TO CONVERSE WITH HIM AND HE LOVES ME RIGHT BACK. HE SO ENJOYS HIS CREATION AND LOVES ALL TIME SPENT WITH US. HE IS SO NOT INTIMIDATING, HE MAY LAUGH AT SOME OF THE THINGS WE SAY, BUT NOT TO HURT US. HE WILL ALWAYS TAKE YOU SERIOUS EVEN WHEN YOU DON'T. HE MAY EVEN GIVE HEAVEY CORRECTION IF YOU LOSE THE THREAD. DO YOU SEE I AM ON HIS SIDE, HE SO WISE. I CAN'T WAIT TO BE WITH HIM FOREVER. HE AND JESUS ARE BOTH OF THE SAME WITT AND MENTAL SHARPNESS. THEY KNOW WHERE AND WHEN YOU ARE UP FRONT. NO MESSING WITH HIM. YOU KNOW.... I JUST LOVE HIM. I AM SO GLAD HE IS MINE AND I AM HIS, FOR ALL ETERNITY. YOU JUST CAN'T DO BETTER THAN THE CELEBRITY OF HEAVEN. THE LORD JESUS CHRIST AND THE LORD GOD ALMIGHTY, CREATOR OF ALL THINGS SEEN AND UNSEEN. ARE WE IN FOR THE TIME OF OUR ETERNAL LIFE? YOU BETTER BELIEVE IT. I PLAN TO CELEBRATE MY ENTRANCE INTO THE MOST HIGH HEAVEN. CRY LIKE A BABY WHEN I SEE MY HEAVENLY FATHER AND HIS GLORIOUS SON. JUST TO WRITE THIS GETS MY HEART TO FLUTTER. O' WHAT A DAY OF

REJOICING THAT WILL BE. I AM READY TO GO RIGHT NOW. THE WAIT IS SO HARD, I HAVE NO DOUBT THAT ALL THINGS ARE READY FOR THE RAPTURE. HOWEVER, HE IS IN CHARGE AND DOESN'T NEED ANYONE'S APPROVAL. HMMM. O' REJOICE. AGAIN, I SAY REJOICE. LET'S ALL GO HOME. I DID A WRITE LAST WEEK "A LETTER FROM HOME", SO GOOD. YOU KNOW, HOME BEING HEAVEN. SO GOOD. HE TOO IS LOOKING FORWARD TO THE HOMECOMING OF HIS OWN. "W.O.W" WONDERFUL O' WONDERFUL. YES, I WANT ALL WHO ARE WAITING FOR THE RIGHT TIME, BE READY. THAT WILL GET YOUR JUICES FLOWING. I AM WRITING MYSELF HAPPY, REAL HAPPY. O' HALLELUJAH. AMEN. NO DOUBT HERE, AND WITH YOU, DON'T LET DOUBT TAKE YOU OUT. O' HALLELUJAH, AND AGAIN. ARE YOU PREPARED FOR THE JOURNEY? BE READY, LISTEN FOR THE TRUMPET.

NOT GOD FIRST, GOD ONLY. HE WILL BE ONLY OR HE WON'T BE ANY. BOW AND WORSHIP. GLORY O' GLORY. BOW AND WORSHIP.
I SAY REJOICE. WHAT A DAY OF REJOICING THAT WILL BE. AGAIN, I SAY REJOICE.

MORE GRACE

AND GOD IS ABLE TO MAKE ALL GRACE ABOUND TOWARD YOU: THAT YE,
ALWAYS HAVING ALL SUFFICIENCY IN ALL THINGS, MAY ABOUND TO EVERY
GOOD WORK. 2 COR. 9:8

WHEN UNBELIEF COMES CREEPING IN,
AND I THINK IT COULD BE TEMPTING SIN.

I WON'T LOSE HEART ONLY GAIN STRENGTH.
GOD IS WITH ME, HE WILL GO THE LENGTH.

EVEN THE BEST, GOD WILL HAVE TO HELP.
SOMETIMES I JUST DON'T FIND WHAT ELSE.

GO WITH HIM, FOLLOW CLOSE, HE HAS A PLAN.
HE'S LAID OUT POWER FOR HIS HOLY MAN.

AS I ENTER INTO HIS PRESENCE IN PRAYER.
I FEEL HIS LOVE, HIS ARMS AROUND ME, HIS TENDER CARE.

JUST WALKING AND TALKING AND SITTING WITH ME.
THERE'S NO ONE MORE PRECIOUS AND GRACIOUS THAN HE.

THERE IS NO FEAR, ALL IS HIS GRACE.
HE HOLDS ME SO CLOSE. HIS TENDER EMBRACE.

SO WARM AND SO TENDER HIS TOUCH. HE IS CLOSE. HE
LOVES ME SO MUCH.

SO PEACEFUL, HE GIVES ME SWEET REST.
MY VIGILANT SHEPHERD, SECURE UNDER HIS DILIGENT BEST.

HIS GRACE, HIS GRACE. HIS AMAZING GRACE. HOW ON
EARTH DO I DESERVE THIS BEAUTIFUL PLACE?

THE HOLY GHOST IS HERE AT THE READY. WILL ALWAYS
UPHOLD ME, HE LEADS ME STEADY.

ONLY MORE GRACE **** ONLY MORE GRACE

HE IS REAL, SUPERNATURALLY, REAL.
O' THE MIGHTY LOVE AND GRACE OF GOD THRU HIS
GLORIOUS SON, AND THE HOLY GHOST.
THE "MAGNIFICENT" THREE IN ONE.

O' THANK YOU, MY "SO" BEAUTIFUL, LORD JESUS CHRIST.
GRACE THROUGH FAITH 5-18-22

COMMUNION

*

TAKE IT EVERY DAY IN REMEMBERANCE OF THE SACRIFICE
OF OUR LORD AND SAVIOR.
OUR LORD JESUS CHRIST, THE LORD'S REDEMPTIVE
SALVATION.

*

BREAD OF LIFE JESUS' BODY

THE BODY OF OUR LORD JESUS CHRIST BROKEN ON THE
WHIPPING POST, FOR MY HEALING.
BY HIS STRIPES I AM HEALED, WHOLE AND HEALTHY.
HIS BODY IS THE BROKEN, BREAD OF LIFE.

*

THE WINE

THE REDEEMING BLOOD OF JESUS
HIS BLOOD WASHED ALL MY SIN AWAY. HE BLED IN THE
GARDEN OF GETHSEMANE,
SWEAT AND BLOOD RAN DOWN HIS FACE WHEN HE PRAYED
FOR HIS FATHER TO TAKE THE CUP AWAY.
HE BLED ON THE WHIPPING POST. HE BLED WHEN THEY PUT
THE CROWN OF THORNS ON HIS HEAD.
HE BLED WHEN HE HUNG ON THE CROSS.
HE BLED OUT WHEN THEY PUT THE SPEAR IN HIS SIDE, TO BE
SURE HE WAS DEAD.
HE BLED OUT WHEN WATER AND BLOOD PROVED HIS DEATH.
THE SPEAR IN HIS SIDE BROKE HIS HEART.

**THANK YOU, MY BLESSED HEAVENLY FATHER,
FOR MY LORD JESUS CHRIST**
AMEN
5-21-22

MATT 26:26 – 29, MARK 14:22 – 25, LUKE 22:14 – 20, 1 COR 11:23 - 27

PRAYER

I BOW MY KNEE, I BOW MY HEAD
TO THANK YOU FATHER FOR EVERY WORD YOU'VE SAID.

I AM AT MY BEDSIDE READY TO SLEEP, BUT I MUST!
THANK YOU FOR THE LOVE, IN WHOM I TRUST.

I'VE HAD A DAY OF RUSH, NOW I NEED REST AND PEACE.
I NEED TO GET INTO HIS SWEET RELEASE.

I BELIEVE I NEED PRAYER TO END THE DAY. JUST CAN'T SLEEP
UNTIL I PRAY.

WORSHIP AND PRAISE IS THE GIFT HE GIVES. O' MY JOY TO
KNOW HE LIVES.

HIS VOICE SO TENDER, HE WELCOMES THE PRAYER. THERE'S
SO MANY THOUGHTS, I LOVE HIS CARE.

JESUS, THE NAME I LOVE TO REPEAT, OVER AND OVER,
PRECIOUS AND SWEET.

I SAY AMEN, BUT KEEP ON AND ANOTHER AMEN. IT DOESN'T
BOTHER HIM, I MUST SAY IT AGAIN.

HE IS SO PATIENT WITH ME, OUR TIME TOGETHER. I WILL
NEVER STOP, THERE'S NOTHING BETTER?

HE NEVER SLEEPS, ALWAYS THERE TO HEAR MY NEED HE
ANSWERS EVERY TIME I CALL, "JESUS", TO INTERCEDE.

I COULDN'T COME THIS FAR, EXCEPT MY LORD BE OVER ALL. I
AM SO GRATEFUL WHEN HE ANSWERS MY EVERY CALL.

THERE ARE TIMES THAT TEARS COME AND I WEEP. HIS
COMFORT ENFOLDS ME, HE KNOWS I AM MEEK.

I STOP THIS PRAYER UNDER HIS WATCH AND GRACE. IT'S
OKAY, AMEN. I LOOK UP TO SEE HIS COMFORTING FACE.

I WILL DRIFT OFF AND ENJOY THE PEACE OF HIS KEEP.
BLANKETS SNUGGLE ME, THANKFUL, HIS LOVE IS SO DEEP.
AMEN AND AMEN.

WHEN I GROW UP, I WANT TO BE JUST LIKE YOU, JESUS.
THATS THE CHILD IN ME. HE LOVES ME NOT BECAUSE OF
WHO I AM, BUT BECAUSE OF WHO HE IS.
KING OF KINGS, LORD OF LORDS. THE ONE GOD SENT. OUR
SALVATION. AMEN.

DELIVER US FROM EVIL, AGAIN
BURDEN OF DEBT

MATTHEW 18:19 AGAIN I SAY UNTO YOU, THAT IF TWO OF YOU SHALL AGREE ON EARTH AS TOUCHING ANYTHING THAT THEY SHALL ASK, IT SHALL BE DONE FOR THEM OF MY FATHER WHICH IS IN HEAVEN.

DEUTERONOMY 28:1-14 THE BLESSINGS FOR OBEDIENCE. 1. AND IT SHALL COME TO PASS, IF THOU SHALL HEARKEN DILIGENTLY UNTO THE VOICE OF THE LORD THY GOD, TO OBSERVE AND DO ALL HIS COMMANDMENTS WHICH I COMMAND THEE THIS DAY, THAT THE LORD THY GOD WILL SET THEE ON HIGH ABOVE ALL THE NATIONS OF THE EARTH: 2. AND ALL THESE BLESSINGS SHALL COME ON THEE, AND OVERTAKE THEE, IF THOU SHALT HEARKEN UNTO THE LORD THY GOD.

GALATIANS 3:13 CHRIST HATH REDEEMED US FROM THE CURSE OF THE LAW, BEING MADE A CURSE FOR US; FOR IT IS WRITTEN, CURSED IS EVERYONE THAT HANGETH ON A TREE.

PSALM 107:20 HE SENT HIS WORD, AND HEALED THEM, AND DELIVERED THEM FROM THEIR DESTRUCTIONS.

ROMANS 15:13 NOW THE GOD OF HOPE FILL YOU WITH ALL JOY AND PEACE IN BELIEVING, THAT YOU MAY ABOUND IN HOPE, THROUGH THE POWER OF THE HOLY GHOST.

ISAIAH 10:27 AND IT SHALL COME TO PASS IN THAT DAY, THAT HIS BURDEN BE TAKEN AWAY FROM OFF THY SHOULDER, AND HIS YOKE FROM OFF THY NECK, AND THE YOKE SHALL BE DESTROYED BECAUSE OF THE ANOINTING.

ISAIAH 54: 17 NO WEAPON THAT IS FORMED AGAINST THEE SHALL PROSPER; AND EVERY TONGUE THAT SHALL RISE AGAINST THEE IN JUDGMENT THOU SHALT CONDEMN. THIS IS THE HERITAGE OF THE SERVANTS OF THE LORD, AND THEIR RIGHTEOUSNESS IS OF ME, SAYETH THE LORD.

WHATSOEVER YE ASK IN MY NAME, THAT WILL I DO.

DELIVER ME FROM EVIL, AGAIN

THE BURDEN OF DEBT

VERILY I SAY UNTO YOU, WHATSOEVER YE SHALL BIND ON EARTH SHALL BE BOUND IN HEAVEN: AND WHATSOEVER YE SHALL LOOSE ON EARTH SHALL BE LOOSED IN HEAVEN. AGAIN I SAY UNTO YOU, THAT IF TWO OF YOU SHALL AGREE ON EARTH AS TOUCHING ANYTHING THAT THEY SHALL ASK, IT SHALL BE DONE FOR THEM OF MY FATHER WHICH IS IN HEAVEN. FOR WHERE TWO OR THREE ARE GATHERED TOGETHER IN MY NAME, THERE I AM IN THE MIDST OF THEM. MATT 18:18-20

THE BLESSINGS FOR OBEDIENCE. AND IT SHALL COME TO PASS, IF THOU SHALT HARKEN DILIGENTLY UNTO THE VOICE OF THE LORD THY GOD, TO OBSERVE AND DO ALL HIS COMMANDMENTS WHICH I COMMAND THEE THIS DAY, THAT THE LORD THY GOD WILL SET THEE ON HIGH ABOVE ALL THE NATIONS OF THE EARTH: AND ALL THESE BLESSINGS SHALL COME ON THEE, AND OVERTAKE THEE, IF THOU SHALT HARKEN UNTO THE LORD THY GOD.

BLESSED SHALT THOU BE IN THE CITY, AND BLESSED SHALT BE IN THE FIELD. BLESSED SHALL BE THE FRIUT OF THY BODY, AND THE FRUIT OF THY GROUND, AND THE FRUIT OF THY CATTLE, THE INCREASE OF THY KINE AND THE FLOCKS OF THY SHEEP. BLESSED SHALL BE THY BASKET AND THY STORE. BLESSED SHALT THOU BE WHEN THOU COMEST IN, AND BLESSED SHALT THOU BE WHEN THOU GOEST OUT. DEUTERONOMY 28:1-6.

CHRIST HATH REDEEMED US FROM THE CURSE OF THE LAW, BEING MADE A CURSE FOR US; FOR IT IS WRITTEN, CURSED IS EVERYONE THAT HANGETH ON A TREE. GALATIONS 3:13.

HE SENT HIS WORD AND HEALED THEM, AND DELIVERED THEM FROM THEIR DESTRUCTIONS. OH THAT MEN WOULD PRAISE THE LORD FOR HIS GOODNESS, AND FOR HIS WONDERFUL WORKS TO THE CHILDRED OF MEN! PSALM 107:20-21

NOW THE GOD OF HOPE FILL YOU WITH ALL JOY AND PEACE IN BELIEVING, THAT YOU MAY ABOUND IN HOPE, THROUGH THE POWER OF THE HOLY GHOST. AND I MYSELF ALSO AM PERSUADED OF YOU MY BRETHEREN, THAT YE ALSO ARE FULL OF GOODNESS, FILLED WITH ALL KNOWLEDGE, ABLE ALSO TO ADMONISH ONE ANOTHER. ROMANS 15:13-14

AND IT SHALL COME TO PASS IN THAT DAY, THAT HIS BURDEN BE TAKEN OFF THY SHOULDER, AND HIS YOKE FROM OFF THY NECK, AND THE YOKE SHALL BE DESTROYED BECAUSE OF THE ANOINTING. ISAIAH 10:27.

NO WEAPON FORMED AGAINST THEE SHALL PROSPER; AND EVERY TONGUE THAT SHALL RISE AGAINST THEE IN JUDGEMENT THOU SHALT CONDEMN. THIS IS THE HERITAGE OF THE SERVENTS OF THE LORD, AND THEIR RIGHTEOUSNESS IS OF ME, SAYETH THE LORD. ISAIAH 54:17

WHATSOEVER YE ASK IN MY NAME, THAT WILL I DO.
NOT GOD FIRST, GOD ONLY. HE WILL BE ONLY, OR HE WON'T BE ANY.

MY WALK WITH JESUS

IF I SHOULD WALK IN ALL HIS GRACE

AND LOOK WITH PITY ON JESUS FACE.

THE SCOURGING, WICKED CORDS

THE SPIKES, THE CROWN, THE DEADLY SWORD.

THE CRIMSON FLOWING FROM HIS CROSS,

SEE IT AS GAIN, NOT HIS DEATH ETERNAL LOSS.

HE ROSE AGAIN NO MORE TO DIE,

HE CONQUERED DEATH FOR YOU AND I.

HIS PEACE IS FOREVER MINE

TILL I TRANSLATE, THE END OF TIME.

AMEN

IF ANY MAN WILL COME AFTER ME, LET HIM DENY HIMSELF AND TAKE UP HIS CROSS DAILY, AND FOLLOW ME. LUKE 9:23 KJV AND HE THAT TAKETH NOT HIS CROSS, AND FOLLOWETH AFTER ME, IS NOT WORTHY OF ME. MATT 10:38 KJV YOU MUST FOLLOW, DILIGENTLY WALKING IN HIS ADMONITION. HE IS WORTHY, O THAT I MAY BE WORTHY TO WALK WITH HIM. PRAISE AND WORSHIP, WITH THANKSGIVING. HE IS WORTHY.

JESUS, MY TREASURE

WHAT DO YOU TREASURE? MY WORK, MY JOB? HOUSES, CARS? THAT'S SO NICE. THEY ARE TEMPORARY THOUGH. NOT TO SAY THAT YOU SHOULDN'T VALUE THEM, YOU SHOULD. HERE'S A NEW IDEA. WHERE DOES ALL MY CREATIVE AND PROGRESSIVE THINKING COME FROM? HMMM. I SAY FROM ABOVE. OH YES, IT DOES. I AM HIS AND HE IS MINE AND IT WILL BE THAT WAY TILL THE END OF TIME. I AM HIS MOTHER AND HIS WRITER. I AM THE ONE HE HAS CHOSEN TO PUT HIS WORDS ON THE PAPER. THAT WILL MAKE YOU THINK OUT LOUD. WHEN I AM TOLD TO SIT DOWN AND LISTEN AS HE HAS SOMETHING TO SAY, I WILL OBEY. I SO LOVE TO HEAR HIS ANNOUNCEMENTS. HE HAS SUCH A TENDER VOICE AND, IN A HURRY, AND LET'S GO. HIS URGENT DEMEANOR AND "LET'S GET THIS THING STARTED" IS KINDA SERIOUS AND SO IMPORTANT. IF YOU HAVE HEARD HIM WHEN HE IS IN A HURRY, YOU WILL ALSO BE IN A HURRY. HE IS CONTAGIOUS. IF HE'S IN A HURRY SO AM I. I SO LOVE HIM, AND HE HAS SAID MANY TIMES THAT HE SO LOVES THE WHOLE WORLD AND THAT INCLUDES ME. YOU MAY THINK THAT HE IS RUDE TO PUSH OR GET THINGS MOVING, NOW. WELL, HE KNOWS WHAT HE WANTS AND HE IS LETTING ME KNOW, TOO. I REALLY WANT WHAT HE WANTS, AND HE, I KNOW, IS IN CHARGE. I LOVE HIM SO, I ALREADY SAID THAT, HUH. I LIKE TO TELL THE WHOLE WORLD OF HIS LOVE AND MY LOVE FOR HIM. HE IS THE TRUE AUTHOR OF LOVE. HE IS A COMFORT TO MY WELL BEING AND HOW COULD I EVER IGNORE HIS CALLS OR COMMANDS. I AM HERE TO LIVE FOR HIM, WHAT A PLEASURE, WHAT A TREASURE. YOU KNOW I AM RIGHT. I COULD NEVER DO ANY PART OF A DAY WITHOUT HIM. WE ARE TALKING

ABOUT THE IMPOSSIBLE, UN'DOABLE, UNWISE, ERROR. YOU PROBABLE HAVE SEEN OR READ MY WRITE "NOT GOD FIRST, GOD ONLY. HE WILL BE ONLY OR HE WON'T BE ANY". HIM ONLY. I RECOMMEND YOU KEEP HIM ONLY AS HE IS THE ONLY GOD. THE THREE IN ONE. GOD THE FATHER, GOD THE SON AND GOD THE HOLY GHOST. THE ONLY THREE IN THE ONLY ONE. JESUS WAS SENT BY THE GOD AND FATHER OF THE TRINITY. YOU MAY HAVE READ THE BOOKS I WROTE A FEW YEARS AGO. I AM THE FOURTH MEMBER OF THE TRINITY, THE ONE NECESSARY TO BRING THE SON OF GOD TO THE EARTH. GOD MADE THAT POSSIBLE MORE THAN TWO THOUSAND YEARS AGO. I AM OF AND IN HIS NEED TO SAVE HIS CREATION OF THIRTEEN THOUSAND YEARS AGO. HIS CREATED MAN WAS MOVING VERY QUICKLY TOWARD IDLE WORSHIP AND LOSING HIS/THE RELATIONSHIP WITH THE CREATOR AND FATHER OF ALL CREATION. IT WAS URGENT WHEN GOD CALLED AND THERE WAS NO ANSWER. THE IDLES HAD TAKEN THE PLACE OF THEIR CREATOR AND HE (GOD) COULD'NT ALLOW THAT. HIS MAN WAS HIS GREATEST TRIUMPH AND HE WAS SO PLEASED WITH HIS GENIUS. "ONLY GOD" AND AGAIN I SAY "ONLY GOD". I AM SO PLEASED TO WORK WITH HIM AND FOR HIM. I JUST LOVE HIS "WIT AND WONDER". LOOK AGAIN, HE CREATED EVERYTHING CREATED. FROM THE TINYEST BUG TO THE GIANTS OF THE FIRST CREATION. WHEN SATAN FELL, HE (SATAN) LOST HIS PLACE IN HEAVEN AND WAS CAST DOWN TO EARTH, WHERE HE, IN HIS ANGER WAS KICKING THE DIRT SO HARDILY SO AS TO BLOCK OUT THE LIGHT OF THE SUN AND ALL CREATURES AND PLANT LIFE DIED. THE DINOSAURS WERE OF THE FIRST CREATION. GOD WENT INTO THE DEEP TO MOURN HIS LOSS OF HIS MOST BEAUTIFUL CREATION, THE EARTH AND HIS BEAUTIFUL LUCIFER. ALL OF THE EARTH WAS WITHOUT FORM AND VOID, AND DARKNESS WAS ON THE FACE OF THE DEEP. GEN 1:2. WELL, HERE WE ARE, IT'S BECOME A REAL PAGE TURNER. AFTER ALL THE WATER IS UNDER THE

BRIDGE, WE ARE VERY POSSIBLY ON THE WAY OUT OR ALL WHO ARE GOD'S, BORN AGAIN LOOKING FORWORD TO THE RAPTURE. I AM ONE OF THE SAVED, WHO IS LOOKING UP. ANXIOUS FOR THE TRIP TO THE GOLDEN SHORES. OH, WHAT A DAY OF REJOICING THAT WILL BE. THE CHURCH SAYS MANY, MAYBE MILLIONS WILL BE LIFTED OFF THE EARTH. HMMM I DON'T THINK SO. THE BIBLE REFERS TO "AS THE DAYS OF NOE", THERE WERE ONLY EIGHT SAVED. THERE MAY NOT BE MANY. SEE MATT 24:36-39. YOU WOULD DO WELL TO READ FOR YOURSELF. HE (JESUS) IS THE MOST GLORIOUS OF ALL HUMANITY, GOD'S PRIDE AND JOY, HIS LORD JESUS CHRIST, MY SON AND SAVIOR, JESUS, MY TREASURE. OH, THAT ALL WOULD KNOW AND TREASURE MY BEAUTIFUL SON. AMEN

HE IS WORTHY OF ALL THAT IS WRITTEN OF HIM FROM
GENISUS TO REVELATION. AMEN
SO BELOVED OF ALL WHO KNOW HIM. HE IS TRULY THE
FAVOR OF GOD FOR ETERNITY.
I AM SO BLESSED BY MY ASSIGNMENT, TO HAVE CARRIED HIM
INTO THE WORLD. AMEN.

HOW LONG O LORD?

WE, IT SEEMS, HAVE BEEN WAITING FOR SO LONG FOR THE RETURN OF OUR SAVIOR. MOST ARE GETTING SO IMPATIENT. ME TOO. I GUESS BECAUSE THE WORLD IS SO MESSED UP. SO MANY HIDEOUS GOINGS ON OUT THERE. WE ARE SO FED UP WITH ALL THE WARS, AND SO MANY PEOPLE DYING, NEEDLESSLY. THE HORROR OF THE INSANE DOING STUFF THAT JUST BAFFLES THE MIND. YES, I HAVE ASKED MANY TIMES "HOW LONG O LORD? HE, SOMETIMES WILL ANSWER. BE PATIENT. I WILL COME AT THE APPROPRIATE TIME. MY OWN HAVE ASKED OF ME FOR MANY YEARS, WANTING TO KNOW WITH DESPERATION THE DAY OF THE LORD. THE DAY WE WILL HEAR THE TRUMPET AND HE WILL DESCEND FROM HEAVEN TO GATHER HIS OWN. I AM SOMETIMES IN WONDER, ASKING "WHY SO LONG O' LORD"? CHILDREN BEING KILLED BY ABORTION, CHILDREN AS VICTIMS OF STREET KILLINGS. IT'S AN UNTHINKABLE CRIME. I DO KNOW THEY ARE INNOCENT AND WILL IMMEDIATELY WITH THE FATHER IN HEAVEN. THEY DO NOT HAVE UNDERSTANDING YET, THOUGH THEY SUFFER, OR NOT. YOU KNOW THEY ARE NOT ABLE TO GRASP THE MEANING OF SUCH HORROR. I SAY THAT THEY MUST BE SAYING "WHY ME, WHAT DID I DO"? SO INNOCENT. EVEN THE ADULTS WHO ARE KILLED BY SOME CRAZY MUST ENQUIRE 'WHY ME'? HOW DO YOU ANSWER THEIR CRIES? I KNOW THEY ARE WITH YOU IN THEIR INNOCENCE. WHEN I SEE IT OR JUST HEAR ABOUT IT, IT GIVES ME THE WILLIES. THEY MUST SO SUFFER WAITING TO GO INTO DEATH. THE ONE WHO PERFORMS THE TRAGIC EVENT MOST LIKELY KILLS HIM/HER SELF AS THEY CAN'T FACE THE AFTERMATH. IT'S THE GREAT POPULATION WHO CRIES OUT "WHAT IS GOD THINKING"? IT'S

NOT GOD, SATAN IS THE CAUSE OF THE HORROR THERE ARE SOME OF US WHO ARE SANE AND CHRISTIANS WHO ARE SOMETIMES ASKING THE SAME QUESTIONS. I LOVE THE BEEJEEBIES OUT OF MY GOD, MY MAKER, MY MOST GLORIOUS HEAVENLY FATHER. I HAVE BEEN ASKED BY SOME WHO ARE NOT OF OUR LORD JESUS CHRIST, UNSAVED, WHY DOES GOD NOT PUT AN END TO THIS HORRENDOUS STUFF? GOD KNOWS AND HE IS IN CHARGE OF ALL THE DETAILS. YOU KNOW I AM IN A PLACE WHERE I AM A CHRISTIAN AND SOME WOULD LIKE TO BEAT ME UP BECAUSE MY FATHER DOESN'T DO SOMETHING ABOUT THE STUFF THAT'S GOING ON. IT'S THE REASONING OF THE WORLD, AS IF I MUST HAVE A PART IN THE TORMENT. WHAT A FRIGHTENING SITUATION. THE WORLD JUST WANTS SOMEONE TO PICK ON OR BLAME OR BEAT'UP ON. I BELIEVE THAT'S BEEN GOING ON SINCE TIME BEGAN. HMMM. I AM HIS TOO AND I DON'T AGREE THAT THESE THINGS SHOULD HAPPEN, BUT IT'S NOT MY FAULT. I DON'T AGREE WITH THE CRAZIES OUT THERE REEKING HAVOC ON THE INNOCENT. I PRAY FOR PEACE AND MERCY ON ALL OF GOD'S OWN. I LOVE ALL OF HIS CHILDREN AND FORGIVE AS HE SAYS, WHEN I AM ABLE, SOMETIMES IT'S TOUGH. I AM TO FORGIVE AS HE HAS FORGIVEN ME, AND THAT'S A WHOLE BUNCH. I HAVEN'T KILLED ANYBODY, BUT I HAVE THOUGHT ABOUT IT. I WOULD HOPE THAT I COULDN'T DO SUCH A THING. THE REAL CHURCH IS AT THE FEET OF JESUS, AND DON'T FORGET IT. IT IS THE REMINDER OF THE PRICE HE PAID FOR MY AND YOUR REDMPTION AND SALVATION. HE WENT TO AN AWFUL DEATH ON THAT CROSS FOR ME, FOR THE WHOLE WORLD. THOUGH THE WHOLE WORLD DOESN'T FESS UP TO THE SACRIFICE OFFERED ON CALVERY, DOESN'T CHANGE WHAT HE DID. IT WILL FOREVER STAND AS THE MOST WONDERFUL THING DONE FOR MANKIND. IT WAS/IS THE MOST GENEROUS ACT OF GOD'S GRACE AND FORGIVENESS. HOW CAN WE NOT GET UP EVERY DAY AND BE REMINDED OF THE DEED AND THANK HIM

FOR HIS GOODNESS. DEAREST GOD, SHOW THE MERCY THAT WAS SHONE TWO THOUSAND YEARS AGO. HE FAVORED ALL OF THE BELIEVERS WHILE JESUS HUNG ON THE CROSS PAYING MY DEBT. WHEN THE PAYMENT WAS FINISHED HE, JESUS, SAID "IT IS FINISHED". PAID IN FULL. GLORY TO GOD. YES AND AMEN. JESUS PAID IT ALL, THANK YOU MY PRECIOUS SAVER. NOW THE BEST IS YET TO COME AND I AM SO THRILLED THAT AT LAST WE WILL SEE OUR SAVIOR FACE TO FACE. O' WHAT A DAY OF REJOICING THAT WILL BE. O' HALLELUJAH, LETS ALL BOW AND BLESSS THE KING OF KINGS AND LORD OF LORDS. WE WILL ALL WORSHIP, WE WILL SHOUT HALLELUJAH, WITHOUT END, FOREVER. GOD HAS A PLAN AND WON'T CHANGE IT. AMEN

I WAS WITH GOD 18,OOO YRS AGO, AFTER CREATION. I WAS WITH GOD 13,OOO YRS AGO, DURING CREATION. I WAS WITH GOD 6,OOO YRS AGO, AFTER SECOND CREATION. 2,OOO YRS AGO I GAVE BIRTH TO HIS SON. I HAVE BEEN IN AND OUT OF THIS WORLD MANY TIMES IN THE LAST 6,OOO YRS.

GOD'S THINKING, GOD'S THOUGHTS

WHAT DOES GOD THINK ABOUT ALL DAY, ALL YEAR? PROBABLY YOU. YOU ARE ALWAYS ON HIS MIND. THERE ISN'T A DAY GOES BY THAT HE NEGLECTS YOU. YOU ARE SO IMPORTANT TO HIM. YOU ARE HIS PRIORITY. IF YOU HAVE A NEED JUST CALL OUT TO HIM, HE WILL SEE TO IT THAT YOU ARE SUPPLIED. HE LOVES IT WHEN ONE OF HIS LITTLE ONES CALLS OUT TO HIM, HE SO LOVES TO HEAR FROM ALL OF US EVEN IN THE MIDDLE OF THE NIGHT. YOU KNOW, HE NEVER SLUMBERS OR SLEEPS, SO HE IS ALWAYS AVAILABLE. YOU PROBABLY ALREADY KNEW THAT SO DON'T FUSS OVER ANYTHING. HAVE YOU EVER THOUGHT THAT SOMETHING WAS WRONG SO HE DIDN'T OK IT. DON'T GIVE UP, IT MAY BE JUST POSTPONED. SO BE PATIENT. WE REALLY DON'T KNOW HIS THOUGHTS AND MOSTLY HE DOESN'T WANT TO SHARE WITH US. WE ALL HAVE SECRETS. HE HAS SECRETS THAT WE WILL NEVER UNDERSTAND. YOU MAY SAY "A PENNY FOR YOUR THOUGHTS" BUT THE PENNY WILL NEVER COVER THE DEEP THOUGHTS OF GOD. ALTHOUGH HE WOULD LOVE TO SHARE WHEN YOU WANT TO HEAR HIS THOUGHTS ABOUT HIS SON. HE DOESN'T HAVE ANY MEAN THINKING REGARDING HIS OWN. YOU KNOW WE ARE SO ANXIOUS TO KNOW WHEN THE RAPTURE WILL COME. I THINK I MAY HAVE ASKED HIM A THOUSAND TIMES THIS WEEK WHEN O LORD WHEN? HE LOOKS FORWARD TO THE RAPTURE TOO, HOWEVER, HE HAS MADE A PLAN TO DO IT BUT IT'S HIS SECRET. ALL OF OUR JUMPING UP AND DOWN AND BEGGING REALLY DOESN'T MOVE HIM. HIS PLANS ARE BIGGER THAN MY PLANS AND HE RULES. WE GET SO OVER- WROUGHT AND OUT OF BREATH. HE SAYS SIMMER DOWN BEFORE YOU EXPLODE. HIS MIND IS MADE

UP AND HE PROBABLY WON'T CHANGE HIS THINKING. ISN'T HE WONDERFUL. HE WILL NOT BE MOVED AS HE HAS OTHER REASONS FOR HIS DOINGS. I KNOW, GO INTO YOUR CLOSET AND PRAY ABOUT IT. I'M SO SURE HE WILL TELL YOU WHEN HIS PLANS ARE ACCORDING TO WHAT YOU THINK. NOT! PRAY THAT HE WILL SEND A NEW LOAD OF PATIENCE AND PEACE. I SO LOVE TO WRITE FOR HIM. HE IS SUCH A INTERESTING THINKER AND WE CAN'T FIGURE OUT HIS WAYS, TRY AS YOU MAY, YOU CAN'T. THAT'S THE PLAN, HIS SECRET PLAN. GIVE IT UP YOU WON'T COME OUT ON TOP. IF YOU COME DOWN WITH AN ALMOST EMPTY HEADACHE, HE WILL WANT TO HEAL THE POOR LITTLE EXHAUSTED THINKER, AND HE WILL. I AM SURE HE IS ENTERTAINED BY YOUR BUSY LITTLE THINKER. YOU JUST CAN NOT OUT THINK HIM. HE IS THE CHIEF THINKER OF THE UNIVERSE, AND HAS BEEN AT IT FOR EONS OF TIME. YOU WILL BE AMAZED AT WHAT HE CAN DO WITHOUT YOU. WE ARE SO DETERMINDED TO WANT TO HELP OUT WITH GOD'S BUSINESS. GOD, I SO WANT TO HELP YOU CARRY THE LOAD. HE WILL SMILE AT YOUR GOODNESS. DO YOU KNOW HE SO APPRECIATES THE WILLINGNESS OF YOUR OFFER. HIS THOUGHTS ARE OUR UNTHINKABLE, WE JUST CAN'T THINK THAT HIGH. WE ARE NEW AT IT, WE ONLY HAVE JUST BEGUN IN THE LAST EIGHTEEN THOUSAND YEARS. HE'S BEEN AT IT FOR ETERNITY, HIS THOUGHTS ARE INFINITE. TRY TO WRAP YOUR BRAIN AROUND THAT. DON'T YOU JUST LOVE HIM, ME TOO. WHAT DO YOU THINK? YOU WILL NEVER FIND THE SPACE IN YOUR TINY BRAIN TO EVEN KNOW HOW TO ASK FOR HIS THOUGHTS. HE MAY WANT TO COMMUNICATE WITH YOU BUT THE STUFF COMING OUT OF HIS WITT AND WONDER WOULD BREAK YOUR SMARTS. WHEN ALL IS SAID AND DONE, HE MAY RELEASE SOME WISDOM FOR YOU TO SERMISE, WOULD THAT JUST MAKE YOU COME UNDONE? IF YOU KNEW WHAT HE KNOWS, WOULD THAT MAKE YOU GOD? NO, BUT IT MIGHT GIVE YOU A HEADACHE OR YOU MAY HAVE THE URGE

TO GO JUMP OFF YOUR BED. DON'T DO THAT, YOU MAY JUST BREAK A LEG OR AN ARM. OWEY. HE WILL CAUTION YOU TO SLOW DOWN BEFORE YOUR COMPUTER GOES BELLY-UP. HE WILL BE ABLE TO FIX IT BUT IT MAY COST A FORTUNE. YOUR BRAIN MAY BE A TRAIN-WRECK. DO YOU KNOW YOU CAN'T GET REPLACEMENT PARTS? YOU WOULD HAVE TO PRAY FOR A HEALING. I AM SURE HE WOULD DO IT. HE SO LOVES YOU. TRY IT. TELL ME HOW THAT WORKS OUT FOR YOU. MY WRITES ARE AN EXTENTION OF SCRIPTURES. HE GIVES ME ALL TO PUT ON THE PAGE, HE IS SO GENEROUS. MY WRITES.TOMORROW IS THE DAY OF REJOICING WHEN HE FINISHES. GOD IS MOST REVERENCED IN ME WHEN I AM MOST HOLY IN HIM. BE HOLY, ONLY IN HIM.

KING OF KINGS, LORD OF LORDS. THE ONE GOD SENT. OUR SALVATION. HE LOVES YOU NOT BECAUSE OF WHO YOU ARE BUT BECAUSE OF WHO HE IS.

LIGHT OUT OF DARKNESS

GENESIS 1:3-4

AND GOD SAID, LET THERE BE LIGHT: AND THERE WAS LIGHT. AND GOD SAW THE LIGHT, THAT IT WAS GOOD: AND GOD DIVIDED THE LIGHT FROM THE DARKNESS. O' THANK YOU, GOD, NO MORE DARKNESS FOR THE ONES WHO COME AFTER THE LIGHT. JESUS, IS THE LIGHT OF THE WORLD. SEEK HIM WHILE YOU MAY. WE READ THE SCRIPTURES AND HEAR HOW MARVELOUS OUR BEGINNING WAS AND WONDER IF WE WILL EVER SEE SUCH A THING AGAIN. THE BEGINNING OF GENESIS SAYS THE EARTH WAS WITHOUT FORM AND VOID. DARKNESS WAS ON THE FACE OF THE DEEP. THE SPIRIT OF GOD HOVERED UPON THE FACE OF THE WATERS. GOD CALLED THE LIGHT DAY AND THE DARKNESS NIGHT. THE EVENING AND THE MORNING WERE THE FIRST DAY. HE SAID AN EXPANSE WAS IN THE MIDST OF THE WATERS, AND IT DIVIDED THE WATERS FROM THE WATERS. GOD MADE THE FIRMAMENT, AND DIVIDED THE WATERS WHICH WERE UNDER THE FIRMAMENT FROM THE WATERS WHICH WERE ABOVE THE FIRMAMENT AND IT WAS SO. THE WATERS ABOVE US ARE THE WATERS BELOW US. HE CALLED THE FIRMAMENT HEAVEN. AND THE EVENING AND THE MORNING WERE THE SECOND DAY. AND SO BEGAN THE MARATHON OF CREATION. GOD MADE TWO GREAT LIGHTS, THE LIGHTS OF THE HEAVENS. THE GREATER LIGHT TO RULE THE DAY AND THE LESSER LIGHT TO RULE THE NIGHT. YOU MAY HAVE READ ON THE FOURTH DAY HE MADE THE STARS ALSO. I AM MY FATHERS LITTLE STAR, BORN ON THE FOURTH DAY. FOUR IS VERY IMPORTANT TO ME, YOU WILL SEE WHY. THAT IS THE DAY I RECEIVED MY CREATED NAME, MEZZECHAH. WE ALL HAVE A CREATED NAME. ON THE SIXTH DAY WHEN GOD WAS

CREATING HIS MAN, HE HAD AN ANGEL WRITE OUR CREATED NAMES IN THE LAMB'S BOOK OF LIFE. REVELATION DECLARES THAT IF YOU DO NOT RECEIVE JESUS, (AS YOUR LORD AND SAVIOR), YOUR NAME WILL BE BLOTTED OUT OF THE LAMB'S BOOK OF LIFE. YOU MUST BE SAVED, BORN'AGAIN. GIVE HIM YOUR LIFE, BECOME A LIGHT OUT OF DARKNESS. BE BORN AGAIN, LET YOUR LIGHT SHINE, "SHINE" NOW, GET OUT THERE AND TELL ALL THE WHOSOEVER WILL TO COME INTO THE LIGHT. GIVE YOUR LIFE TO JESUS. WALK WITH HIM AND SEE WHAT A TURN'AROUND WILL DEVELOPE. YOUR SALVATION AND REDEMPTION IS PROVEN WHEN YOU BEGIN TO SHARE HIM WITH ALL YOU COME IN CONTACT WITH. YOU DON'T' HAVE TO HAVE A PULPIT TO GET THE WORD OUT. JUST A FEW ENCOURAGING WORDS MAY TURN SOMEONE TO JESUS. IF THEY WILL ALLOW, PRAY A SHORT PRAYER WITH THEM, WE ALL NEED PRAYER. IF YOU HAVE UNSAVED FAMILY, THROW A PARTY AND LET JESUS BE THE GUEST OF HONOR. HE LOVES PARTIES, MAKE IT A SHORT PARTY BUT ASK AFEW TO STAY AND HELP WITH CLEAN UP, MAYBE THE UNSAVED. IT'S AN OPPORTUNITY FOR ONE-ON-ONE TALK. WHEN THEY ACCEPT JESUS IT WILL BE A JOYOUS END OF EVENING. BE SURE TO DO A FOLLOW'UP, AS THEY WILL WANT TO TALK ABOUT JESUS. I AM SAVED BUT I NEVER TIRE OF TALKING ABOUT HIM. HE IS, BTW, THE LIGHT OF MY LIFE. O'YES. UNLESS WE ARE BORN INTO A GOOD CHRISTIAN FAMILY, YOU WILL HAVE A GREAT TESTIMONY TO SHARE WITH THE WHOSOEVERS. W.O.W WONDERFUL O' WONDERFUL. HE BRINGS LIFE TO/WITH ALL WHO KNOW HIM. I AM OF AN AGE WHERE I MAY HAVE BEEN SEEN WITH JESUS, YES, LAUGH. IT'S POSSIBLE. WHEN I WAS MAYBE TWELVE YEARS OLD, I DID HEAR FROM HEAVEN VIA THE HOLY GHOST. HE STOOD ME STILL IN THE DINING ROOM OF OUR HOME IN PIPESTONE, MN. HE TOLD ME MY NUMBER IS FOUR, THE FOURTH MEMBER OF THE TRINITY. IF THAT BOTHERS YOU, GET OVER IT, IT'S MY STORY. I AM THE CHOSEN

MOTHER OF THE LORD JESUS CHRIST. I WAS TOLD THAT VIA THE LORD JESUS CHRIST. I DIDN'T TELL ANYONE, BUT I DID BELIEVE IT TO BE THE TRUTH. I DID TALK TO THOSE WHO WERE WELL INTO BEING BORN'AGAIN, CLASS MATES WHO WERE CHRISTIANS. IT WAS SO GOOD TO HAVE THEM TO TALK TO. I DIDN'T SHARE THE WHOLE STORY BUT THEY WERE EASY TO GET TO AT LEAST DURING BREAKS. OTHER THAN THAT, THEY WERE MOSTLY CATHOLIC AND I DIDN'T KNOW MUCH ABOUT WHAT THEY BELIEVED. I WOULD LIKE TO GO BACK AND HAVE A TALKATHON WITH THEM NOW. I THINK MOST ARE GONE. MY SISTER WOULD BE A GOOD ONE TO ENGAGE IN A BIBLICAL CHAT. SHE WAS CLOSE TO ME AGE WISE, BUT SHE LEFT AFEW YEARS AGO. I HAVE A MUCH YOUNGER SISTER, SHE IS WONDERFUL. SHE IS A STRONG BELIEVER. BLESS HER HEART. AMEN, AMEN

DEEP CALLETH UNTO DEEP. MY PROPHECY. I GIVE HIM ALL THE GLORY.
THE REAL CHURCH IS AT THE FEET OF JESUS. DEDICATE TO ME YOUR BEAUTY........

THE LIGHT, THE LORD, THE LOVE OF MY LIFE

MY DARLING, MY BELOVED, MY GOD. IN HIM IS ALL I NEED. DEEP CALLETH
UNTO DEEP. PSALM 42:7

THESE ARE THE ASSETS OF FOLLOWING OUR LORD AND
SAVIOR, JESUS THE CHRIST, OUR MESSIAH. YOU MUST GET ON
BOARD WITH JESUS. HE IS THE MOST VALUABLE THING TO
EVER HAPPEN IN YOURS AND MY LIFE. IT WILL BE ETERNAL
LIFE, YOU WILL WANT TO BE BORN'AGAIN. GET A WONDERFUL
BIBLE AND STUDY IT WITH ALL YOUR MIGHT. POUR OUT YOUR
HEART TO HIM, STUDY WHENEVER YOU HAVE A CHANCE. SET
ASIDE TIME FOR JUST STUDYING THE WORD OF GOD. TIME
WELL SPENT. HE SO WANTS TO SPEND TIME WITH YOU. SOME
CALL IT THE QUIET TIME, SOUNDS GOOD. YOU AND JESUS SO
CLOSE. HE WILL BE THE GLORIOUS TEACHER TO SHOW YOU
THE BIBLE. HE WILL SEE TO IT YOU HEAR ALL ABOUT HIS
WONDERFUL SALVATION. THE OFFER OF PEACE AND
TRANQUILITY. HE IS A LIFE CHANGER, FOR THE GOOD, THE
BAD AND THE UGLY. WHEN THE STUDY TIME IS OVER THERE
WILL BE STILLNESS IN YOUR HEART. THAT'S HOW IT'S
SUPPOSED TO BE. YOU MAY WANT TO JUST SIT AND PONDER
THE LESSON. MAYBE KNEEL OR BOW TO TALK TO HIM IN
PRAYER. YOU MAY BREAK INTO SONG TO PRAISE HIM WITH
YOUR BEAUTIFUL VOICE. SING YOUR OWN SONG, YOU CAN
MAKE IT UP AS YOU GO ALONG. HE LOVES THE ORIGINALITY.
TELL HIM THAT IT'S FOR JUST YOU AND HIM, IT'S YOUR SONG,
JESUS AND YOU. DOESN'T THAT SOUND GLORIOUS. O' YOU
BETTER BELIEVE IT. SING IT OUT, SOME MAY GIVE YOU A
STARE, BECAUSE IT'S SO WONDERFUL. THAT'S FOR SURE.
DON'T YOU LOVE THE TITLE, THE FOUR L'S. IS HE FUN OR
WHAT? O'HE IS AND SO BEAUTIFUL. WHO IS MORE

WONDERFUL THAN OUR JESUS? HE IS THE BEST IN EVERYTHING I LOVE TO DO OR SAY. HE IS SO WORTHY IN EVERY INSTANCE AND DOING OF MY LIFE. HE MAKES LIFE SO WORTH LIVING JUST BECAUSE HE LIVES. I AM SO HAPPY TO COMMUNE WITH HIM. HE MAKES ALL WHO COME TO BE COMFORTABLE, TO JUST LOOK INTO HIS FACE, SO PRECIOUS. THIS IS WHAT WE ALL HAVE TO LOOK FORWARD TO. HIS TENDER VOICE IS SO INTRIGUING. HE IS SUCH A HOLY WONDER. HOW DO PEOPLE GET ALONG WITHOUT HIM? I WANT TO HOLD HIS HAND WHILE WE WALK AND TALK. IMAGINE WALKING WITH JESUS AND LISTENING TO HIM EXPOUND ON THE SCRIPTURES. THAT SOUNDS TO ME LIKE HEAVEN, O' YES, IT IS HEAVEN. I REALLY DO LOOK FORWARD TO HEAVEN TWENTY-FOUR + SEVEN, IT WON'T BE BORING, JESUS ISN'T BORING. WE WILL HAVE QUESTIONS AND FOR SURE, HE WILL HAVE ALL THE ANSWERS. JESUS KNOWS EVERYTHING, HE MADE IT ALL AND HE KNOWS ALL ABOUT EVERYTHING. MY PLEA IS THAT THINGS HURRY'UP. I WANT TO BE WITH MY JESUS AND HE WANTS TO BE WITH ME. I DO NOT BOAST OF ANYTHING. O' I DO BOAST THAT I KNOW HIM. WHAT A BLESSING. IS THAT THE MOST GOOD (GOD) FORTUNE OF ANYTHING YOU CAN IMAGINE, JUST TO KNOW HIM, JUST TO BE WITH HIM AND WALK WITH HIM. HE SO LOOKS FORWARD TO ALL OF THE ONES WHO CHOSE TO FOLLOW HIM AND SPEND ETERNITY WITH HIM. WOW, WHAT A DAY OF REJOICING THAT WILL BE. I HAVE LOOKED FORWARD TO THIS PLACE IN TIME SINCE I FOUND OUT ABOUT JESUS AND HEAVEN, AND WE ARE (I AM) GOING TO LIVE IT, FOREVER. WHAT A SHAME THAT NOT ALL BELIEVE AND LOOK AT THE BELIEVERS AS THOUGH WE ARE FOOLISH. IT BREAKS MY HEART, BUT WE HAVE TO LET THE DOUBTERS GO. WE WON'T SEE THEM AFTER THE RAPTURE AND I DON'T THINK WE WILL REMEMBER THEM EITHER. THERE IS NO SADNESS IN HEAVEN SO WE WILL NOT KNOW OF

THEM. WE MUST GET AFTER THE FAMILY, MOM, DAD, BROTHERS AND SISTERS. COME TO JESUS, HURRY. AMEN

ALL GLORY AND HONOR TO OUR LORD AND SAVIOR, GOD'S SACRIFICE. MY DADDY IS SO GOD, GOD GAVE HIS BEST. INDEED, THE LORD JESUS CHRIST IMPRINT ON ME YOUR LOVE. BLESS ME TO MY KNEES. I BOW TO HIM, WORSHIP

WHAT GARDEN, WHOSE GARDEN

THERE IS A GARDEN MENTIONED IN SCRIPTURE, GARDEN OF GETHSEMANE. THE GARDEN WHERE JESUS WENT TO PRAY WHEN HE WAS ON HIS WAY TO THE CROSS. HE DID TAKE THREE (PETER, JAMES AND JOHN) OF HIS DISCIPLES WITH HIM AND INSTRUCTED THAT THEY WATCH WHILE HE WENT TO PRAY. HE DID ASK THEM TO WATCH, BUT THEN THEY FELL ASLEEP. HE CAME TO THEM AND FOUND THEM SLEEPING. HE DID ASK PETER, COULD YOU NOT WATCH WITH ME FOR ONE HOUR? HE WENT AWAY AGAIN TO PRAY, SAYING TO HIS FATHER, "O FATHER, IF THIS CUP MAY NOT PASS AWAY FROM ME, EXCEPT I DRINK IT, THY WILL BE DONE". WHEN HE CAME AGAIN TO THE DISCIPLES, THEY WERE ASLEEP, AGAIN. HE WENT AWAY A THIRD TIME SAYING THE SAME WORDS. WHEN HE CAME BACK, THEY WERE ASLEEP AND HE SAID "SLEEP ON NOW, AND TAKE YOUR REST: BEHOLD, THE HOUR IS IS AT HAND, THE SON OF MAN IS BETRAYED INTO THE HANDS OF SINNERS. RISE, LET US BE GOING: BEHOLD, HE IS AT HAND THAT DOTH BETRAY ME". WHILE HE WAS SPEAKING, JUDAS, ONE OF HIS DISCIPLES CAME WITH A GREAT MULTITUDE HAVING WEAPONS, FROM THE CHIEF PRIESTS AND THE ELDERS OF THE PEOPLE. JUDAS DID BETRAY WITH A SIGN SAYING, HIM WHOSOEVER I SHALL KISS THAT SAME IS HE: HOLD HIM FAST. AND FORTHWITH HE CAME TO JESUS, AND SAID, "HAIL, MASTER" AND KISSED HIM. JESUS DID ASK "WHOM DO YOU SEEK"? THEY ANSWERED HIM, JESUS OF NAZARETH AND WHEN HE ANSWERED THEM "I AM HE" THEY ALL FELL TO THE GROUND. HE TOLD THEM I AM HE, SO LET THESE MEN GO. JESUS WAS BETRAYED WITH A KISS. JESUS DID ASK JUDAS, "FRIEND, WHEREFORE ART THOU COME"? THEY CAME AND

LAID HANDS-ON JESUS, AND TOOK HIM. WE KNOW THAT PETER, ONE OF JESUS' DISCIPLES, DID TAKE A SWORD FROM ONE OF THE SERVENTS OF THE HIGH PRIEST AND CUT OFF THE SERVANTS EAR. JESUS DID REBUKE PETER FOR HIS DOING, THAT IF YOU LIVE BY THE SWORD YOU MAY DIE BY THE SWORD. THEY DID TAKE JESUS AWAY, THEY HAD THE ONE THEY WANTED. ALL THE DISCIPLES RAN AWAY, DIDN'T WANT TO WATCH THE TRIAL OF THEIR LEADER, LEST THEY SUFFER THE SAME PUNISHMENT COMING TO JESUS. DOES IT MAKE YOU WONDER IF YOU WOULD RUN AWAY, TOO? HMMM THAT'S A HARD ONE TO THINK ON. I WOULD HOPE TO THINK I WOULDN'T, BUT I BELIEVE YOU WOULD HAVE TO BE THERE. SOME SAY THE GARDEN OF GETHSEMANE IS THE SAME AS IT WAS TWO THOUSAND YEARS AGO. I DON'T THINK IT IS, BUT WE WON'T DEBATE THAT NOW. JESUS WAS PUT ON TRIAL AFTER THE GARDEN INCIDENT. IT WAS SO HORRIBLE, BUT THAT WAS THE WAY IT WAS TO BE AS IT WAS TOLD IN THE O T. ALL THAT HAPPENED TO OUR JESUS WAS PROPHESIED, PSALM 41:9. WE DO SEE THE THINGS IN OUR SCRIPTURE, NEW TESTAMENT PREDICTED IN THE OLD TESTAMENT. WHENEVER YOU SIT DOWN TO READ THE SCRIPTURE, YOU WILL REMEMBER, O' YES, SEEING THAT SOMEWHERE ELSE. I SO LOVE TO READ THE BOOK. EVEN THE BOOKS IN THE O T THAT HAVE NAMES WE CAN'T EVEN PRONOUNCE ARE SO GOOD TO READ. THE GARDEN IN THE BEGINNING, GARDEN OF EDEN, IS RIGHT UP THERE WITH GARDEN OF GETHSEMANE. BOTH VERY IMPORTANT TO THE SCRIPTURE. BTW, HAVE YOU EVER WONDERED WHERE HIS EARTH FATHER WAS WHEN THIS WAS HAPPENING TO MY JESUS? HE IS NOT MENTIONED IN THE THE SCRIPTURES AFTER THE BIRTH OF JESUS. HE MAY HAVE DIED AND JESUS TOOK CARE OF HIS WIDOWED MOTHER AND THE YOUNGER CHILDREN. I WAS RIGHT THERE WHEN THEY NAILED HIM TO THE CROSS. MY HEART WAS BROKEN, EVEN THOUGH I KNEW HE WOULD RISE AGAIN, BUT WHERE WAS

HIS FATHER. EVEN AFTER THE CRUCIFIXION HE IS NOT MENTIONED. I HOPE SOMEDAY YOU WILL COME SEE MY GARDEN. MY GARDEN IS IN MY FRONT YARD, EVERYWHERE. I AM THE MOTHER OF THOUSANDS. I HAVE A CERTAIN PLANT CALLED, MOTHER OF THOUSANDS, AND I AM. COME AND SEE. IT'S FASCINATING. EVERY ASSIGNMENT GIVEN TO ME FROM THE TIMES OF THE OT TILL THE BIRTH OF JESUS WAS FOR MY PROVING. GOD HAD TO TEST WHETHER I WOULD BE THE RIGHT ONE TO MOTHER HIS SON? I WAS, I AM. 'GLORY TO GOD'. JESUS WAS MY ASSIGNMENT AND MY PLEASURE, AND STILL IS. WHATEVER WOULD I DO W/O MY JESUS? I WILL NEVER KNOW, HE IS MINE. NOW.

DEDICATE TO ME YOUR BEAUTY, SWEET HOLY GHOST. SO BE IT. DEEP CALLETH UNTO DEEP, AMONEE TRIESS.
HIS LOVE IS ETERNAL, HIS LOVE HAS NO EXPIRATION DATE.
HIS LOVE IS FROM EVERLASTING TO EVERLASTING. HE COVERS US ALL.

DID YOU HEAR THAT?

1 THESSALONIANS 4: 16-18

DID YOU HEAR THAT? DID I IMAGINE WHAT I HEARD. I THOUGHT I HEARD A TRUMPET SOUND. I HAVE BEEN WAITING FOR THAT FOR A VERY LONG TIME. IT'S THE SOUND OF THE TRUMPET WAILING AS MY LORD JESUS CHRIST RETURNS TO THE EARTH TO CLAIM HIS OWN, ALL WHO ARE READY TO GO WITH HIM TO OUR NEW HOME. THE FORMAL WORD IS THE RAPTURE. IT'S BIBLICAL. HAVE YOU READ ABOUT IT? WELL, HAVE YOU? I HAVE BEEN LOOKING FORWARD TO THIS SINCE I WAS IN SUNDAY SCHOOL. O' I BELIEVE I HEARD THE TRUMPET SOUND AS TOLD IN THE SCRIPTURES. HE SHOULD BE HERE ANY SECOND NOW. SURE IS PEACEFUL. DID HE COME FOR ONLY A FEW? I AM SO SURE HE IS COMING FOR ME. MAYBE IT WASN'T THE CALL I THOUGHT IT WAS. I AM SO SURE I AM GONNA GO WITH HIM WHEN HE COMES. I GUESS I MUST BE HEARING THINGS WRONG. MAYBE I AM A LITTLE OVER ANXIOUS. SOMEBODY COULD BE MESSING WITH ME TOO. I AM READY AND HE IS STILL ON HIS WAY. O" HALLELUJAH, I DIDN'T MISS THE CALL. IF I HEAR IT AGAIN, I WILL BE SURE TO PAY BETTER ATTENTION. THERE ARE SO MANY FALSE ALARMS GOING ON/OFF. I BELIEVE VERY STRONGLY THAT I WILL GO WITH HIM WHEN THE TIME IS RIGHT. I DON'T BELIEVE THAT THERE WILL BE MILLIONS OR BILLIONS GOING UP TO MEET HIM IN THE AIR. SOUNDS GOOD THOUGH. I PRAY THAT THERE WILL BE A GLORIOUS CLOUD OF BELIEVERS TAKEN UP. THAT'S THE WAY TO GO AFTER IT. PRAY, PRAY THAT ALL WILL BE SAVED. DO GET ON YOUR KNEES AND PRAY THAT ALL THE LOST SOULS COME TO KNOW OUR BEAUTIFUL LORD JESUS CHRIST. HE IS SO WONDERFUL, DON'T MISS THE CALL. COME SEE ME, LET ME CHANGE YOUR MIND, THAT YOU BECOME A TRUE FOLLOWER

OF THE ONLY SAVIOR WHO FATHER GOD ORDAINED TO SAVE THE WHOSOEVER WILL. YOU MUST AND JUST BELIEVE HIS WORD. THAT'S A LONG ONE TO TAKE IN. I HAVE TO TELL YOU HOW IMPORTANT IT IS TO BE FOUND SAVED WHEN HE COMES. YOU MUST DIE TO THE THINGS OF THE WORLD, THE THINGS OF SATAN, THE LIAR. BE BORN AGAIN, INTO THE KINGDOM OF THE SAVED, THE KINGDOM OF GOD. I SEEM TO REPEAT MYSELF, I DO, BUT WE MUST NOT ALLOW THE "MANY OR ANY" TO BE LEFT BEHIND. WE MAY NOT BE ABLE TO SAVE THE WHOLE WORLD BUT WE MUST GIVE IT A GOOD TROJAN TRY. THERE ARE SOME WHO THINK IT WOULD BE FUNNY AND FUN TO GET HOLD OF A TRUMPET AND DO A FEW BLASTS TO SEE THE CRAZY CHRISTIANS GATHER TO BE LIFTED OFF THE EARTH. THAT'S NOT FUNNY NOR WISE , YOU COULD GET HURT. I KNOW THAT HE IS ON HIS WAY SO DON'T MESS WITH US WHO BELIEVE. MAYBE IF YOU THINK YOU WOULD GET A KICK OUT OF A FALSE ALARM IT JUST MAY TURN OUT TO BE TRUE AND YOU MAY BE LEFT BEHIND. NOW, THAT'S A HEART'BREAKER. MAYBE WE WILL PLAN A PICNIC AND HAVE ALL THE TRUMPET PLAYERS COME FOR A CONCERT. O' SOUNDS LIKE FUN. WE WILL SEND OUR JESUS AN INVITATION. MANY WILL HAVE A FRONT ROW SEAT TO WATCH THE RAPTURE. SOUNDS LIKE A MOCKERY TO SOMETHING SO IMPORTANT AND HOLY. BETTER RETHINK THAT BAD IDEA. DON'T MESS WITH GOD, IT COULD BE FATAL. LET'S BE SERIOUS NOW, LET'S GET OUT AND SAVE SOME SOULS. GOD IS SO READY TO COME FOR THE SAVED AND THAT IS REALLY GOOD NEWS. MAKE THAT A PRIORITY, HE WILL BE SO PLEASED WITH ALL WHO SPREAD THE GOOD NEWS. IT'S SO VERY URGENT SINCE THE LORD IS SO CLOSE TO COMING, AS WE HAVE BEEN TOLD. MY BIBLE SAYS SO. THE BOOK OF TRUTH, THE BOOK OF REDEMPTION AND SALVATION. ALL MUST HAVE A BIBLE TO WARN OF THE NEED OF ANSWERING THE CALL OF GOD THROUGH THE LORD JESUS CHRIST. HE MAY BE SENDING THE LAST CALL AS WE READY

THIS WRITE. I SO LOVE TO WRITE FOR MY LORD. HE IS SO PATIENT TO DICTATE WHAT HE WANTS ON THE PAPER. I SO WANT TO DO IT WRITE/RIGHT. HE IS THE MASTER OF THE PEN AND PAPER. HE IS SO MY INSTRUCTOR. I MUST GET IT DONE IN TIME FOR THE WHOLE WORLD TO BE SAVED. I AM HERE TO PLEASE HIM. I BELIEVE HE IS GLAD HE CHOSE ME TO WORK FOR HIM AS HE IS ALSO PLEASED FOR ALL WHO PREACH THE WORD TO THE MASSES ON SUNDAY. I SO LOVE TO GO TO CHURCH, WHAT A WONDERFUL START TO THE WEEK. THEY ARE MY FAMILY, MY CHURCH FAMILY. BEAUTIFUL PEOPLE, I VALUE THEM TO BE GREATER THAN PRECIOUS JEWELS. I WOULD LOVE TO BE RAPTURED FROM THE SUNDAY SERVICE. I WILL TAKE MY DOG TO CHURCH ON THAT SPECIAL DAY. LET'S ALL GO HOME. DID I HEAR A TRUMPET???

NOT GOD FIRST, GOD ONLY. HE WILL BE ONLY OR HE WON'T BE ANY. AMEN
WE WHICH ARE ALIVE SHALL BE CAUGHT UP TO MEET THE LORD IN THE AIR. AMEN

TIMES UP, YES

THOSE ARE THE WORDS I AM WAITING TO HEAR. I BELIEVE THAT WE WILL BE CALLED TO THE RAPTURE. WE WILL LOOK UP TO SEE THE LORD IN THE CLOUDS. O'WHAT A DAY OF REJOICING THAT WILL BE. THE TIME OF THE RAPTURE. THEN WE WHICH ARE ALIVE AND REMAIN SHALL BE CAUGHT UP TOGETHER WITH THEM IN THE CLOUDS, TO MEET THE LORD IN THE AIR: AND SO SHALL WE BE WITH THE LORD. WHEREFORE COMFORT ONE AND ANOTHER WITH THESE WORDS. CAN YOU IMAGING THAT SCENARIO, WITHOUT THE WEEPIES?. IT'S GOT TO BE SOON OR I MAY MELT. I SO WANT TO HEAR THE WORD'S "TIMES UP". YES, I DO. WE HAVE TO GET OUT THERE AND EVANGELIZE THE POPULATION SO WE CAN GET CLOSER TO THE DAY OF THE LORD. I WANT TO TO IT THAT ALL MY BILLS ARE PAID AND THERE ARE NO RUFFLED FEATHERS IN THE HOUSE OR THE NEIGHBOR HOOD. THERE MUST NOT BE ANY REASON FOR A RAPTURE REVERSE. WE HAVE KNOWN ABOUT THE END TIME FOR A WHILE NOW SO WE DON'T WANT ANY SETBACKS. GET YOUR SHOWER OUT OF THE WAY, BRUSH YOUR TEETH AND EMPTY THE TRASH. WHEN HE COMES O'PLEASE BE READY. I KNOW THAT THOSE THINGS DON'T MATTER BUT JUST DO IT. WHEN THE TRUMPET SOUNDS WE MUST BE IN MOTION. LET'S BE CAREFUL THAT WE ARE KIND AND IN ORDER WITH ALL THE SAVED. NO MESSING WITH THE WAYTHE LINE IS FORMED. WE ALL ARE IMPORTANT TO OUR SAVIOR. SO BE NICE. I SO WANT THE TRANSITION TO GO SMOOTHLY. WHEN WE SEE HIS BEAUTIFUL FACE THERE WILL BE PERFECT SILENCE. JUST TO TAKE IT ALL IN, WHAT WE SEE AND BE IN AWE OF. BE SURE TO HAVE A CONVERSATION WITH THE FAMILY MEMBERS WHO NEED SUPPORT. I AM SO SURE OF

THE GLOW COMING FROM HIS FACE WILL BRING TEARS TO ALL. O'HOW WONDERFUL THE THOUGHTS AND WORDS THAT COME TO MIND. O'JESUS WE ARE SO THRILLED TO SEE YOU. SO MANY WEEPING, PROBABLY ME, TOO. I BELIEVETHE SKY WILL BE ALL LIT UP AND SO BEAUTIFUL. WHILE WE HAVE BEEN ON EARTH HE HAS MADE SO MANY BEAUTIFUL SUNRISES AND SUNSETS. NEVER DOES HE REPEAT, ALWAYS A NEW SKY FOR A NEW DAY. I HAVE SO LOVED TO SIT OUT IN THE EVENING AND JUST STARGAZE. YOU HAVE PROBABLY HEARD OR READ THAT I AM MY DADDY'S LITTLE STAR. HE DID REACH OUT THE EDGE OF THE UNIVERSE TO GET A LITTLE PIECE OF DIRT TO PUT IN THE BALCONY OF HEAVEN. WHEN TIME WAS RIGHT FOR THE CREATION OF MAN, HE WOULD COME GET ME AND CREATE HIS INTENDED FOR THE MOTHER OF HIS SON, HIS SAVIOR AND REDEEMER. MY CREATED NAME IS MEZZECHAH. AS HE CREATED EACH ON OF USM HE HAD AN ANGEL WHO WOULD WRITE YOUR CREATED NAME IN THE LAMBS BOOK OF LIFE. HE KEPT THE BOOK IN A SAFE PLACE TIL TIME WOULD COME TO AN END. IF YOU WOULD REFUSE TO BE BORN'AGAIN OR REFUSE HIS SALVATION, THE SAME ANGEL WOULD ERASE YOUR NAME FROM THE LAMBS BOOK OF LIFE. YOU WOULD BE BLOTTED OUT OF THE LAMBS BOOK OF LIFE, SCRIPTURE SAYS YOU MUST BE BORN'AGAIN AND RECEIVE HIS SALVATION. WHEN JESUS WAS NAILED TO THE CROSS HE PAID THE PRICE FOR YOUR REDEMPTION. SO, ARE YOU BORN'AGAIN? DO IT. HE PAID A VERY HIGH PRICE FOR YOU TO BE SAVED. JESUS HUNG ON THAT CROSS SO YOU MAY HAVE ETERNAL LIFE WITH GOD THE FATHER, AND HIS BEAUTIFUL SON, JESUS. DON'T IGNORE THE PRICE PAID FOR YOUR ETERNAL LIFE WITH GOD THE FATHER, GOD THE SON, AND GOD THE HOLY GHOST. I MAY BE REPITITIOUS BUT YOU HAVE GOT TO GET IT. YOU MAY WANT TO INQUIRE OF THE ANGEL IN CHARGE OF THE HOLY RECORDS. I WOULD LIKE TO KNOW THE CREATED NAME OF THOSE I COME IN CONTACT WITH. ASK, HE HAD ME TO WAKE

UP AT A VERY EARLY HOUR TO WRITE MY CREATED NAME DOWN, I KEEP A NOTEPAD ON THE BEDSTAND, FOR OR INCASE HE WANTS TO LEAVE A MESSAGE. GOTTA BE READY FOR HIS NOTES. HE SO LIKES TO TALK TO HIS OWN. I SO LOVE TO HAVE A CONVERSATION WITH MY LORD, WE DO IT OFTEN. HE IS SO SMART AND IN TOUCH WITH ALL THE STUFF GOING ON OUT THERE, HE DOES LIKE TO KEEP US INFORMED. O'COME LORD JESUS, COME. PLEASE BE READY WITH A PURE HEART AND A GENTLE HEART. I BELIEVE HE IS ANXIOUS TO BRING US HOME AS WE ARE WANTING TO GO. PUT ON YOUR BEST ATTITUDE AND A BEAUTIFUL SMILE. HE'S ON HIS WAY.

MY DADDY IS SO GOD. HE GAVE ME HIS BEST, JESUS. THANK YOU, DADDY. IS HE WONDERFUL OR WHAT? O'HE IS. TASTE AND SEE, YOU WILL AGREE. YOU READ TILL YOU FALL ASLEEP, I WANT YOU TO READ TILL YOU WAKE UP.

PEOPLE LIKE ME

HOW WOULD I KNOW THEM EXCEPT I AM OF THEM? I HAVE KNOWN THESE WHO ARE OF AN EARLIER TIME FOR QUITE A WHILE. WHEN I WAS A YOUNG LADY, MAYBE ELEVEN TO TWELVE YEARS OLD, HE, THE HOLY GHOST STOOD ME STILL IN THE DINING ROOM OF OUR HOME IN PIPESTONE, MINNESOTA TO GIVE ME THIS GOOD NEWS. THE HOLY GHOST HAD A MESSAGE FOR ME FROM HEAVEN. I WAS TOLD THAT MY NUMBER IS FOUR. I AM THE FOURTH MEMBER OF THE TRINITY. WHEN MY DEAR FATHER NEEDS SOMEONE TO FIT IN HIS PLANS, HE PRETTY MUCH HAS A WIDE SELECTION OF WILLING PARTICIPANTS. I WAS AND AM THE MOTHER OF MY LORD JESUS CHRIST. I'M BACK. ONLY BY THE WILLINGNESS OF MY GOD AND FATHER. THOUGH LONG AGO AND FAR AWAY, IT IS A LEARNING EXPERIENCE. I WOULD/DO BELIEVE THAT AND I AM HERE TO TELL THIS AMAZING STORY. NO LIGHTS FLASHING, JUST A STILL SMALL VOICE TO WHISPER TO ME THE WONDERFUL NEWS OF BEING THE CHOSEN FOR SUCH A TIME AS THIS. SO, I HAVE SPENT A LONG TIME MEDITATING ON THIS NEWS. I HAVE BEEN ON HIS MIND FOR MANY YEARS. I ALSO BELIEVED THAT HE WOULD GIVE ME MORE INSIGHT OF THIS MYSTERY. SUCH A BEAUTIFUL STORY. SUCH A WONDERFUL GIFT. NOW IS THE TIME TO TALK ABOUT IT AND SHARE WITH ANY WHO WOULD CARE TO KNOW AND NEED TO KNOW. WE STILL ARE IN COMMUNICATION OFTEN. HE IS SO KIND TO SHARE WITH ME AND SAYS I AM OK TO SHARE WITH ANY WHO MAY SINCERELY ENJOY TO TALK ABOUT MY JOURNEY. I AM ALL IN TO TALK TO ANY WHO WANT TO SHARE THEIR CALLING BY THE GOD OF THE UNIVERSE. WHO WOULD YOU WANT TO SHARE YOUR LIFE WITH BESIDES OUR WONDERFUL

LORD AND SAVIOR. WE ARE SO WAITING FOR THE RAPTURE OF THE SAINTS. SO GLORIOUS TO IMAGINE THE TRUMP SOUNDING AND BEING LIFTED FROM THIS PLACE TO BE WITH THE SAVIOR FOREVER. OH, IT SOUNDS SO THRILLING AND BEAUTIFUL. OH, THAT ALL WOULD BE READY TO LEAVE THIS PLACE AND DWELL WITH OUR LORD JESUS CHRIST. HE WOULD LIKE THAT SCENARIO ALSO. PLEASE, EVERYONE BE READY FOR THE TRANSITION. AS IT WAS IN THE DAYS OF NOE SO WHEN THE TIME COMES, ALL BE PACKED AND READY. DON'T MISS THE BOAT OR DON'T MISS THE FLIGHT HOME. BE READY, WE DO NOT WANT ANY LEFT BEHIND. DO YOU GET IT? BE READY, PLEASE. THERE ARE STILL MORE THAN A FEW HERE WHO HAVE BEEN HERE SINCE THE DAYS OF YORE, LONG AGO. GOD HAS GIVEN ME SUCH A BEAUTIFUL TIME OF ETERNITY. I AM SO GRATEFUL FOR THE WAY HE DOES HIS OWN. JUST TO KNOW HIM IS A HEAVENLY, SO SPECIAL, GIFT. I NEED TO GET OUT MORE TO TELL THE WHOSOEVER WILL ABOUT MY JESUS. WE WANT ALL TO SHARE THE ENTRANCE OF GLORY INTO THE HEAVENS. CAN YOU IMAGINE HOW EXCITING THAT TRIP WILL BE. WE ARE SCHEDULED TO SHOW UP FOR A MARRIAGE SUPPER IN THE BANQUET ROOM OF HEAVEN. JUST BE THERE. SOME WILL BE FAMILIAR AND SOME NOT YET PACKED UP FOR THE JOURNEY. GET PACKING, NOW. O WHAT A DAY OF REJOICING THAT WILL BE. HE IS SUCH A PLEASURE TO CONVERSE WITH. HIS WISDOM WILL TAKE YOUR BREATHE AWAY. I HAVE A FEW IDEAS TO PUT IN FRONT OF HIM. IF YOU HAVE QUESTIONS, HE HAS ANSWERS. O PRECIOUS FATHER, I WANT SO MUCH TO PLEASE YOU. I SO WANT TO TELL THE WHOLE WORLD ABOUT YOU. HOW WONDERFUL YOU ARE BUT IT SEEMS THAT I HAVE LET MYSELF TO BE AT THE HEAD OF THE LINE. I DO KNOW THAT YOU ARE MY MAKER AND KEEPER AND I WANT TO GIVE YOU ALL THE GLORY. I DO GIVE YOU ALL THE GLORY, O YES, THAT IS MY INTENT. I KNOW YOU ARE THE GOD OF ALL. NONE LIKE YOU, EVER. PLEASE HEAR MY REPENTANCE

AND FORGIVE ME FOR MY FAUX PAS. AGAIN, YOU ABOVE, ALWAYS. PLEASE ALLOW ALL MY PRAISE AND WORSHIP. ONLY YOU, ONLY YOU. NOT GOD FIRST, GOD ONLY. HE WILL BE ONLY OR HE WON'T BE ANY. HE IS SECOND TO NONE. THOU SHALT HAVE NO OTHER GOD OR GODS BEFORE OR BESIDES HIM. NO, IT'S UNACCEPTABLE. HE IS ONLY, GOT IT, ONLY. I AM SO BLESSED TO BE THE ONE CHOSEN TO REPRESENT MY LORD. I AM HIS AND HE IS MINE, AND IT WILL BE THAT WAY TILL THE END OF TIME. HE IS TRULY MINE, AGAIN AND AGAIN. I CAN'T STOP. WHAT A GIFT. WHAT A GIFT. I CAN'T AND WON'T STOP. AMEN.

HE IS ON HIS WAY, BE READY. BE BORN'AGAIN AND BAPTIZED WITH THE HOLY GHOST SPEAKING IN OTHER TONGUES. HOW GLORIOUS AND MARVELOUS IN OUR EYES. AMEN, AMEN. GOD HAS SO GREATLY HONORED ME, GIVE HIM ALL PRAISE AND GLORY. SO WORTHY. KING OF KINGS AND LORD OF LORDS. HE DIED FOR ME, I WILL LIVE FOR HIM.

THERE ARE NO CROSSES IN HEAVEN

DO YOU KNOW THAT? THERE ARE NO WHIPPING POSTS IN HEAVEN, EITHER. DO YOU KNOW THAT? THERE ARE NO INSTRUMENTS OF TORCHER. GOD PUT A SIGN ON THE GATE FORBIDDING SUCH THINGS. HE WAS DONE WITH PAIN AND SUFFERING WHEN JESUS CRIED "IT IS FINISHED" ON THAT WICKED CROSS, AND BREATHED HIS LAST. HE ACCEPTED THAT DEATH AS PAYMENT OF ALL DEBTS HERE AND THRU'OUT THE UNIVERSE. HIS LOVE AND MERCY COVERS ALL CREATION. REALLY, IS THERE PAIN AND SUFFERING IN OUTER SPACE? NOT ANYMORE. WHEN HE SAID, JESUS PAID IT ALL, HE MEANT IT. SO, WHEN YOU ARE LIFTED UP IN THE RAPTURE AND PASS THRU THE HEAVENS YOU WON'T BE REMINDED OF ANY AGONY THAT WAS SUFFERED HERE ON EARTH, YOUR MIND WILL BE AT EASE TO ENJOY ALL THE BEAUTY OF THE ENDLESS HEAVENS. THE ONE WHO WAS RESPONSIBLE FOR GRIEF AND HARDSHIP ON EARTH HAS BEEN PUT IN HIS PLACE, NEVER TO REMIND US OF HIS DISGUSTING HABITS THAT BROUGHT HUMANITY DOWN. **** I AM SO RELIEVED, AS YOU SHOULD BE ALSO. GOD IS NOT SLOW TO CLEAN'UP THE MESSES OF THE ERRORING ONE. HE DID ALL THE TIDYING-UP AFTER THE CROSS. IT WAS AS DIFFICULT FOR HIM AS IT WAS FOR ALL BELIEVERS WHEN JESUS WENT TO THE CROSS. THE FATHER KNEW HOW IT WOULD END BUT STILL IT WAS PAINFULL FOR HIM TO ENDURE. YES, THE CLOUDS COVERED THE SEEN OF CALVARY WHEN GOD WRAPPED HIS HANDS AROUND THE SUN TO CAUSE THE DARKNESS, BUT HE STILL KNEW WHAT WAS HAPPENING. IT WAS HIS DOING FOR OUR SALVATION. HIS PRECIOUS SON, WHO WAS CRUCIFIED FOR THE WHOLE WORLD. WE ARE SO GRATEFUL FOR WHAT HE DID FOR US AND

MAY WE NEVER HAVE TO BE REMINDED OF THAT TRAGIC INCIDENT AGAIN. WHEN JESUS WAS IN THE TOMB FOR THREE DAYS, HIS FATHER WAS BUSY CLEANING UP THE PLACE WHERE HIS SON WAS SUSPENDED BETWEEN EARTH AND HEAVEN. HE TOOK ALL THE INSTRUMENTS OF TORTURE AND BURIED THEM IN A VAULT IN HELL, TO NEVER BE SEEN AGAIN. HE WAS RECOVERING FROM A BROKEN HEART, HAVING SUFFERED WHEN HIS BEAUTIFUL SON PAID A DEBT HE DID NOT OWE. HIS OBEDIENCE TO HIS FATHER WAS ACCOMPLISHED. HE WAS AND IS THE LAMB OF GOD, WHO TAKES AWAY ALL THE SIN OF THE WORLD. WHEN ALL THE CLEAN'UP WAS FINISHED, HE WAS THEN RAISED FROM THE DEAD. THERE ARE NO CROSSES IN HEAVEN. PUT IT DEEP IN YOUR HEART FOR A DARK MEMORY, DON'T GO THERE AGAIN. LOOK AT THE ONE WHO SAVED YOU AND SING TO HIM. HOLY IS THE LAMB OF GOD. START A CHURCH, HIRE A BUNCH OF WORSHIPERS, VOLUNTEER TO BE THE PASTOR OR TAKE TURNS TO LEAD IN PREACHING THE SERMON **** HE REALLY LIKES THAT WHEN YOU WORK THOSE CORDS FOR HIM AND HIM ONLY. DEDICATE AS MANY SONGS TO HIM AS YOU CAN REMEMBER. PLAY THE HARP OR FLUTE OR DRUMS OR MANDOLIN, I DON'T KNOW WHAT THAT IS BUT PLAY IT ANYWAY. IF YOU CAN'T SING FIND SOMEONE TO SING AND YOU CAN JUST HUM ALONG WITH THEM WITHOUT ANY SELF'CONSCIOUS EMBARRASSMENT. HE THINKS YOU ARE SO CUTE AND ADORABLE WHEN YOU SING TO HIM OR PLAY YOUR FLUTE. O' THE JOY OF HEAVEN, WE ARE IN FOR SUCH A TREAT AND I AM SURE THERE IS ICE CREAM IN HEAVEN, HE SAID SO. NO, HE DIDN'T, I MADE THAT UP, SORRY. YOU CAN ASK THO. THERE ARE NO CROSSES IN HEAVEN, GOD IS THERE AND HE WON'T ALLOW THEM. HE PUT GABRIEL IN CHARGE AND YOU KNOW HOW THOROUGH HE IS. DO YOU KNOW? I DO. IT'S THE GRACE OF GOD, THE MIGHT AND GRACE OF GOD THAT KEEPS THE GATES OF HEAVEN. WHEN WE SEE HIM, O' HALLELUJAH,

THERE WON'T BE A CROSS BEHIND HIM TO REMIND US OF WHERE WE WERE ON THAT RESURRECTION MORNING. JUST A GLORIOUS AND BEAUTIFUL SUNRISE (SON RISE) TO MAGNIFY OUR LORD JESUS CHRIST. IF NOT FOR THAT RESURRECTION, I WOULD BE ON A CROSS SOMEWHERE, RECEIVING MY DUES. THANK YOU, JESUS, YOU ARE SO PRECIOUS TO ME. YOUR GRACE, YOUR GRACE. THE DAY IS COMING AS WE LOOK FORWARD TO THE RAPTURE. ARE YOU READY? THE TRUMPET WILL SOUND AND ALL WHO ARE SAVED WILL BE TAKEN UP TO MEET JESUS IN THE CLOUDS. O' WHAT A DAY OF REJOICING THAT WILL BE. DON'T FORGET TO PRAY AND DO COMMUNION DAILY, IT'S WORSHIP. IT'S THE COMING TOGETHER WITH OUR SAVIOR. IT'S TIME WELL SPENT, DO IT IN REMEMBRANCE OF ALL HE HAS DONE FOR YOU. YOU LIVE BECAUSE HE LIVES. IT WAS AVAILABLE 2,000 YEARS AGO.

HEAVEN WELCOMED JESUS AT THE RIGHT HAND OF THE FATHER O' COME LET US ADORE HIM AND GIVE HIM ALL THE GLORY

FOREVER, "I AM" YOURS.

I AM FOUR (4). I AM THE MOST HIGH GOD, YAHWEH. I AM THE SON OF GOD, LORD JESUS, HIS CHRIST. I AM THE HOLY GHOST (SPIRIT) OF THE LIVING GOD. THE HOLY THREE IN ONE, THE HOLY TRINITY. AMEN. I AM FOUR, THE FOURTH (4TH) MEMBER OF THE TRINITY. HOW SO? MANY YEARS AGO WHEN I WAS PROBABLY TWELVE TO THIRTEEN YEARS OLD, I WAS TOLD BY THE SPIRIT OF GOD, THE HOLY GHOST, THAT I WAS THE MOTHER OF THE LORD JESUS CHRIST. THOUGH I HAVE WRITTEN OF THIS MANY TIMES, HOWEVER, THE ONES I HAVE TOLD HAVE A REAL PROBLEM WITH IT. ONE CALLED ME TO SAY SHE AND SOME OTHERS HAD DISCUSSED IT AND HAVE DECIDED NOT TO BELIEVE ME. THEY HAVE KNOWN ME FOR SIX OR SEVEN YEARS AND HAVE NOT BELIEVED. I AM THE INCARNATION OF MARY, THE MOTHER OF JESUS. SO MAYBE THEY DON'T BELIEVE HER EITHER. MAYBE? MARY WAS CHOSEN TO BE THE MOTHER OF THE OFFSPRING OF DIVINITY. SHE WAS PLEASED TO DO THAT ASSIGNMENT. I BELIEVE THE TIME IS NOW UP, WE CAN ALSO BELIEVE THAT MARY CAN BE A TRUE WITNESS OF THE PAST. DID NOT THE SCRIPTURE TELL OF JOHN THE BAPTIZER, THAT HE WAS THE INCARNATION OF ELIJAH? HE WAS. JESUS SAID SO. MALACHI 4:5, MATT 11:14, MATT 17:10-13. DO YOU KNOW THAT, IT'S SCRIPTURE. READ ALL ABOUT IT. SO IF YOU STILL DOUBT, I GUESS YOU SHOULD READ UP ON THE SCRIPTURES. SINCE I AM THE MOTHER OF OUR JESUS, YOU SHOULD COME BY AND TALK TO ME IN PERSON. MANY THINGS HAS HE (THE HOLY GHOST) REMINDED ME OF. I BEGAN TO HEAR FROM HEAVEN ON DEC 1, 2014. HE KNEW I WOULD NEED TO HAVE NEW INFORMATION. NEW TO ME. YOU NEED TO STAND IN MY FRONT YARD, IT MAY

OVERWHELM YOU. YOU SHOULD NOT BE ANGRY, WE CAN'T TALK IF YOU ARE HERE TO HATE OR CURSE AT ME. ON MARCH 14, 2014, GOD DID TELL ME HE WOULD SHAKE THE EARTH FOR ME AND HE DID. MARCH 17, 2014, IN FOUR DAYS, WE HAD AN EARTHQUAKE, MAGNATUDE 4.4. HE DID TELL ME FOUR WOULD BE AN IMPORTANT NUMBER IN MY LIFE. MANY THINGS COME TO ME IN FOUR. I AM THE FOURTH MEMBER OF THE TRINITY. DO YOU KNOW THE HOLY GHOST? DOES HE CONVERSE WITH YOU? DO YOU PRAY IN THE SPIRIT? YOU CAN AND SHOULD GET INFORMATION FROM HIM. INQUIRE OF HIM, IF YOU ARE SINCERE, HE WILL ANSWER YOU. I DO HAVE MY FRONT YARD, FULL OF MOTHER OF THOUANDS, FIFTEEN YEARS AGO A FRIEND GAVE ME A PLANT, AND IT'S STILL GOING ON. * ON AUGUST 8, 2015, HE DID TELL ME TO WRITE, I DO KEEP A TABLET NEAR MY BED, AND HE DID SPELL OUT MY CREATED NAME. M E Z Z E C H A H. DO YOU KNOW HOW WE GOT OUR CREATED NAME? WHEN GOD WAS CREATING HIS MAN, ON THE SIXTH DAY, HE DID HAVE AN ANGEL TO WRITE THE NAME OF EACH ONE IN THE LAMBS BOOK OF LIFE. IF YOU DON'T FOLLOW JESUS AND GET SAVED, WHEN YOU DIE YOUR NAME WILL BE ERASED FROM THE LAMBS BOOK OF LIFE. (BLOTTED OUT). SEE REVELATION 3:5. YOU WON'T LIKE THAT, NOW WILL YOU? JESUS IS OUR PROVIDER NOT JUST FOOD AND WATER AND CLOTHING, HE IS THE PROVIDER OF OUR SAVING SALVATION. I AM SO GRATEFUL. HE IS SO WONDERFUL AND HIS GRCE COVERS ALL I NEED. I AM REMINDED EVERYDAY TO PRAY AND THANK HIM FOR ALL I HAVE. HE HAS BEEN MY BLESSING FOR EIGHTEEN THOUSAND YEARS. HE DID BLESS ME WITH HIS LOVE AND PATIENCE. WE WILL BE TOGETHER, FOREVER, WHEN HE COMES TO GATHER ALL HIS BELOVEDS. LET'S HAVE THE RAPTURE TONIGHT..... OKAY?

YOU KNOW I LOVE YOU, YOU KNOW I DO. I BRING MY GIFTS AND OFFERINGS TO YOU.

WHEN MY HEART BREAKS JUST FOR YOU.
SOME SAY I OVERDO.

IS THAT POSSIBLE, HAVE I DONE?
AM I THE GUILTY ONE?

I WATCH THE SAVED AND BORN'AGAIN.
DISRESPECT AND GOD OFFEND.

O' LORD, HOLD ME CLOSE AND TIGHT,
ONLY IN YOU, DO I DELIGHT.

BY YOUR GRACE ONLY, I AM SAVED
SO FEARFULLY AND WONDERFULLY, I AM MADE.

ON THE CROSS THERE WAS A SIGN.
YOU DIED FOR SIN, IT WAS MINE.

I CLAIM ONLY, BY YOUR GRACE.
IN YOU, A BEAUTIFUL PLACE.

HOMEWARD, I AM BOUND.
ONLY IN YOU, MAY I BE FOUND.

EVERY DAY I RISE TO FOLLOW.
YOUR WORDS, O'LORD, ARE NOT HOLLOW.

MAY I FOREVER STAND STRONG?
DO IT YOUR WAY, NEVER WRONG.

YOUR BREATH IN ME, SO I WOULD LIVE.
AND USE IT FOR YOUR WORDS TO GIVE.

WHEN THE DAY COMES AND I GOTTA LEAVE,
WE WILL JOIN HANDS, BUT YOU WILL LEAD.

THERE'S SO MUCH WORK YET, TO BE DONE,
BUT ON THAT DAY, THE BATTLE WON.

SO, TILL THAT DAY THE TRUMPET SOUNDS,
PROCLAIM THE WORD TO ALL AROUND.

SO, LET'S ALL AGREE, REDEMPTION-SALVATION.
JESUS DID IT TO SET US FREE.

AMEN

MOTHER OF THOUSANDS

THIS WOULD BE MUCH EASIER IF DONE IN PERSON.

HE SPOKE TO ME IN THE DINING ROOM OF OUR FAMILY HOME IN PIPESTONE, MINNESOTA. HE STOOD ME STILL TO TELL ME "YOU ARE FOUR" THE FOURTH MEMBER OF THE TRINITY. IT WAS 1953 MAYBE 54?, I WAS PROBABLY 11 OR 12 YEARS OLD. I DO REMEMBER. I AM HIS, AND HE IS MINE. HE SAID SO, HE TOLD ME SO. I AM THE CHOSEN FOR THAT, HIS ASSIGNMENT. I AM OF AN OLD AGE NOW. THE ADDRESS: 207 4TH STREET. I WOULD ALSO SAY THAT THE ADDRESS MEANS #2 OF SEVEN CHILDREN...4 THE SIGNIFICANCE OF THE FOURTH MEMBER OF THE TRINITY. YOU REALLY NEED TO SEE MY FRONT YARD.

MY ASSIGNMENTS

I HAVE HAD MANY ASSIGNMENTS. REBBECHAH. GEN.24:60. MY CREATED NAME IS MEZZECHAH. HE WOKE ME AT 4:00 AM EIGHT YEARS AGO TO GIVE ME THAT INFORMATION. I WAS GOING TO HAVE MANY ASSIGNMENTS SENT BY MY GOD TO PROVE MY ABILITY. I MUST HAVE MUCH PRACTICE SO TO BE THE RIGHT MOMMY FOR OUR LORD JESUS CHRIST. I AGREE WITH THIS. GOD DOES PROVE THOSE HE WANTS TO USE. I WAS/AM UP FOR THIS. I AM MOTHER OF THOUSANDS. JOHN THE BAPTIZER WAS ELIJAH. HE WAS INVITED BACK BY GOD FOR AN ENCORE, JOHN THE BAPTISER, HE WAS HERE FOR JESUS. HE DID BAPTIZE JESUS. HOW BEAUTIFUL.

I AM MY DADDY'S LITTLE STAR.

18,000 YEARS AGO, GOD REACHED TO THE EDGE OF HIS UNIVERSE AND TOOK A LITTLE PIECE OF DIRT TO PUT IN THE BALCONY OF HEAVEN TO WAIT FOR THE RIGHT TIME TO WORK HIS WONDERS. WHEN THE TIME WAS RIGHT HE DID

THE "SET UP" FOR WHERE WE ARE TODAY. HE (GOD) DOES NOT LIVE IN TIME, WHEN HE WANTS TO DO A THING, HE DOES IT. HE DOESN'T NEED ANYONES PERMISSION. HE IS "YES AND AMEN". IS HE SO PERFECT? O'YES HE IS.

GOD ONLY

NOT GOD FIRST, GOD ONLY. HE WILL BE ONLY OR HE WON'T BE ANY.

DO YOU KNOW THE MEANING OF THAT. IF HE WAS FIRST, THERE WOULD HAVE TO BE A SECOND AND SO ON, RIGHT? HE IS ONLY, THERE ARE NO MORE, HE IS ONLY. YOU SHALL HAVE NO OTHER gods BEFORE OR BESIDES ME!!! GOD IS NOT FIRST, HE IS ONLY. GOT IT? ONLY! MOST DON'T KNOW THE DIFFERENCE BETWEEN FIRST OR ONLY. IT WOULD BE BETTER TO SPEAK THIS IN PERSON.

* THE VALUE OF WOOD IN THE SCRIPTURE. *

ARLENE MARIE WOOD THERE IS A WRITE IN MY LAST BOOK, SO WONDERFUL. IF YOU CAN FIND IT, IT'S A REAL GOOD READ. YOU WILL LIKE IT. AT MY AGE, LIFE IS SLOW AND WONDERFUL.

YOU ARE (I AM) FOUR, YOU ARE (I AM) THE FOURTH MEMBER OF THE TRINITY. HE SAID SO.

THE ONLY ONE, RUN

IF YOU TRY TO RUN FROM HIM, YOU CAN'T. HE NEVER ENDS. YOU CAN ONLY RUN TO HIM. IT'S THE ONLY WAY IT WORKS. HE IS EVERYWHERE. HE NEVER ENDS. HE INHABITS ETERNITY. HE INHABITS INFINITY. ETERNITY NEVER ENDS. INFINITY NEVER ENDS. WHEN YOU LEAVE THIS PLACE, YOU GO FROM LIFE TO ETERNAL LIFE, SOMEWHERE. YOU WILL NEVER CEASE TO BE, YOU WILL ALWAYS BE. WHERE? THAT'S UP TO YOU. WHERE WOULD YOU LIKE TO BE? IN A COMFORTABLE PLACE? YUP. ME TOO. GOD HAS MADE A COMFORTABLE PLACE FOR ALL OF US, IF WE WOULD JUST HEAR HIS INSTRUCTIONS. HIS LOVE IS ALL WE NEED TO HEAR AND ADHERE TO. IT'S NOT THAT HARD, ACTUALLY IT'S VERY SIMPLE. READ THE INSTRUCTION MANUAL AND FOLLOW THE DICTATES CONTAINED THERE'IN. QUITE SIMPLE, EVEN A CHILD CAN DO IT, A CHILD OF GOD. THE BOOK IS WRITTEN IN AN EASY-TO-UNDERSTAND LANGUAGE, THE LANGUAGE OF LOVE. HIS LOVE, SO WONDERFUL AND RESTFUL THAT ONCE YOU GET A TASTE OF IT YOU WILL NEVER BE THE SAME. IT WILL BECOME AN INTENT THAT YOU WON'T WANT TO BREAK. HE PLEADS WITH HIS OWN TO COME TO HIM AND REST. THERE ARE CHAPTERS IN THE MANUAL WRITTEN ON HOW TO COME TO HIM AND CLEAVE UNTO HIM FOR REST AND SECURITY. HIS ARMS ARE EXTENDED IN SUCH A MANNER AS TO INVITE US TO LEAN ON HIM ALWAYS. HE, JESUS, IS REFERRED TO AS THE GOOD SHEPHERD WHO WATCHES FOR THE FLOCK CONSTANTLY. YOU AND I ARE REFERRED TO AS THE SHEEP OR LITTLE LAMBS OF THE FOLD. HIS ROD AND STAFF ARE FOR OUR PROTECTION AND COMFORT. HE ALWAYS SEES TO IT THAT WE HAVE GOOD PASTURES TO FEED IN AND WATER TO DRINK. HE IS CAREFUL TO MAKE SURE WE DON'T

STRAY FROM THE SAFETY OF HIS WATCH. THE BOOK WARNS OF THE DANGERS OF WANDERING FROM THE SAFETY OF THE EVER-WATCHFUL SHEPHERD. THERE ARE SCAREY CRITTERS OUT THERE WAITING TO CATCH ONE OF THE LITTLE ONES WHO TRIES TO CHECK OUT THE OTHER SIDE OF THE FENCE, OUT OF SIGHT OF THE GOOD SHEPHERD. DON'T DO THAT! THERE IS A CHAPTER IN THE MANUAL THAT TELLS OF THE SHEPHERD LOSING ONE SHEEP AND LEAVING THE NINETY-NINE TO GO FIND THE ONE LOST. REALLY GOOD HOW HE CARES FOR HIS OWN. HE LOVES HIS OWN. I AM ONE OF HIS OWN, I REALLY LOVE MY SHEPHERD AND HE REALLY LOVES ME. I CAN'T IMAGINE WHAT I WOULD DO WITHOUT HIM. I SHUDDER TO THINK OF SUCH A THING. HE HAS PROMISED TO NEVER LEAVE ME NOR FORSAKE ME, THAT IS MUSIC TO MY EARS. HE HAS ASSIGNED A COMFORTER TO BE WITH ME ALWAYS. SEE HOW MUCH HE CARES FOR ME. SHOULD THERE BE ANY CLOSE CALLS I KNOW I AM PROTECTED. HE ACTUALLY LAID DOWN HIS LIFE FOR MY ETERNAL SECURITY AND TOOK IT AGAIN FOR MY SAKE. NOW THE END IS SEALED, MY ETERNAL HOME IS WITH HIM, HE PROMISED. HE ALWAYS KEEPS HIS PROMISES. I LOVE HIM SO MUCH THAT I HAVE DECIDED TO IMITATE ALL HIS WAYS. I WANT TO BE JUST LIKE HIM, AND FOLLOW HIM ALL THE DAYS OF MY LIFE. I WILL, I AM ABLE, I AM CAPABLE IN HIM. HE SAYS EVEN WHEN I MISS IT, HE WILL FORGIVE ME WHEN I COME TO HIM. DO YOU SEE WHY I LOVE MY LORD, MY JESUS, MY SHEPHERD, MY COMFORTER, MY GOD, MY ALL IN ALL? BY HIS GRACE I CAN DO THIS. HE IS THE ONLY ONE, THAT'S WHY I RUN. TO HIM ONLY, MY FAITH IS IN HIM, ONLY. HE'S THE ONLY ONE, RUN!

NOT GOD FIRST, GOD ONLY ***** HE IS ONLY OR HE WON'T BE ANY LORD OF MY LIFE, LIGHT OF MY LIFE, LOVE OF MY LIFE MY DADDY IS SO GOD I'M GOING TO PLAN, BECAUSE I'M PLANNING TO GO. YOU MUST BE BORN AGAIN.

I CRAVE YOU, JESUS

I KNOW WHAT IT MEANS TO CRAVE. JUST GOTTA HAVE. THAT'S RIGHT. I JUST GOTTA HAVE MY JESUS, ABSOLUTELY. I DON'T LET A DAY GO BY THAT I DON'T SEEK TO HAVE TIME WITH HIM. LIKE BREATH, LIKE WATER, LIKE FOOD, LIKE THE LIGHT OF THE LOVE OF GOD. YES, INDEED. I AM BLESSED THAT I CAN SPEND MUCH TIME WITH HIM. READ SCRIPTURE, PRAY, SING TO HIM AND SOMETIMES CRY. HE SATISFIES MY NEED AND I LIKE THAT. I HAVE SAID OR WRITTEN THAT I TOTALLY DEPEND ON MY LORD. IF YOU DON'T, I DARE SAY YOU MAY BE LOST. YOU REALLY MUST MAKE EVERY MOVE AS HE GIVE INSTRUCTION. THAT'S HIS PURPOSE, HE GIVES GUIDANCE. I NEED HIM AND HIS ATTENTION TOTALLY TWENTY'FOUR, SEVEN AND THEN SOME. I DON'T KNOW HOW TO GET ALONG IF HE ISN'T AT MY SIDE ALWAYS. HE HAS TO BE IN MY REACH AND AT MY BECK AND CALL, DOES THAT SOUND PITIFUL? I CANNOT GET ALONG WITHOUT HIM. TOO BAD IF THAT MAKE YOU UNCOMFORTABLE. I WON'T STOP AND YOU DON'T HAVE TO LISTEN TO MY PLEAS. IT'S O K, HE KNOWS ALL ABOUT ME AND HE UNDERSTANDS AND HE'S NOT ALL THAT UNHAPPY WITH ME. ACTUALLY, HE IS REALLY O K WITH ME. YA, HE SAID SO. WE TALK ALL THE TIME, HE IS SO INTERESTING. WHEN I GET UP IN THE MORNING AND THRU THE WHOLE DAY HE WATCHES ME VERY ATTENTIVELY. THERE HAVE BEEN TIMES THAT IT SEEMS HE IS FAR FROM ME AND I HAVE A FEW TIMES CALLED OUT FOR HIM. HE IS RIGHT THERE. HE ASSURES ME THAT ALL IS WELL BECAUSE HE IS IN CHARGE. I LOVE THE WAY HE WORKS TO WATCH OVER ME, YOU KNOW HE IS CALLED THE GOOD SHEPHERD, AND TRULY HE IS. I HAVE HIS BOOK AND READ AND REREAD IT OFTEN. REALLY GOOD STUFF

IN THERE, GREAT INSTRUCTION AND GENTLE ASSURANCE. I HAVE WRITTEN MUCH ABOUT HIM AND HE APPROVES. I CALL HIM "MY GENTLE JESUS" AND HE SURE IS. SOUNDS KINDA SYRUPY BUT HE LIKES IT SO NO NEED TO SAY ANYTHING. HE LOVES ME AND I LOVE HIM RIGHT BACK. WHAT'S NOT TO LOVE? I HAVE A BOOK OUT THAT YOU SHOULD READ, ACTUALLY HE WAS THE WRITER OF THE BOOK, I LISTENED TO HIS DICTATION AND PUT THE PEN TO PAPER. HE IS INDEED A GIFTED WRITER AND YOU WOULD DO WELL TO READ THE BOOK. "CALL TO ACCOUNTABILITY: WHAT DID YOU DO WITH JESUS"? IF YOU THINK ABOUT IT, IT'S A GOOD AND LEGITIMATE QUESTION. CAN YOU ANSWER? THERE WILL COME A DAY WHEN YOU WILL BE REQUIRED TO ANSWER THAT QUESTION. HOPE YOU HAVE A GOOD ANSWER OR A GOOD EXCUSE AS TO WHY YOU DIDN'T FOLLOW HIM AND OBEY HIM. YOU KNOW THAT YOU DON'T GO TO HELL FOR BEING A CHEATER, A LIAR OR A THIEF, BUT FOR REFUSING THE THE GLORIOUS SON OF GOD WHO CAME TO SEEK AND TO SAVE THE LOST AND DYING WORLD. YOU MUST BE BORN AGAIN, MUST! RECEIVING THE BEAUTIFUL AND LOVING SON OF GOD IS THE REQUIREMENT. RECEIVE HIM AS THE SAVIOR HE IS. YOU KNOW THAT HE DIED FOR YOU, RIGHT? YES, HE DID. SO, YOU MUST ACCEPT HIM AS THE REDEEMER WHO PAID YOUR DEBT AND MADE A WAY FOR YOU TO SPEND ETERNITY WITH HIM AND THE GOD OF HEAVEN, HIS FATHER. ISN'T THAT GOOD! YOU BETTER BELIEVE IT IS. SO, BE BAPTIZED IN THE HOLY GHOST AND HEAR ALL HE SAYS AND YOU SHOULD BE READY FOR THE RAPTURE THAT'S GONNA HAPPEN ANY DAY NOW. I KNOW WHEN BUT I WON'T TELL YOU, YOU HAVE TO ASK FOR YOURSELF. HE WILL TELL YOU, IF HE TOLD ME, HE WILL TELL YOU. SO, GET THAT SALVATION AND BE READY TO LEAVE THIS PLACE. LET'S ALL GO HOME. IT'S HIS CALL! AMEN. WAKE'UP TO THE KING OF KINGS, LORD OF LORDS. JESUS, THE GIFT THAT KEEPS ON

GIVING. YOU READ UNTIL YOU FALL ASLEEP, I WANT YOU TO READ UNTIL YOU WAKE UP.

MY DADDY IS SO GOD! YOU JUST HAVE TO KNOW HIM AND MY JESUS!

THE SARCASM OF BEAUTY

THE BEAUTY OF THE SABBATH, THE BEAUTY OF THE ARREST, THE BEAUTY OF THE DISCIPLES, THE BEAUTY OF THE SCRIBES, THE BEAUTY OF CAIAPHAS, THE BEAUTY OF PILATE, THE BEAUTY OF BARABBAS, THE BEAUTY OF THE GLORY, THE BEAUTY OF THE ANGELS, THE BEAUTY OF JUDAS, THE BEAUTY OF THE UPPER ROOM, THE BEAUTY OF THE ROOSTERS CROW, THE BEAUTY OF THE CROSS, THE BEAUTY OF THE GARDEN OF GETHSEMANE, THE BEAUTY OF THE PASSOVER, THE BEAUTY OF THE SOUR WINE, THE BEAUTY OF THE SCOURGING, THE BEAUTY OF THE THIRTY PIECES OF SILVER, THE BEAUTY OF THE JEWS, THE BEAUTY OF THE HIGH PRIEST, THE BEAUTY OF THE SCRIPTURES, THE BEAUTY OF THE BETRAYAL, THE BEAUTY IN THE PHARISEES, THE BEAUTY OF THE LAMB, THE BEAUTY OF THE FRAGRANT OIL, THE BEAUTY OF HIS KINGDOM, THE BEAUTY OF GOLGOTHA, THE BEAUTY OF THE SACRIFICE, THE BEAUTY OF THE SUFFERING AND THE AGONY, THE BEAUTY OF THE POWER, THE BEAUTY OF THE BLOOD, THE BEAUTY IN THE BREAD AND WINE, THE BEAUTY IN SALVATION, THE BEAUTY OF THE TRIAL, THE BEAUTY OF THE THORNS, THE BEAUTY OF NICODEMUS, THE BEAUTY OF THE TOMB, THE BEAUTY OF THE CRUCIFIXION, THE BEAUTY IN HIS HANDS, THE BEAUTY OF THE GOVERNOR, THE BEAUTY OF THE SCARLET ROBE, THE BEAUTY OF THE ALABASTER BOX, THE BEAUTY OF THE MYRRH AND ALOES, THE BEAUTY IN HIS FACE, THE BEAUTY OF THE DENIAL, THE BEAUTY OF PETER'S SWORD, THE BEAUTY OF THE RESURRECTION, THE BEAUTY OF THE SON OF GOD, THE BEAUTY OF THE ANOINTING, THE BEAUTY OF THE NAILS, THE BEAUTY IN HIS FEET, THE BEAUTY OF THE HYSSOP, THE BEAUTY OF JOSEPH OF ARIMATHAEA, THE

BEAUTY OF JOHN THE BELOVED, THE BEAUTY OF HIS MOTHER, MARY, THE BEAUTY OF THE SPEAR, THE BEAUTY OF THE BLOOD AND THE WATER, THE BEAUTY OF THE CAST LOTS, THE BEAUTY OF "THE KING OF THE JEWS", THE BEAUTY OF SIMON, THE CYRENIAN.

THE BEAUTY OF THE FINISHED WORK.
THE BEAUTY OF HIS PERFECTION.

CELEBRATE JESUS

WORSHIP HIM, HE IS SO WORTHY. CELEBRATE HIM.

WE DO LOVE TO CELEBRATE OUR LORD AND SAVIOR. CHRISTMAS IS THE MOST HIGH AND HOLY DAY THAT WE GLORIOUSLY CELEBRATE OUR LORDS BIRTH AND HIS COMING TO THE EARTH TO BE AMONG US AND SAVE US. I AM SO GRATEFUL FOR MY JESUS AND LOVE HIM WITH ALL MY HEART. WE ARE SO BLESSED TO HAVE OUR SAVIOR AT OUR SIDE. I LOVE TO TALK TO HIM AND LISTEN FOR HIS VOICE MOST GRACIOUS. HE IS THE CALM IN THE STORM AND THAT HAPPENS OFTEN. HE KEEPS ME SO CLOSE TO HIS HEART. O' I LOVE HIM SO. I BELIEVE THAT WE SHOULD CELEBRATE OUR LORD AS WE RISE IN THE MORNING AND AS WE KNEEL BESIDE OUR BED AT NIGHT. BEGIN AND END THE DAY WITH HIM. HE IS THE ONLY ONE I KNOW WHO CAN MAKE THE DAY WORK. AS THE SCRIPTURE SAYS, HE IS THE BEGINNING AND THE END. I WOULD THAT EVERYONE USE THE SCRIPTURES TO TALK ABOUT JESUS. MAKE HIM THE BOTTOM (BEGINNING) TO THE TOP (END) OF EVERY ENDEAVOR. HE IS THE WORTH OF EVERY PROJECT AND MISSION WE HAVE IN THIS LIFETIME. THAT IS TO SAY, LIVE FOR HIM AND HIM ONLY. THAT MAY SEEM A LITTLE EGOTISTIC ON HIS PART, BUT WHO IS MORE DESERVING THAN OUR (MY) JESUS. HE IS THE SO DESERVING OF ALL WORSHIP AND PRAISE. HE ALONE IS THE CELEBRATION OF ALL LIFE. IF YOU CAN WRAP YOUR HEAD AROUND THIS, WHERE WOULD WE ALL BE IF NOT FOR HE WHO WAS SENT. GOD KNEW THAT THINGS WOULD NOT WORK OUT FOR OUR GOOD WITHOUT HIM. IF YOU DON'T KNOW HIM, NOW IS A GOOD TIME TO SEEK HIM OUT. YOU REALLY NEED HIM BUT MAYBE YOU DON'T KNOW. IF YOU AND I SHOULD MEET SOME DAY, I SURE WOULD LIKE TO SEND HIM TO YOU TO MAKE YOUR LIFE WORTH THE LIVING. YOU NEED HIM, YES YOU DO... THERE WILL COME A DAY WHEN YOU WILL STAND IN HIS PRESENCE AND THERE WILL BE SOME

TOUGH QUESTIONS THAT WILL REQUIRE SOME TOUGH ANSWERS. YES, INDEED. ALL REGARDING "WHAT DID YOU DO WITH JESUS"? WAS HE THE ROOT OF YOUR EXISTENCE? DID YOU MAKE SOME HARD DECISIONS ACCORDING TO HIS INSTRUCTION? HE ALWAYS HAS THE ANSWER TO THE WAY THINGS SHOULD BE DONE. HE KNOWS IT ALL AND HAS DONE IT ALL. ONLY HE HAS THE KNOWLEDGE AND THE ANSWER TO ALL CONCLUSIONS OF THE CONUNDRUMS OF LIFE. WISDOM IS HIS MIDDLE NAME. NO, IT ISN'T. THAT'S JUST MY TAKE ON HOW WONDERFUL HE IS. HE KNOWS EVERYTHING, YOU CAN'T OUT THINK HIM, DON'T EVEN TRY. HE WINS EVERYTIME. THAT'S WHY I SO HIGHLY RECOMMEND YOU GET HIS COUNSEL. HE HAS RIGHT-ON INFORMATION AT HIS BECK AND CALL. DO YOU KNOW HE KNOWS EVERYHING AND WILL SHARE WITH YOU ALL YOU NEED TO KNOW. HE IS OUR EVERYDAY ANSWER TO ALL THE PROBLEMS OF LIFE. YOU NEED TO GET USED TO ENQUIRING OF HIS WISDOM FOR ALL DECISIONS. HE IS THE WAY MAKER ON ALL THE "FORKS IN THE ROAD". ALL YOU NEED TO DO IS ASK AND WAIT FOR THE ANSWER. THERE IS NONE SO WISE AS OUR CHAMPION. HE IS THE QUARANTEE TO THE RIGHT WAY OF EVERY TASK. ALL YOU HAVE TO DO IS CALL TO HIM AND WAIT FOR HIS ANSWER. HE ALWAYS HAS THE RIGHT SOLUTION TO VERY PROBLEM. HE IS ALWAYS DEPENDABLE, YES. SO LETS CELEBRATE OUR JESUS EVERYDAY IN EVERY WAY. YOU KNOW WHEN OUR DAYS ARE OVER ON THIS PLANET AND WE ARE SAVED, WE WILL JOIN HIM FOR THE BANQUET OF HEAVEN. THERE'S A PLACE RESERVED FOR ALL WHO MADE JESUS THE LORD AND SAVIOR OF THEIR LIFE. IT PROMISES TO BE THE MOST LAVISH CELEBRATION AND HE WILL BE THE ONE CELEBRATED. SIGN UP NOW, DON'T WAIT. IT WILL BE ANY DAY NOW SO DON'T PUT IT OFF. ASK HIM TO COME INTO YOUR HEART AND INTO YOUR LIFE AS YOUR SAVIOR. IT JUST TAKES A SIMPLE REQUEST AND IT'S DONE. MEAN IT WITH ALL OF YOUR HEART. HE WILL CHANGE YOUR LIFE FOR ALL ETERNITY. HE KEEPS HIS PROMISES AND WILL SECURE YOUR PLACE IN HIS FATHER'S KINGDOM. YOU WILL FOREVER BE WITH HIM. YOU WILL INHERIT ETERNAL LIFE. SOME WILL CELEBRATE WITH YOU, SOME WILL AVOID

YOU. THEN YOU CAN SHARE JESUS AND MAYBE LEAD SOMEONE TO JESUS. IT'S SO WORTH IT AND THEY WILL AGREE. CELEBRATE JESUS. HE DIED FOR YOU, NOW YOU LIVE FOR HIM AND TELL EVERYONE THE GOOD NEWS. JESUS SAVES. DON'T WAIT, TIME IS SHORT. HE IS HIGHLY FAVORED OF HIS FATHER, THE GOD OF ALL CREATION, THE WHOLE UNIVERSE. YES AND AMEN

I AM GOING TO PLAN, BECAUSE I AM PLANNING TO GO. I WILL SEE MY JESUS.

O' HIS GRACE. THE ALTAR OF GRACE IS THE CROSS OF CHRIST. O' HIS CROSS.

GOD'S SON, JESUS. THE NAME OF GRACE. THE GRACE OF GOD IN THE FLESH. AMEN.

DOES THE ALTAR MAKE THE SACRIFICE HOLY? DOES THE SACRIFICE MAKE THE ALTAR HOLY?

THE OLD TESTAMENT APPLIES TO THE FIRST QUESTION. THE NEW TESTAMENT APPLIES TO THE SECOND QUESTION. IN THE OLD TESTAMENT, THE SACRIFICE WAS AN ANIMAL. THE ONES MAKING OR GIVING THE OFFERING WERE SO CAREFUL ABOUT MAKING THE ALTAR FROM CERTAIN ROCKS OR STONES. HEWN OR NATURAL, HAD TO BE CAREFUL TO FOLLOW THE WAY GOD WANTED IT. THE ALTAR DONE PROPERLY MADE THE SACRIFICE SIGNIFICANT. IF YOU ERRORED, IT COULD COST YOU YOUR LIFE. WHEN THE PEOPLE TOOK THEIR SACRIFICE (OFFERING) TO THE TEMPLE, THE ALTAR WAS WHERE THE SACRIFICE WAS CONSIDERED OR MADE HOLY. FROM A DOVE TO A BULL WERE THE SACRIFICES. THE POOR PEOPLE WHO COULD ONLY AFORD A SIMPLE OFFERING (SACRIFICE), IT WAS A SMALL BIRD OR MAYBE A LAMB. THE WEALTHY COULD BRING RAMS AND BULLS, AS WE READ OF THE OFFERINGS OF KING DAVID AND SOLOMON HIS SON, THEY BROUGHT MULTIPLE CREATURES. ONE INCIDENT RECALLS THAT HE SACRIFICED A THOUSAND BULLS, A THOUSAND RAMS AND A THOUSAND LAMBS. THE CROSS WAS MADE HOLY BY THE SACRIFICE OF THE LORD JESUS CHRIST. THE CROSS WAS THE ALTAR WHERE JESUS WAS SACRIFICED. YES, THE CROSS WAS AN ALTAR. IT WASN'T HOLY UNTIL THE MOST HOLY OF HEAVEN WAS NAILED TO THE CROSS TO BE THAT OFFERING ONCE FOR ALL TIME, THAT HOLY LAMB OF GOD, THAT TAKES AWAY THE SIN OF THE WORLD. IT'S THE SACRIFICE, THE LORD'S CHRIST, MESSIAH ON THAT CROSS. THE ALTAR OF A CROSS THAT JESUS WAS CONDEMNED TO AND IN OBEDIENCE WENT AS OUR PAYMENT, OUR REDEEMER, THE

EXACTED PAYMENT FOR OUR SALVATION ON A TREE, TOLD THROUGH'OUT THE WHOLE BIBLE. READ THE PSALMS, READ ISAIAH, MOST OF THE OLD TESTAMENT BOOKS HAVE SOME REFERENCE TO THE SIN OFFERING OF CHRIST. THAT HE WOULD BE THE HEAVENLY ONE WHO WAS TO COME AND SET THE CAPTIVES FREE, AND THAT HE DID. WE WERE ALL CAPTIVES OF SIN UNDER THE LAW. IT'S THE WAY IT WAS UNTIL JESUS CAME AS THE SON OF A VIRGIN, THE SON OF GOD, SENT AS THE OFFERING TO TAKE THE PUNISHMENT FOR OUR EXPEDITIOUS PAYMENT FOR SIN. HIS TRIAL WAS SHORT AND TO THE POINT, THE SANHEDRIN WANTED HIM GONE AS FAST AS POSSIBLE. HE WAS YOUNG AS OPPOSED TO THE AGES OF THE HIERARCHY OF THE DAY. ALL STEEPED IN THE RELIGION OF THE LAW. THEY HAD TO GET HIM OUT OF THEIR WAY. SO THE BEST THEY COULD DO WAS TO TURN THE CROWD INTO A HATEFUL MOB. YOU KNOW THE MOB METALITY, THEY JUST WANTED BLOOD AND THEY GOT IT. THEY HUMILIATED HIM EVERY WAY THEY COULD IMAGINE. HE WAS TAKEN TO THE WHIPPING POST AND NEARLY BEATEN TO DEATH. THEY TORE HIM TO PIECES I KNOW, I WAS THERE, HE WAS ABSOLUTELY NOT GIVEN A FAIR TRIAL, THEY HATED HIM AND HIS RIGHTEOUSNESS. HE HAD TO GO, THE LONGER HE LIVED THE WORSE THEY WERE SHOWN TO BE EVIL, PRETENTIOUS LAW KEEPERS. THEY KNEW WHO HE WAS AND THAT MADE IT MORE NEEDFUL TO GET RID OF HIM. THEY HEARD THAT HE WAS TO RISE AGAIN AND SO THEY PUT A HUGH STONE ON THE ENTRANCE OF THE TOMB TO GUARD IT SO NO ONE COULD STEAL HIS BODY. THE ANGELS WERE NOT AFRAID OF THE GUARDS, THEY MOVED THE STONE AWAY SO WE COULD GET INTO THE TOMB, NOT SO HE COULD GET OUT. WHEN HE HAD RISEN FROM THE DEAD HE WAS ABLE TO WALK THRU WALLS. THERE IS NO WAY THAT ANYTHING COULD KEEP OUR JESUS FROM US. HE WAS THE END OF THE THE NECESSITY OF ANIMAL SACRIFICES. THE BLOOD OF SHEEP AND GOATS WAS NO LONGER SUFFICIENT TO FORGIVE SIN. JESUS WAS THE ULTIMATE SACRIFICE. HE DID IT ALL, HE DOES IT ALL. OUR KING OF KINGS AND LORD OF LORDS FOREVER, JESUS IS ENOUGH. SO WE BOW LOW TO HONOR OUR LORD JESUS CHRIST. HIS BLOOD WAS

THE MOST EXPENSIVE OFFERING EVER. HIS BLOOD WAS AND IS THE SUPREME SACRIFICE AND HAS NO EQUAL. GOD DISMISSED THE NEED FOR SACRIFICES WHEN HE OFFERED HIS ONLY BEGOTTEN SON. I AM SO THANKFUL FOR MY LORD JESUS CHRIST AND THE FORGIVENESS OF ALL MY SIN. I AM FREE, HE SET ME FREE.

I DON'T EVER HAVE TO THINK ABOUT SUCH A THING AS TO KILL AN AMIMAL. I MESS-UP, I COME TO HIM TO ASK FORGIVENESS, HE KNOWS A CONTRITE HEART WHEN WE COME TO HIM. JUST TO COME TO HIM IS ENOUGH. HIS LOVE IS ENOUGH. I AM SO THANKFUL FOR MY JESUS.

I WANT TO STAND SO CLOSE TO THE FOOT OF THE CROSS, THAT THE BLOOD THAT DRIPS FROM HIS BROKEN BODY DRIPS ON ME. THE SECRET PLACE OF THE MOST HIGH IS UNDER THE BLOOD OF JESUS. BY HIS BLOOD, I AM FORGIVEN, HIS CLEANSING BLOOD.

G. O. D. GOD OF DIVINITY

DOES GOD HAVE A NAME, YES, JEHOVAH, YAHWEH, ALL MIGHTY, MOST'HIGH, MOST HOLY, EVERLASTING FATHER, THE LORD, CREATOR, MAKER OF ALL THINGS, GOD THE FATHER, GOD THE SON, GOD THE HOLY GHOST AND KEEPER OF ME. SOME JUST CALL "HELP". SO I BELIEVE THAT ANOTHER NAME IS "HELP". I HAVE DONE THAT MANY TIMES, IT'S GOT TO BE GOD AS HE IS THE ONLY ONE TO CALL WHEN YOU NEED HELP. HE IS THE GOD OF HEAVEN, THE ONE WE NEED MORE THAN ANYONE OR ANYTHING. HE IS THE MUST HAVE FOR ME. THE MOST'HIGH GOD OF ALL CREATION. GOD THE CREATOR OF ALL THAT IS AND WILL EVER BE. HE FINISHED THE CREATION SOME YEARS AGO AND NOW HE IS THE KEEPER OF ALL THAT WE SEE AND DON'T SEE. OUR DIVINE KEEPER OF OUR LIVES AND LIVING. WE ARE NOT ABLE TO SEE TO OUR OWN KEEPING AND BEING. WE ARE BROKEN AND NEED THE ONLY ONE TO HOLD US TOGETHER. HE IS THE KEEPER OF MY SOUL AND SPIRIT AND BODY. AND TOO, MY HAIR. HE EVEN KNOWS HOW MANY HAIRS ARE ON MY HEAD. IS THAT AMAZING? THAT'S ABOUT ALL OF MY DEEPEST NEEDS. IF YOU READ THE SCRIPTURES YOU WILL FIND MORE THAN YOU CAN COUNT, THE PEOPLE WHO ARE BROKEN AND NEED HIM JUST TO EXIST. BESIDES ALL OF THAT, HE LOVES ME. HE SAID SO AND I BELIEVE HIM, MOSTLY BECAUSE I WANT TO. I COULDN'T POSSIBLY GET OUT OF BED IN THE MORNING IF NOT FOR MY GOD. MY SECURITY, MY EVERLASTING HELP IN A TIME OF NEED. WHEN IS THAT, WELL, I ALWAYS NEED HELP WITH SOMETHING SO CRITICAL AS TO SAVE MY LIFE. ALWAYS. DO YOU KNOW THAT EVERYTHING DEPENDS ON HIM? IT SEEMS THAT WE ARE IN CHARGE BUT NOT SO. HE IS. THAT'S A VERY GOOD THING

SINCE I AM NOT GOOD AT BEING IN CHARGE. HE IS THE BEST "IN CHARGE" THAT COMES TO MIND, OH YES. AS I KNEEL BY MY BED AT NIGHT TO TALK WITH HIM BEFORE I SLEEP, I MUST THANK HIM FOR ALL HE DOES SINCE HE DOES IT ALL. YES, HE DOES. I AM SO GRATEFUL FOR HIS HAND TO DO IT ALL AND BE IT ALL FOR ME. NOW FOR THE BEST PART, HE IS MY MOST HIGH AND MOST HOLY. HE, THE DIVINE OF MY LIFE. LIFE IS SACRED AND HE SEES TO IT THAT I HONOR HIM, AS HE REMINDS ME OF HIS DEITY AND HOLINESS. LEST I SHOULD BE CASUAL ABOUT MY ATTITUDE TOWARD HIM. MUST TREAT HIM AS THE MOST HIGH AND HOLY WITH MUCH REVERENCE. BEND THAT KNEE AND BOW THAT HEAD TO HIM WITH ALL MY HEART. I LOVE HIM WITH ALL MY HEART AND MUST LET HIM KNOW THAT I WILL ALWAYS BOW REAL LOW TO HONOR HIS KINGSHIP AND DIVINITY. MUST GO TO CHURCH TO WORSHIP WITH THE BELIEVERS IN OUR CITY. TO SING HYMNS TO HONOR MY PRECIOUS LORD. READ THE WORD AND PRAY WITH REVERENCE AND GLORIFY HIS NAME. HE GAVE SO MUCH AND FOR SURE, HE IS WORTHY. HIS SON WAS THE RANSOM PAID BY THE FATHER TO REDEEM ME AND THE WHOLE WORLD, WHETHER I OR THEY RECEIVE OR NOT. HE DIED THAT WE MAY BE SAVED, IF YOU DON'T HONOR HIM AND RECEIVE HIS SACRIFICE, YOUR FUTURE MAY NOT BE AS GOOD AS THE ONES WHO HAVE. HE DID IT BEFORE THE FACT. SO ALL YOU HAVE TO DO IS ACKNOWLEDGE HIS WORK AND WORSHIP HIM. THAT BANNER OR STANDARD OVER ME IS HIS LOVE AND IS THE LORD JESUS CHRIST, HE ON THAT CROSS IS THE TYPE OR SHADOW ON THE POLE. THE SERPENT ON THE POLE, WHEN THEY LOOKED ON IT THEY WERE HEALED. JESUS IS THE HEALER, THE DIVINE HEALER. IS THIS THE MOST WONDERFUL THING YOU HAVE EVER HEARD? DO YOU LOVE HIM SO MUCH AND ARE YOU SO GRATEFUL FOR HIS LIFE AND DEATH? ME TOO. HE IS MY WHOLE LIFE, I AM POSSESSED, AND JOYFULLY SO. HE SO DESERVES EVERYTHING I CAN DO TO WORSHIP HIM AND HIS

FATHER AND THE BLESSED HOLY GHOST. ALL THEY, SO GOD, SO GOD. THANK YOU, MY PRECIOUS LORD AND SAVIOR. NOT GOD FIRST, GOD ONLY. HE WILL BE ONLY OR HE WON'T BE ANY. IF GOD HAD AN IDEA, HIS IDEA WOULD BE GOD. MY CREATOR, MY EVERYTHING. I LOVE THE SONG "WORTHY". WE SING IT OFTEN IN CHURCH. IT'S ONE OF THE BIGGIES, BECAUSE MY GOD IS THE ONLY BIGGIE. NO DISRESPECT INTENDED, HE KNOWS. I LOVE HIM SO MUCH AND IT'S SO WONDERFUL TO HAVE A WORSHIP SERVICE THAT SOMETIMES TAKES MORE THAN HALF OF THE MESSAGE TIME. IT'S ALL GOOD, HE SAID SO, I HEARD HIM. AMEN.

MY DADDY IS SO GOD. GOD GAVE HIS BEST, INDEED. THE LORD JESUS CHRIST.
HE LOVES YOU NOT BECAUSE OF WHO YOU ARE BUT BECAUSE OF WHO HE IS.

MY ARK

THE SUN HAS SET, THE NIGHT SO DARK.
I AM SAFE IN MY JESUS, MY ARK.

NO MOON TO GLOW OR SHINE TONIGHT.
A MILLION STARS BUT GIVE NO LIGHT.

I GUESS THEY ARE TOO FAR AWAY.
SO GLAD TO HAVE HIM NEAR TO STAY.

I HUG MY PILLOW AND GO OFF TO SLEEP.
TO DREAM OF TOMORROW AND COUNT THE SHEEP.

THE WINDOW OPEN, I FEEL A BREEZE.
IT'S COOL AND FRESH, GOOD TO PLEASE.

NOW I WAKE TO A PASSING THOUGHT.
SHOULD I BOTHER, MAYBE NOT?

THE DAYS ARE COMING TO AN END.
MUST GET OUT AND WITNESS TO A FRIEND.

I SO LOOK FORWARD TO JESUS RETURN.
SOME DON'T KNOW THE LORD, THEY MUST LEARN.

HE THE ONE TO BRING US HOME.
HE IS OUR SAVIOR, HE ALONE.

GOD SENT HIS PRECIOUS SON,
WE KNOW HE IS THE ONLY ONE.

MY SAFETY PROMISED IN HIS ARMS.
TO KEEP ME SAFE FROM ANY HARM.

HE IS MY STRENGTH, A SOLID MARK.
HE THE STRONGHOLD, TENACIOUS ARK.

HE IN ME AND I IN HIM,
NO STORM OR WIND CAN COME WITHIN.

THERE IS NO FEAR OR ANY DOUBT.
JESUS, MY ARK, WILL KEEP IT OUT.

HE IS MY ARK, I AM SAFE IN HIM.
ALL MY LOVE TO HIM, HIS NOE.

IF I PLACE MYSELF WITH YOU, JESUS, I AM IN A GOOD PLACE
***** HE LOVES ME, I LOVE HIM BACK. *****

THE PRESENCE AND ESSENCE OF GOD

THE PRESENCE OF GOD IS THE FACT OF THE PERCEIVED IMPRESSION. WHEN YOU ARE PARTAKING OF THE BODY OF OUR LORD JESUS CHRIST - THE BREAD OF LIFE - YOU MUST SEE HIM AS THE BATTERED, BROKEN BODY ON THAT WHIPPING POST. HE SAID "EXCEPT YOU EAT MY FLESH AND DRINK MY BLOOD YOU HAVE NO LIFE IN YOU. JOHN 6:53-56. HIS PRESENCE IS IN THE BREAD AND IN THE CUP. WHEN I TAKE COMMUNION, AS ALSO THE ESSENCE (POWER) IS IN THE BREAD AND IN THE CUP. MANY LEFT OFF FOLLOWING JESUS WHEN HE MADE THAT ANALOGY, SAYING "THIS IS A HARD SAYING; WHO CAN HEAR IT". JOHN 6:66 KJV (NOTICE THE 666). HOW APPROPRIATE! YOU MAY NOT UNDERSTAND BUT YOU BETTER BELIEVE IT. THERE IS LIFE IN HIM AND HIM ONLY. IT'S THE POWER OF LOVE, IT'S THE POWER OF GRACE, IT'S THE POWER OF GOD. THE PRESENCE AND ESSENCE OF GOD.THE ESSENCE OF GOD IS THE POWER OF GOD. WHEN HIS ESSENCE (POWER) IS ALL AROUND, THE WORK IS DONE. "THY WILL BE DONE", HIS WILL IS HIS WORK. PROOF IS WHEN YOU GRATE THE PEEL OF A LEMON OR WHATEVER, BREAK AND MANGLE THE SKIN OR PEEL, IT'S PURE ESSENCE IS RELEASED. WHEN THEY SCOURGED AND LACERATED JESUS' BODY IT RELEASED THE POWER OF HEALING. ISAIAH 53:5 AND BY HIS STRIPES WE ARE HEALED. WHEN GOD'S SON WAS BEATEN AND HUNG ON THAT CROSS, IT WAS A WORK OF COMPASSION. IT RELEASED THE PURE ESSENCE (POWER) OF GOD THRU THE DEATH OF THE PURE AND SPOTLESS LAMB OF GOD, HIS PRECIOUS SON, JESUS. THE HEALING AND FORGIVING POWER THAT WOULD LAST THRU THE END OF THE AGE. THANK YOU, JESUS.THE ESSENCE OF GOD TOO, IS THE FORGIVING POWER IN THE BLOOD. THE BLOOD SHED ON THAT CROSS BY THOSE SPIKES AND THAT CROWN OF THORNS WAS SO NECESSARY FOR THE FORGIVENESS OF SIN. THO THE (TEARS) OF BLOOD SWEAT AND SHED

IN THE GARDEN OF GETHSEMANE WERE EVIDENCE THAT WE NEED NOT SUFFER MENTAL ANGUISH, HE DIDN'T WANT TO DRINK THAT CUP OF OUR SIN, YOURS AND MINE. HE ASKED THE FATHER IF THE CUP COULD PASS FROM HIM. HOWEVER, THE FATHER INSISTED THAT HE DRINK IT. HE WAS REMINDED THAT FOR THIS PURPOSE WAS HE SENT. WE MUST FOREVER BE THANKFUL FOR THAT CROSS, THAT HAD HE NOT FULFILLED THE WORK WE WOULD STILL BE IN OUR SIN AND FOREVER LOST. WE BLESS HIS HOLINESS AND HOLY NAME, OUR LAMB OF PERFECTION, WHO TOOK AWAY THE SIN OF THE WORLD. ESPECIALLY MINE. THANK YOU, JESUS. WHEN I TAKE THE BREAD AND THE CUP I AM REMINDED OF HIS LOVE AND SACRIFICE. HOW CAN I NOT? THANK YOU, JESUS, ALWAYS. SEE YOU ABOVE THE CLOUDS. AMONEE TRIESS! SO BE IT BY THE HOLY GHOST. JUST WORSHIP HIM! HE IS WORTHY! I THINK I HAVE GIVEN A COMPLETED WORK OF THE ESSENCE AND PRESENCE OF THE BODY AND BLOOD OF JESUS. YOU MAY WANT TO GO FARTHER WITH THAT STUDY AND YOU SHOULD. WE ALL NEED TO DO A LONG STUDY OF THE SUFFERING OF JESUS. HOW CAN WE NOT APPRECIATE HOW HE SUFFERED FOR ALL OF HUMANITY AT THE HANDS OF HIS ACCUSERS? THAT'S A GOOD WAY TO STUDY TO SHOW YOURSELF APPROVED. WE ALL WHO DEEPLY LOVE OUR SAVIOR DO SO APPRECIATE THE WORK FINISHED ON THE CROSS. I COULD GO ON AND ON, AS THAT'S WHERE I LOVE TO BOAST IN HIM. O HOW HE LOVES ME, O HOW I LOVE HIM.ASCENDING LOVE IS LESS THAN DESCENDING LOVE. YOU CAN'T OUT LOVE THE GOD OF HEAVEN. DO YOU KNOW THAT? YOU DO NOW. I KNOW THAT I AM WORDY, I KNOW IT, BUT I CAN'T HELP IT. THIS IS MY LOVE STORY THAT GOES ON AND ON TILL MY SAVIOR COME TO GET ME. THE LONGER YOU KNOW HIM THE MORE YOU LOVE HIM. JUST DO IT. TRUE LOVE IN YOUR HEART, THE THE LONGER, THE STRONGER YOUR LOVE. AMEN

PRESENCE: PRECEIVED IMPRESSION, TO BECOME AWARE OF THE DIFFERENCE MADE BY THE ACTION OF SOMEONE OR SOMETHING. JESUS, MY LORD!
ESSENCE: POWER OF ABSOLUTE REALITY, SUBSTANCE. POWER OF CHRIST WAS RELEASED WHEN HIS BODY WAS BROKEN. HIS FRAGRANCE, HIS PERFUME. HIS POWER: ANOINTING OIL, HEALING POWER WAS RELEASED. JESUS, MY LORD!
THE PRESENCE AND THE ESSENCE OF GOD IS THE LORD JESUS CHRIST THROUGH THE HOLY GHOST. IS THAT THE MOST BEAUTIFUL THING YOU EVER HEARD? YES!
HE WALKS WITH ME AND HE TALKS WITH ME. THAT'S WHAT HE DOES.

AD'INFINITUM

THE STATE AND STATEMENT OF OUR GOD

HIS REAL ESTATE, TOO

IN REFERENCE TO THE STATE OF OUR GOD, HE IS THE MOST ELITE OF ALL MEMBERS OR BEINGS OF HEAVEN. ABSOLUTELY. THE MOST HIGH, NONE OTHER HIGHER THAN HE. DON'T THINK YOU CAN EVEN COME NEAR HIS HIGH'NESS. NOPE. UNTOUCHABLE. THIS ALSO IS THE FORMAL ACCOUNT OF HIS STATE AND STATEMENT. WE ALL STAND BACK IN DEEPEST REVERENCE BEFORE HIM WHO SITS ON THE THRONE OF HEAVEN. JESUS, THE SON, THE HOLY GHOST (SPIRIT) HAVE PRIORITY AND THE SAVED ARE ALLOWED. THERE IS NO ROYALTY REGAL ENOUGH TO APPROACH HIS THRONE. YOU WOULD DISSOLVE IMMEDIATELY IF YOU TRIED. HIS THRONE IS HIS DWELLING, HE WILL NEVER EVER STEP DOWN FOR ANY REASON. WE HAVE THE LORD JESUS CHRIST, OUR MESSIAH WHO WE HONOR AS THE GOD (KING OF KINGS, LORD OF LORDS) OF ALL THE HEAVENS, ABLE TO BE WITH US IN THE FLESH. YES, HE IS GOD IN THE FLESH. WHEN GOD NEEDED TO BE AMONG HIS PEOPLE, HIS HIGHEST CREATION, HE BEGOT AN OFF'SPRING IN THE FLESH TO WALK WITH US, TO REPRESENT HIS REGAL AND UNTOUCHABLE SELF. WE ARE SO ECSTATIC (IMMEASURABLEY HAPPY) TO HAVE OUR JESUS TO BE OUR LORD AND KING, OUR GOD IN THE FLESH. THE ONE WHO WAS ABLE TO FEEL OUR HUMANITY AND COMMONNESS. THAT MAY NOT BE A WORD, UNTIL NOW. AS WE ARE ENLIGHTENED BY THE READING OF THE SCRIPTURES, WE ARE TOLD THAT OUR LORD JESUS WAS BROUGHT TO THE EARTH AS A NEW BORN WHEN THE ANGEL GABRIEL ANNOUNCED TO MARY, A YOUNG VIRGIN, THAT SHE WOULD BEAR A SON AND HE WOULD BE OF THE HOLY GHOST. HE WAS INDEED, BORN THROUGH A VIRGIN VIA THE SPIRIT OF GOD. HE WAS VIRGIN BORN. HE WAS A BABY WHO WAS DELIVERED IN A STABLE, PROPHESIED AND ORDAINED TO BE OUR MESSIAH. WHEN HE

WAS OF AN AGE TO BE OUR MOST HIGH AND HOLY TEACHER AND BEGAN HIS MINISTRY, HE WAS DESPISED BY THE JEWISH HIERARCHY AND THEY SET ABOUT TO HAVE HIM KILLED. HE WAS CRUCIFIED. THEY DID SUCCEED HOWEVER, HIS FATE ORDAINED OF HIS FATHER AND HAVING BEEN IN THE GRAVE FOR THREE DAYS GOD RAISED HIM FROM THE DEAD TO DIE NO MORE. BY HIS DEATH WE INHERIT ETERNAL LIFE. WE BOW LOW TO OUR LORD JESUS CHRIST AS OUR SAVIOR AND REDEEMER, SENT BY THE ONE WE HONOR AS THE SUPREME OF ALL BEING. WE SOMETIMES DON'T HAVE WORDS TO GIVE TITLE OF OUR GOD. HIGH AND LIFTED UP, WHO HAS NO EQUAL. AMEN. HIS STATEMENT IS THAT HE IS SO HIGH, SO HOLY AND WE MUST HAVE NO REVERENCE EXCEPT THE THRONE OF THE GOD OF ALL THAT IS, IS. WE ARE IN AWE OF HIS MULTI UNIVERSES. IT GOES ON AND ON, FARTHER THAN ANYONE CAN POSSIBLY SEE. YOU MAY BUILD ALL THE TELESCOPES YOU PLEASE, NOT ENOUGH. DO YOU EXPECT THAT YOU MAY LOOK THROUGH A GLASS AND SEE A GLORIOUS DOMAIN AND A THRONE? I DON'T THINK SO. HE IS TOO BIG TO SEE HIM, THAT WILL MAKE FOR A GOOD DISCUSSION AND DISCOURSE. YOU WILL NEED FIFTY MILLION SUPER TELESCOPES TO COVER THE AREA OF OUR GOD. MAYBE EVEN THAT'S NOT ENOUGH. PLEASE DON'T LOSE SLEEP OVER IT THOUGH, THERE IS NO COMPETITION. IT'S ONE OF THOSE THINGS THAT CAN'T BE DONE. SO, GET OVER IT. THEN WE NEED TO HAVE A LOOK AT HIS REAL ESTATE. ON EARTH, WE CELEBRATE HIS REAL ESTATE, ISRAEL. LITTLE ISRAEL IS HIS AND HE IS SO IN LOVE WITH HER. WHEN JESUS COMES BACK THE SECOND TIME HE WILL PUT HIS FEET DOWN ON THE TEMPLE MOUNT. HE WILL DECLARE THAT SHE IS THE HOLY CITY OF OUR GOD. HIS PROPERTY, HIS ONLY. ALL WHO THOUGHT THEY HAD A CLAIM TO IT WILL FIND THEY ARE BEING EVICTED. THEY WILL NOT BE ASKED TO LEAVE, THEY WILL BE MADE TO LEAVE, PERMANENTLY. SHE WILL BE, SHE IS THE HOLY CITY OF GOD. IT'S BEEN THE PLAN FOR, FOREVER. HER WIDTH, HER LENGTH. HER DEPTH ALL EQUAL. SHE IS THE FOUR'SQUARE CITY OF GOD. ISN'T THAT EXCITING. I CAN'T WAIT FOR THE FULFILLING OF THIS EVENT. IT'S SO MARVELOUS IN MY EYES,

AND I AM GONNA BE ONE WHO SHOUTS FROM THE HOUSETOPS THE TRUTH OF ALL THAT HAS GONE BEFORE US. WE ARE GONNA HAVE A CELEBRATION TO END ALL CELEBRATIONS. HE OUR GRAND HOST, JESUS, WILL BE THERE FOR THE WELCOMING OF ALL WHO ACCEPTED HIM AS SAVIOR AND REDEEMER. WE WILL LIVE FOREVER WITH OUR SAVIOR, WITH NO TIME OR CLOCK TO WATCH. HALLELUJAH! I AM HIS LITTLE STAR. AMEN.

NOT GOD FIRST, GOD ONLY. HE WILL BE ONLY OR HE WON'T BE ANY. MY DADDY IS SO GOD. HIS STATE, HIS STATEMENT AND REAL ESTATE STAND FOREVER.
YOU CAN'T DISPUTE ANY OF HIS HISTORY. IT WAS, IT IS, ETERNAL AND INFINITE.

YOU ARE MY PLEASURE

TOGETHER FOREVER, MY PLEASURE

MY DEAREST HEAVENLY FATHER, LORD JESUS, BLESSED HOLY GHOST, MY BELOVED THREE IN ONE. YOU, AND ONLY YOU, ARE MY HOLY PLEASURE. LIFE IS SO TOUGH SOMETIMES AND I HAVE TROUBLE FOCUSING ON WHAT'S IMPORTANT. BY IMPORTANT, I MEAN THE LORD JESUS CHRIST AND MY FAITH THAT MAKES ALL THINGS POSSIBLE. THE ENEMY COMES TO ACCUSE THAT I AM NOT DOING MY PROMISES TO MY LORD. HOW WOULD HE KNOW, HE DOESN'T? HE'S JUST AN OPPORTUNIST. HE COULD CARE LESS HOW I AM DEDICATED TO MY LORD. HE JUST LOOKS FOR ANYTHING TO ANNOY ME. O YAH, THAT'S HIS JOB. NASTY LITTLE PEST THAT HE IS. I MUST NOT GIVE HIM ANY TIME. MAY I ALWAYS GIVE THE LORD ALL MY ATTENTION. HE IS MY OUTSTANDING PLEASURE AND WONDERFUL FRIEND. EVEN IN TOUGH TIMES AND ASIDE FROM PROBLEMS THAT POP'UP, HE IS GOOD THINKING AND A PLEASURE TO PONDER. HIS BOOK IS THE INSTRUCTION BOOK, THE "HOW TO" BOOK, THE "MUST'READ" BOOK. YOU CAN'T DO BETTER THAN "THE BOOK". DO YOU KNOW THAT I AM TALKING ABOUT THE BIBLE? I HAVE FOUND OUT SO MUCH IN MY SHORT STAY HERE, JUST READING DAILY OR WHEN EVER THERE WAS TIME BEFORE I KNEW HOW URGENT IT WAS AND IS. MUST READ EVERYDAY OR MAYBE THREE OR FOUR TIMES A DAY, DEPENDING ON HOW CRITICAL THE NEED. THERE ARE TIMES THAT THE NEED IS EVEN MORE NEEDY. YAH, I DO LOVE TO READ MY BOOK, MY BEAUTIFUL BIBLE OR BIBLES. I HAVE QUITE A FEW, THANK YOU LORD. I LOVE EVERY ONE OF THEM. BY HIS MERCY AND GRACE, I AM UP EARLY AND SOMETIMES LATE, TOO. I GET SO INVOLVED IN MY WRITING, I HAVE TO STAY WITH HIM WHEN HE WANTS TO VISIT AND WRITE WHAT SAYS. HE IS SOMETIMES QUITE LONG WINDED. DON'T TELL HIM I SAID THAT. YES, I KNOW HE KNOWS. ACTUALLY, IT'S MY PLEASURE TO BE UP WITH HIM AND TO GET UP EARLY TO MEET HIM IN THE MORNING.

YOU JUST GOTTA LOVE HIM. O HIS GRACE, O HIS GRACE. WHERE WOULD WE BE WITHOUT HIM, WHERE WOULD I BE WITHOUT HIM? THAT'S A HARD THOUGHT. BY HIS GRACE, MUST NOT GO THERE, IT'S UNTHINKABLE. HE IS SO GOOD AND BRINGS WONDERFUL MEMORIES. HE'S BEEN WITH ME ALL MY LIFE, NOT ALWAYS AS CLOSE AS I SHOULD HAVE ALLOWED. I WAS BORN INTO A CHURCH FAMILY, WE WENT OFTEN BUT WE WERE NOT REAL STEADY. I HAVE GOOD MEMORIES OF EVERY SUMMER VACATION BIBLE SCHOOL. I AM GRATEFUL FOR MY CHRISTIAN HERITAGE. MOM AND DAD WERE GOOD AT MOTIVATING US CHILDREN TO WORSHIP. THANK YOU, MOM AND DAD, THANK YOU HEAVENLY FATHER FOR GOOD PARENTING. THESE THINGS ARE NOT BY ACCIDENT, THEY ARE ON PURPOSE, GOD'S PURPOSE. MY DADDY IS SO GOD. NOT GOD FIRST, GOD ONLY. HE WILL BE ONLY OR HE WON'T BE ANY. TASTE AND SEE. HE CALLS US BY THE NAME GIVEN AT CREATION. YOU WILL KNOW WHEN HE CALLS, YOU KNOW THAT NAME. YOU MAY NOT KNOW HOW TO CALL IT BUT YOU WILL RECOGNIZE IT. I THINK A LITTLE LIGHT COMES ON INSIDE, A LITTLE EXTRA HEADS'UP. WHAT A WONDERFUL SAVIOR I HAVE. BE SURE YOU TAKE HIM WITH YOU EVERYWHERE YOU GO. TO BE SURE YOU WON'T BE GOING ANYWHERE INAPPROPRIATE. FOR SUCH A TIME AS THIS, WE CERTAINLY ARE VERY NEAR OUR GOING HOME CALL. STAY ALERT! I THINK WE PROBABLY WILL BE IN CHURCH OR IT MAY BE IN THE MIDDLE OF THE NIGHT OR IN OUR PRAYER CLOSET. I KNOW I WILL BE SO HAPPY TO SEE MY LORD, MY JESUS, MY KING, SO MAJESTIC, COULD I HAVE A MORE DESIRABLE, ADORABLE FRIEND. I HAVE BEEN WAITING A LONG TIME. O HIS GRACE AND GLORY. WE WILL TALK ABOUT HIS GRACE AND GLORY, HE LIKES THAT. TOGETHER FOREVER, MY PLEASURE. LORD JESUS, YOU ARE MY PLEASURE. I WILL ENJOY MY GENTLE JESUS. HE LOVES ME AND I LOVE HIM BACK. BY HIS GRACE I AM SAVED. ASCENDING LOVE IS LESS THAN DESCENDING LOVE, THAT'S WISDOM. DADDY GAVE ME HIS BEST, "JESUS" GLORIOUS WISDOM. I WILL WANT TO SING TO HIM OR WITH HIM WHILE WE WAIT TO BE SEATED AT THE WEDDING SUPPER. WHAT A DAY OF REJOICING THAT WILL BE. HIS GRACE, HIS CROSS, HIS RESURRECTION,

HIS REDEMPTION, HIS SALVATION. IT'S ALL HIM, IT'S ALL HIS GRACE, YOU CAN'T HELP BUT LOVE HIM. HE'S THE GREATEST CHRISTMAS GIFT EVER. GET OUT THERE AND BOAST OF HIS LOVE FOR YOU. TELL ALL WHO WILL LISTEN. AMEN AND AMEN

I'VE PICKED ALL MY FLOWERS, MADE A BIG BOUQUET
SO NOW I AM READY, IF JESUS COMES TODAY
WE ALL KNOW HE'S ON HIS WAY. ON TIME, HE WON'T DELAY!

HEAVEN LOOKED AWAY

EVEN ON THE DAY OF BETRAYAL, WHEN JESUS AND THE DISCIPLES CAME TOGETHER FOR THE PASSOVER, JESUS KNEW THE CROSS WAS IMMINENT. HE ALWAYS KNEW HIS PURPOSE FOR BEING HERE. HE KNEW WHY THE FATHER SENT HIM AND HOW THE END WOULD COME TO PASS. IT HAD TO BE OR WE WOULD BE HOPELESS AND LOST. JUDAS TOO, WAS PART OF THE PLAN OF OUR REDEMPTION AND SALVATION, THO I AM SURE HE WAS A WILLING PARTICIPANT. MATT 26: 14-16. HE DID ACCEPT THE 30 PIECES OF SILVER, HOWEVER HE TRIED TO GIVE IT BACK BUT THEY HAD THEIR INTENDED VICTIM AND THERE WAS NO GOING BACK. HE HANGED HIMSELF AFTER THE HORRENDOUS DEED. WE DON'T REALLY KNOW WHAT HE WAS THINKING. WHEN HE REALIZED THE HORROR OF WHAT HE HAD DONE, HE WAS BROKEN. HE COULDN'T REVERSE IT THO, AS HE LOST HOPE. HE REPENTED AND GAVE THE MONEY BACK BUT THAT DIDN'T WORK OUT. OLD TESTAMENT FORETOLD THAT THIS WAS THE WAY HE WOULD GO. THE PSALMS TELL US THAT HE WOULD LIFT HIS HEAL AGAINST JESUS AND BETRAY HIM. PSALM 41:1-13. AMAZING HOW THE SCRIPTURES, O T TELLS THE STORY OF OUR LORD JESUS CHRIST. THAT'S HOW WE KNOW GOD WROTE THE BOOK. THE BIBLE, BEGINNING TO END. AND WE KNOW IT'S TRUE, GOD CANNOT LIE.

HEAVEN LOOKED AWAY

THE END WAS NEAR. JESUS KNEW IT. WHEN HE WAS IN THE GARDEN OF GETHSEMANE HE ASKED THE FATHER IF THE CUP OF HIS TORTURE COULD PASS AND NOT HAVE TO DRINK IT. MARK 14:36. GOD HIS FATHER, SAID NO. IT WAS FOR THIS PURPOSE WAS HE SENT. THANK YOU, JESUS, WHAT WOULD WE DO IF YOU DIDN'T. WHAT WOULD I DO IF YOU DIDN'T? THE TRIAL, THE DENIAL, THE BEATING, THE CROSS. THE LOVE, THE LOVE, THE LOVE. FOR ME. JESUS WALKED TO THE HILL TOP OF COMDEMNATION FOR ME. HIS HANDS WERE PIERCED, HIS FEET WERE PIERCED. HIS CROWN OF THORNS TO MOCK HIS KINGSHIP PIERCED HIS BROW AND THE HOLY BLOOD RAN DOWN HIS FACE AND DRIPPED TO THE GROUND. THE GROUND SO HONORED TO RECEIVE IT. AS I WATCHED, THE TEARS OF DREAD RAN DOWN MY FACE MIXED WITH THE BLOOD OF MY BELOVED SON. THE SKY DARKENED AND THE CLOUDS BECAME THICK AND HEAVY. GOD WRAPPED HIS HANDS AROUND THE SUN. HEAVEN LOOKED AWAY. ALL THE SIN OF THE AGES CAME TO SEE HOW THE JUDGEMENT WOULD PLAY OUT. THE CROWD HISSED AND MOCKED HIM AS HE ENDURED THE BEGINNING OF HELL. ALL THE SIN GATHERED FROM EDEN TO OPENING OF THE BOOK OF LIFE WAS ON HIM. HE HAD FINISHED THE CUP OF OUR GUILT. THE FATHER, THE HOLY OF HEAVEN, COULD NOT WATCH AS HIS SON ABSORBED ALL THE SIN OF THE AGES IN HIS BODY. THEN SAID "IT IS FINISHED". SCRIPTURE SAYS GOD CANNOT AND WILL NOT LOOK ON SIN. JESUS TOOK IT ALL TO HELL AND HE LEFT IT IN THE PIT, HE PAID IN FULL THE STORAGE FEES WITH HIS LIFE. WE ARE ETERNALLY GRATEFUL, JESUS. DEBT PAID IN FULL, HE IS RISEN, HE IS RISEN INDEED.

HEAVEN WELCOMED JESUS AT THE RIGHT HAND OF THE FATHER
HE LOVES YOU, LOVE HIM BACK, HEAVEN AND EARTH, REJOICE
I LOVE MY LORD AND HE TRULY LOVES ME, AMONEE TRIESS

I HAVE WRITTEN
WHAT I HAVE WRITTEN

ISA. 45:22-25 & 46:8-13 TURN TO ME AND BE SAVED, ALL YOU ENDS OF THE EARTH. FOR I AM GOD AND THERE IS NO OTHER. BY MYSELF I HAVE SWORN, MY MOUTH HAS UTTERED IN ALL INTEGRITY A WORD THAT WILL NOT BE REVOKED. BEFORE ME EVERY KNEE WILL BOW, BY ME EVERY TONGUE WILL SWEAR. THEY WILL SAY OF ME, "IN THE LORD ALONE ARE DELIVERANCE AND STRENGTH". ALL WHO HAVE RAGED AGAINST HIM WILL COME TO HIM AND BE PUT TO SHAME. BUT ALL THE DESCENDANTS OF ISRAEL WILL FIND DELIVERANCE IN THE LORD AND WILL MAKE THEIR BOAST IN HIM. REMEMBER THIS, AND KEEP IT IN MIND, TAKE IT TO HEART. REMEMBER THE FORMER THINGS, THOSE OF LONG AGO, I AM GOD, AND THERE IS NO OTHER, I AM GOD AND THERE IS NONE LIKE ME. I MAKE KNOWN THE END FROM THE BEGINNING, FROM ANCIENT TIMES, WHAT IS STILL TO COME. I SAY, 'MY PURPOSE WILL STAND, AND I WILL DO ALL THAT I PLEASE. FROM THE EAST I SUMMON A BIRD OF PREY (AN EAGLE, CYRUS) FROM A FAR-OFF LAND, A MAN TO FULFILL MY PURPOSE. WHAT I HAVE SAID, THAT WILL I BRING ABOUT. WHAT I HAVE PLANNED, THAT I WILL DO. LISTEN TO ME, YOU STUBBORN-HEARTED, YOU WHO ARE NOW FAR FROM MY RIGHTEOUSNESS. I AM BRINGING MY RIGHTEOUSNESS NEAR, IT IS NOT FAR AWAY AND MY SALVTION WILL NOT BE DELAYED. I WILL GRANT SALVATION TO ZION, MY SPLENDOR, MY GLORY, TO ISRAEL.

NONE CAN CHANGE OR ERASE MY WORD. THERE IS NOT NOW NOR EVER WILL BE "COMPROMISE". TRY IT. IT'S MY

WORK THAT I FINISHED. DON'T PUT PEN TO PAPER TO REDO ANYTHING OF MINE. I WILL BREAK YOUR ARMS, CRUSH YOUR MIND, STOP YOUR HEART, STRANGLE YOUR TONGUE, BLIND YOUR EYES, REMOVE YOUR EARS. HANDS OFF. IF YOU DON'T BELIEVE MY WORD (MY JESUS), LOVE MY COMMANDS, AND HEAR MY SAYING "THUS SAYETH THE LORD". PLEASE READ PSALM 10:1-18.

STAY IN BED SO WHEN YOU DIE YOU WON'T HAVE FAR TO FALL. I AM GOD AND THERE IS NO OTHER. EXCEPT I GIVE YOU WORD, BE QUIET. SSHHH...

I HAVE WRITTEN WHAT I HAVE WRITTEN
NO COMPROMISE
I AM HONORED TO WRITE FOR HIM
HE IS REAL, SUPERNATURALLY, REAL
O THE MIGHTY LOVE AND GRACE OF GOD BY THE HOLY
GHOST
I KNOW THE DAY OF HIS RETURN, JUST ASK HIM, HE WILL
TELL YOU

www.ingramcontent.com/pod-product-compliance
Lightning Source LLC
Chambersburg PA
CBHW032222050726
47591CB00001B/220